Waltharius

DALLAS MEDIEVAL TEXTS AND TRANSLATIONS

EDITOR
Philipp W. Rosemann
(University of Dallas)

EDITORIAL BOARD

Denis M. Farkasfalvy, O.Cist. (University of Dallas);
Theresa Kenney (University of Dallas); James J. Lehrberger, O.Cist. (University of
Dallas); J. Stephen Maddux (University of Dallas); John R. Sommerfeldt
(University of Dallas); Francis R. Swietek (University of Dallas);
Bonnie Wheeler (Southern Methodist University)

BOARD OF EDITORIAL ADVISERS

Charles S. F. Burnett (Warburg Institute); Marcia L. Colish (Yale University);
Thérèse-Anne Druart (Catholic University of America); Kent Emery, Jr.
(University of Notre Dame); Hugh Bernard Feiss, O.S.B. (Monastery of the Ascension);
Bernard McGinn (University of Chicago); James McEvoy (†);
James J. Murphy (University of California, Davis);
John T. Noonan, Jr. (U.S. Court of Appeals for the Ninth Circuit, San Francisco);
Edward M. Peters (University of Pennsylvania); Carlos Steel (Katholieke
Universiteit Leuven); Baudouin van den Abeele (Université catholique de Louvain);
Nancy van Deusen (Claremont Graduate University)

SPONSORED BY

UNIVERSITY OF DALLAS

DALLAS MEDIEVAL TEXTS AND TRANSLATIONS
22

Waltharius

EDITION, TRANSLATION, AND INTRODUCTION
BY

Abram Ring
(Battle Ground Academy)

PEETERS
LEUVEN - PARIS - BRISTOL, CT
2016

Cover illustration: Ekkehard composing the *Waltharius*. Drawing by Hermann Vogel for Otto von Leixner's *Illustrirte Geschichte des deutschen Schriftthums in volksthümlicher Darstellung*, vol. 1: *Von den ersten Anfängen bis zum Ende des siebzehnten Jahrhunderts* (Leipzig and Berlin: Otto Spamer, 1880), after p. 36.

A catalogue record for this book is available from the Library of Congress.

© 2016 – Peeters – Bondgenotenlaan 153 – B-3000 Leuven – Belgium.
ISBN 978-90-429-3354-5
D/2016/0602/119

Doctori semper et maxime desiderato William Sadler Bonds,
qui mihi ignem Latinae accendit.
Et uxori carissimae et optimae, Melinda, cui omnia bona vitae meae debeo.

Frontispiece: Strips from fragments of the *Waltharius* found in the binding of an incunable at the University of Chicago at Urbana-Champaign, University Library, Pre-1650 MS 0148. The fragments date to the second third of the eleventh century. Courtesy of the Rare Book & Manuscript Library, University of Illinois at Urbana-Champaign.

Foreword

We all know, or at least have heard of, Odysseus, Aeneas, Beowulf, King Arthur, Siegfried … the heroes of epic poems or romantic literature whose existence is more legendary than historical, and yet who have, to a considerable extent, shaped the western imagination. Walter, the main protagonist of the *Waltharius*, is not such a household name. Nonetheless, the *Waltharius* occupies a firm place in the list of great western epics. Its afterlife continues into the twentieth century, as one particularly successful adaptation, by the German poet and novelist Joseph Victor von Scheffel, has spawned translations into many other languages, operas, and even a film.

It is easy to imagine the material of the *Waltharius* in a contemporary movie starring Sylvester Stallone or Arnold Schwarzenegger. Special effects would be crucial to convey the carnage that is at the center of the work—a merciless battle between Walter and a series of opponents which leaves the latter with their brains split, guts spilled, and invariably decapitated … with eyes torn out of their sockets still quivering on the ground.

But there is more. The *Waltharius* is also a story of love between its hero and a beautiful woman, it is a story of honor and virtue, of betrayal, of power and wealth. Replete with lively dialogue, the poem rarely bores—even outside the ferocious battle scene. So, material for Stallone and Schwarzenegger?

Yes, but as Abram Ring shows in his scholarly introduction and notes, there is a further dimension to the *Waltharius*, in addition to its film-worthy story line. The poet (still ultimately unknown, though there have been educated guesses) brilliantly weaves together the strands of at least three distinct traditions, which meet and sometimes conflict in every line of the poem. The *Waltharius* resounds with references to pagan literature, especially the *Aeneid*, which its author has read through the lens of the commentary by the fourth/fifth-century Roman grammarian Maurus Servius Honoratus. The origins of the Walter legend are Germanic, however; there are similarities, for example, with the Anglo-Saxon *Waldere* fragments. Our hero and his opponents, then, are medieval Germanic warriors who are conceived and depicted by means of ancient language.

Christianity is the third crucial element in the mix. Walter not only decapitates his enemies; on occasion he is quite devout and can be found in prayer. As he flees with his betrothed, he easily resists erotic temptations, since the two are not yet married. The Christian influences in the poem derive from Scripture, to be sure, but also from Prudentius's *Psychomachia*, which is one of the work's most important sources.

Dr. Ring has given us a new edition of the text of the *Waltharius* in this volume, an edition whose scholarly apparatus sums up the fruits of more than a century of philological work on the poem. More than that, the recent discovery of manuscript fragments in the library of the University of Illinois has made it worthwhile to reexamine the textual evidence. Dr. Ring's translation, in prose, conveys well the linguistic complexity of the poem, which often plays with Graecisms and Germanisms that reflect its varied sources. Finally, his copious notes document in great detail the different traditions on which the *Waltharius* draws, pointing the interested reader to secondary literature that further investigates the poem's language, author, sources, and historical background.

Philipp W. Rosemann
August 14, 2015

Table of Contents

Introduction

The Poem and Its Hero

Here is a medieval Latin epic of nearly fifteen hundred lines that inherits and revitalizes the classical Latin tradition of Vergil, Ovid, Horace, Statius, Lucan, and Silius Italicus, as well as the Christian poetic tradition of Juvencus, Prudentius, Sedulius, Arator, and Venantius Fortunatus.[1] Its author is apparently a young monk and talented poet capable of comprehensively reinterpreting a rich Germanic saga about historical and legendary figures such as Attila the Hun and the mythical Germanic smith Weland—all in allusive Latin language, spiced with select Greek and Germanic words. The reader finds a smorgasbord of allusions to the classical and Christian poets mixed in with biblical references and select words harvested from the poet's reading of ancient scholars such as Servius and Isidore.[2] Indeed, the scholarly depth of poetry with its dense, complex, and at times confusing allusions has led some to call it a medieval epyllion because it displays the meticulous crafting that is characteristic of classical epyllia, such as Catullus 64.[3]

---

[1] For an apparatus with parallels from earlier Latin literature, see Strecker and Schumann, *Nachträge* (1951). For other lists of parallels and sources, see Grimm and Schmeller, *Lateinische Gedichte* (1838), 65–8; Peiper, *Ekkehardi Primi Waltharius* (1873), xxxi–xxxiv; and Althof, *Waltharii Poesis* (1899), 48–9. For Vergil as a model, see Strecker, "Ekkehard und Vergil" (1898) and Wagner, *Ekkehard und Vergil* (1939). For Silius Italicus, see Schieffer, "Silius Italicus in Sankt Gallen" (1975). For Statius, see Schumann, "Statius und *Waltharius*" (1950). For Lucan, see D'Angelo, "La 'Pharsalia' nell' epica latina medievale" (1999), esp. 422, and Segaert, "De invloed van Lucanus' *Pharsalia* op het *Waltharius*" (2008), 57–130. For a good general discussion of the poetic models of the *Waltharius*, see Zwierlein, "Das Waltharius-Epos und seine lateinischen Vorbilder" (1970) or, more recently, Bisanti, "Il Waltharius fra tradizioni classiche e suggestioni germaniche" (2002).

[2] The highly allusive style of the poem has gained increasing attention from scholars. Ziolkowski (2001) praises "the Latin author's alternatingly reverential and combative use of intertexts" (29). In another recent examination, Schuhmann, "Dichtersprachliches im *Waltharius* (2006), after reviewing several of the poet's classical borrowings, concludes (456) "dass das Werk als qualitativ hochwertig bezeichnet werden muss" ("that the work must be described as high-quality"). Others who emphasize the poet's creative use of allusion are Ebeling-Koning, *Style and Structure in Ekkehard's Waltharius* (1977); Kratz, "*Quid Waltharius Ruodliebque cum Christo?*" (1977); Kratz, *Mocking Epic* (1980); Kratz, *Waltharius and Ruodlieb* (1984); and D'Angelo, *Waltharius* (1998). This positive view of the author's use of intertextual references stands against an earlier treatment of the poem as little more than a convenient patchwork of earlier works.

[3] See Baumbach and Bär (ed.), *Brill's Companion to Greek and Latin Epyllion and Its Reception* (2012), 504–05.

Modern scholarship generally agrees that the *Waltharius* is a Latin version of an older Germanic saga.[4] However, exactly how much of the story was invented by our Latin poet is subject to debate. The fragmentary Old English *Waldere*, which tells the same story as our poem, is probably independent of the *Waltharius*, but this is not universally agreed, and both poems have eluded conclusive dating. Nevertheless, stylistic connections between the *Waltharius* and the poetic tradition of the Old English *Waldere* and *Beowulf*, as well as other Germanic analogues, have been illustrated in my commentary, since the immediate source of the *Waltharius* surely came from a similar Germanic tradition. Indeed, the *Waltharius*, though written in Latin, shows quite a strong relationship to early Germanic poetry both linguistically and formally.

The numerous references to the poem in medieval library catalogs show that it was popular with medieval readers.[5] As for its literary heirs, the *Waltharius* and its tale had significant influence on the French Roland tradition,[6] the German *Nibelungenlied* (a chief source for Wagner's famous opera, *the Ring*),[7] the Spanish Gaiferos tradition,[8] and many other medieval works such as the Latin *Ruodlieb*,[9] a poem which along with the *Waltharius* prefigures the later medieval romance tradition. The best overview of the *Waltharius'* substantial medieval afterlife is by Surles, who traces all the various strands in detail.[10] Grimm's excellent edition, published in 1838, showed the *Waltharius* to be one of the great primary sources for Germanic legend. His solid scholarship and enthusiasm about Germanic folk history ensured the poem's popularity in German society and academia. Following Grimm, the nineteenth-century novel of Joseph Victor von Scheffel incoporates the poem into a fictional narrative about a tenth-century monk.[11] Von Scheffel even includes his own translation of the *Waltharius* at the end of his novel, along with a lengthy note revealing his debt to its

---

[4] See below under "Other Versions of the Story and the Germanic Source."

[5] See Strecker and Schumann, *Nachträge* (1951), 2–9, on lost and extant manuscripts. See also Glauche, *Schullektüre im Mittelalter* (1970), 94–5.

[6] See Tavernier, "*Waltharius, Carmen de prodicione Guenonis* und Rolandepos" (1914) and Heintze, "Gualter de Hum im Rolandslied" (1986).

[7] Hagen is a character in the *Nibelungenlied* (see esp. 39.2344, ed. Bartsch). See Renoir, "*Nibelungenlied* and *Waltharii Poesis*" (1964). For the *Waltharius'* connections with Germanic bridal quest narratives, see Bornholdt, "The Bridal-Quest Narratives in *Þiðreks saga* and the German *Waltharius* Poem" (2000).

[8] See Millet, *Waltharius—Gaiferos* (1992).

[9] The *Ruodlieb*'s indebtedness to the *Waltharius* is treated in the introduction (xxv–xxxiii) and notes (207–09) of Kratz, *Waltharius and Ruodlieb* (1984).

[10] See Surles, *Roots and Branches* (1987).

[11] See von Scheffel, *Ekkehard. Eine Geschichte aus dem zehnten Jahrhundert* (1855). The text of the original edition is freely available in digital format at http://www.deutschestextarchiv.de/book/show/scheffel_ekkehard_1855 (accessed August 5, 2015).

author.[12] The novel's titular character is Ekkehard, who is depicted reading the poem, since von Scheffel subscribes to Grimm's influential view that Ekkehard I of St. Gall was the author—see the section below on "The Authorship and Dating of the *Waltharius*."[13]

The novel has been often reprinted in German, including a recent illustrated version following the text edited by the medievalist Friedrich Panzer; this edition includes almost three hundred interpretative notes treating its historical sources.[14] Furthermore, von Scheffel's *Ekkehard* has been translated into many other languages, including English, since it was well researched, charming, and quite influential on the development of modern historical fiction.[15] It has even been interpreted in poetry and music and turned into a German television film, a German opera, and an English stage play.[16] The *Waltharius'* inspiration of this influential work of historical fiction is no surprise since our poet has incorporated historical details in a traditional tale that he has richly embellished in his allusive verses.

The *Waltharius* poem itself with its black humor, its conflicted hero, and its strange Hollywood-style happy ending has much to offer a contemporary audience,

---

[12] Scheffel also collaborated in a later critical edition of the poem; see Scheffel and Holder, *Waltharius* (1874).

[13] For more on the novel's recreation of Ekkehard's world, see Wunderlich, "Medieval Images: Joseph Viktor von Scheffel's Novel *Ekkehard* and St. Gall" (1998).

[14] See von Scheffel, *Ekkehard. Eine Geschichte aus dem 10. Jahrhundert* (2000). Other German editions include those edited by Karl Siegen (1925), Friedrich Düsel (1925), Gustav Manz (1929), Friedrich Panzer (1935), Karl Stratil (1938), Joseph Witsch (1944), Hans Reiber (1982), Walter Klemm (1989).

[15] As one reviewer of an English edition put it, "Von Sheffel [sic] was not only the first to put historical facts into the vital form of a novel, but has also proved to be one of the most successful. Neither Dumas nor Scott excels him in animation, and his ready wit, local color, and discernment of character give an ease and familiar interest to 'Ekkehard' that is often lacking in the later and in some respects greater historical novels" (*The Literary World: A Fortnightly Review of Current Literature* [Boston] 27.3 [February 8, 1896]: 46). English translations include those by Sofie Delffs (1872), Herman Hager (1890), Carla Wenckebach (1893), W. H Carruth (1895), Nathan Dole (1895), Helena Easson (1911), and Rudolf Tombo (1965). Other translations include the French by R. Scherdlin (1934) and Gisèle Vallerey (1941), the Danish by Johannes Magnussen (1879), the Norwegian by Ingeborg Konow (1903), the Lithuanian (Vilnius: Žaltvykslė, 1994), and the Estonian by Uno Liivaku (2004).

[16] The 1988 German television film in six episodes was written by Diethard Klante, and the script was published as *Ekkehard: nach dem Roman von Victor von Scheffel* (1990). The German opera in five acts is by Adolf Kröner, Wilhelm Hertz, and Carl Hecker—for a recording, see Jonas Kaufmann, Nyla van Ingen, Susanne Kelling, Jörg Hempel, Mihoko Fujimura, and Peter Falk, *Ekkehard* (Capriccio 60080 [CD], 2000, recorded 1998). It is adapted from the earlier opera by Johann Joseph Abert, *Ekkehard. Oper in fünf Akten* (1878). For an earlier musical interpretation by H. Hofmann, see *The Musical Times* 481 (1883): 162. The English play is by Rebecca Sophia Ross, *The Monk of St. Gall: A Dramatic Adaptation of Scheffel's Ekkehard* (1879). For a poem inspired by the novel, see Adele Elisa von Bredow-Goerne, *Ekkehard* (1868).

as Townsend suggests through his favorable comparison of the poem to modern
action films and thrillers.[17] Yet, outside of Germany, it remains somewhat obscure
compared to classics such as the *Aeneid* and *Beowulf*. Still, it has been growing in
popularity with English-speaking scholars as the bibliography of this edition shows.
Besides the literary-historical importance of the poem, its curious and colorfully
crafted story surely warrants its own respect. Upon careful reading it reveals itself to
be a complex literary creation that presents a highly self-conscious portrait of a toil-
ing, troubled man who sometimes finds himself fighting his own faults. That is the
serious side of the poem—its continual alternation between earnest praise and blame
for a hero who is human, and thus imperfect.

On the other hand, as much recent work has shown, the poet has infused the epic
with playfulness and irony.[18] The ancient rhetorical term "irony" (*ironia*) is most simply defined as "saying one thing while meaning another." Whether the prologue that
appears in some manuscripts of the *Waltharius* was written by the author or only by a
careful reader and editor of the poem, it correctly suggests how to read the work as a
whole: "It requires one to play rather than pray to the Lord. When read through, it
shortens the undistinguished hours of the long-aged day" (ll. 19–20). That is, the poem
should be viewed as a source of educated entertainment. However, a number of scholars have understood the *Waltharius* as presenting a moralizing Christian message,[19] and
they are right to emphasize the poem's Christianity, since, despite the poet's playfulness, the intertextual references to the Bible and Prudentius's *Psychomachia* (a popular
poetic Christian allegory about the soul's battle between the Virtues and Vices) keep
the reader aware of a deeper message that questions the ideals of pagan heroism and
reveals the vices inherent even in its Christian hero.

Thus Edoardo D'Angelo does well to emphasize the hero's twofold nature (*duplic-
ità*) as evidenced by the poet's frequent vacillation between the Christian Walter,
who is pious, wise, and caring, and his pagan heroic alter ego, who is cruel, violent,

---

[17] See Townsend, "Ironic Intertextuality" (1997), esp. 69–71.

[18] On this trend, see Wehrli,"*Waltharius*" (1965); Morgan, "Walter the Wood-Sprite" (1972); Parkes,
"Irony in the *Waltharius*" (1974); Kratz, "*Quid Waltharius*" (1977); idem, *Mocking Epic* (1980); idem,
Waltharius and Ruodlieb (1984); Ziolkowski, Review of *Mocking Epic* (1983); idem, "Fighting Words"
(2001); idem, "Blood, Sweat, and Tears" (2006); and Townsend, "Ironic Intertextuality" (1997). Green,
in *Irony in the Medieval Romance* (1979), cites (21) the explicit use of the term *ironia* in the *Waltharius*
(*per hyroniam*, at l. 235) to show how aware medieval poets were of this narrative technique, which, as
Green shows, became popular and pervasive in medieval romance. Medieval readers of the *Waltharius*
understood the playfulness of such language; recently discovered fragments of a *Waltharius* manuscript
show a medieval German gloss for *hyroniam*, namely, "spot," which can be translated as "sarcasm"—see
Green, "'Waltharius' Fragments from the University of Illinois at Urbana Champaign" (2004).

[19] On this view, see Wolf, "Zum *Waltharius christianus*" (1954–55); Katscher, "*Waltharius*—Dichtung
und Dichter" (1973); Ernst, "Walther—ein christlicher Held?" (1986).

yet terribly fascinating.[20] Though D'Angelo's Freudian analysis and existential interpretation of the poem range far from its historical background, he is absolutely right to see Walter as a hero at war with himself. Indeed, one of the poem's chief models, Prudentius's *Psychomachia*, allegorically illustrates precisely the kind of inner battle which occurs in Walter. Surely too the conflicted hero has numerous parallels in both classical and Christian literature. Does Achilles not kill countless Greek allies and his friend Patroclus through his arrogance? Does Aeneas not abandon Dido and fall prey to rage when he strikes down Turnus? Does Peter not thrice deny Christ? Does Christ himself not call out on the Cross, "My God, My God, why have you forsaken me?"[21] A hero must have faults or his triumphs seem too easy.

THE PLOT OF THE *WALTHARIUS*

The *Waltharius* begins with action-packed pseudo-historical background. After making a scholarly reference to the three divisions of the earth (a classical doctrine much repeated in early medieval literature), our poet tells us that Huns once ruled much of this and that their reign lasted for a thousand years, a bit of grand hyperbole. Then, transported back in time by the narrator, we hear that Attila the Hun, the infamously bloody king, is invading western Europe. The Hunnish monarch swiftly overwhelms his enemies and takes hostages and tribute from three kings: King Gibicho of the Franks, father of Gunther, King Hereric of Burgundy, father of Hildegund, and King Alphere of Aquitaine, father of Walter. The hostages are the noble youth Hagen—because prince Gunther is too young—Hildegund, and Walter. We learn that young Walter and Hildegund have already been betrothed by their parents. Attila raises the hostages in the Hunnish court as his own children, and Hagen and Walter swiftly distinguish themselves in his service. Indeed, Walter apparently becomes Attila's greatest general. Soon we see Hagen secretly slip away and abandon his prominent role in the Hunnish court in order to join Gunther, his rightful king, who has rebelled from the Huns after the death of his father Gibicho. Attila's wife, Ildico, warns her husband that Walter may want to follow his friend Hagen, so he should be married to a Hunnish bride in order to secure his loyalty. In a clever rhetorical ploy, Walter denies the queen's accusation and convinces Attila that a wife would only prevent him from being an effective warrior for his king.

---

[20] See D'Angelo, *Waltharius* (1998), 18–19.

[21] It is interesting that Christ says this at the ninth hour (Mt 27:46, Mk 15:34), for Walter's final battle with Gunther and Hagen also comes to its climax at the ninth hour (see l. 1343), a probable allusion.

Walter leads Attila's army to victory against rebels so as to quell any lingering doubts as to his loyalty. Then, immediately after returning from the battle, he meets privately with Hildegund to plot their escape. There is some tension in the scene, especially for the original Christian audience, because the young man and woman are not married but are meeting in private and making secret plans to run away together. Together they sponsor a lavish feast and get all the Huns drunk. Meanwhile, Hildegund steals the king's treasure according to Walter's instructions. Together Walter and Hildegund flee with the treasure and Walter's war horse, Lion, while the Hunnish court sleeps off their binge drinking. Attila wakes late the next day with a horrible hangover and a worse temper, offering generous rewards to his Hunnish vassals if they can catch Walter, but to no avail. His most talented servant has outsmarted and outsped them while they slept.

Forty days later when they cross the Rhine by ferry, Walter gives the ferryman some fish he had caught along the way, presumably from the Danube or another eastern river. The ferryman takes the strange foreign fish (perhaps Danube sturgeon) to Gunther's royal cook, who prepares them for the king. His curiosity roused by the odd fish, King Gunther summons the ferryman and hears his tale about a hero outfitted for battle, his beautiful female companion, and his horse laden with treasure. Hagen, sitting at Gunther's table, recognizes that the ferryman has described Walter. Then Gunther dismisses Hagen's obvious interest in his friend, whom he hopes to see again, and plots to attack Walter and seize the treasure for himself, since he knows it comes from Attila and deems it payment for what the Huns took from his father Gibicho. Not once does Gunther consider that Walter's father had likewise lost his fortune to Attila, nor, in fact, does the Frankish king show concern for anyone but himself.

Hagen tries but ultimately fails to dissuade the avaricious Gunther, who takes Hagen and eleven other selected warriors to hunt down Walter and his treasure. When they catch up with him, Hagen refuses to fight his friend and stands by while Gunther's eleven other warriors, including Hagen's own nephew Patavrid, fight Walter and die one by one. The next day Hagen, grieved at the loss of his nephew, joins Gunther to fight Walter, and in a climactic battle they each lose a part of their body: Gunther a leg, Hagen an eye (and some teeth), and Walter his right hand. Finally, they quit their strife. Hildegund tends to their wounds, and Walter and Hagen banter away making jests about each other's injuries. After this scene rife with black humor and biblical resonance (Mark 9:42: "And if your hand causes you to sin, cut it off …"), the poet briefly tells of Hagen and Gunther returning to Worms, while Walter and Hildegund arrive home to be married and live happily ever after. Finally, we close with the poet's request for indulgence on account of his young age and then the last line with its pious prayer: "This is the *poésie* of Walter. May Jesus save you!"

OTHER VERSIONS OF THE STORY AND THE GERMANIC SOURCE

The *Waltharius* is the earliest complete version of the Walter saga.[22] Because of its Germanic features and because of the many Germanic poems that deal with the story and its characters, scholars rightly assume that it is based on an older, no longer extant Germanic source. However, it is unclear how much the poet took from his source, and how much he has changed or invented. The two extremes would be that the *Waltharius* is a translation of a Germanic saga, or that it is entirely inspired by classical and late antique works such as the *Aeneid*, the *Thebaid*, and the *Psychomachia*.[23] Neither extreme is really tenable; for, while the poem is packed full of echoes and adaptations of Vergil and others, it also contains a great number of undeniably Germanic features, which Jones discusses in detail.[24] The most commonly held view is that much of the poem is based on a Germanic source while the poet has added and embellished the story in various ways due to his classicizing and Christianizing tendencies. Certainly, the *Waltharius* sometimes agrees with and sometimes diverges from other versions of Walter's story that appear in the *Nibelungenlied* and elsewhere. Even where one finds similarities, it does not necessarily prove a common Germanic source, since direct or indirect knowledge of the plot of *Waltharius* could have influenced later vernacular literature. Moreover, the *Waltharius* cannot be a literal translation of a Germanic saga—not only because of the many differences from other versions of the story, but also because various aspects of its language and style, not to speak of its themes and scenes, obviously reflect the influence of Latin models.

Other sources for Walter's story include the Anglo-Saxon *Waldere* fragments (8th–10th century, thus possibly earlier than *Waltharius*), the Italian *Chronicon Novaliciense* II.7–12 (mid-11th),[25] the Middle High German poems *Walther und Hildegund* (13th century) and the *Nibelungenlied* (ca. 1200), and Polish accounts, including the earliest in the *Chronicon Poloniae* (late 14th century) under the year 1135.[26] Other

---

[22] Perhaps the most detailed, if overly speculative, attempt to reconstruct the original saga is Carroll (1952). There is no scholarly consensus about the nature of our poet's source.

[23] The key proponent of this radical view was Panzer, "*Waltharius* in neuer Beleuchtung" (1948) and *Der Kampf am Wasichenstein* (1948).

[24] See Jones, "The Ethos of the *Waltharius*" (1959).

[25] This manuscript combines selected quotations (sometimes with minor changes) from the poem with a prose story about a certain Waltharius of royal blood who eventually repents and becomes a monk! Thus it clearly confuses the original tale with some later Waltharius, but the confusion may be intentional and certainly tells us about the readership of the poem in the eleventh century.

[26] See Learned, *The Saga of Walther of Aquitaine* (1892), for texts of many of these sources and Magoun/Smyser, *Walther of Aquitaine* (1950), for translations and discussion. See also Strecker and Schumann, *Nachträge* (1951), 20–2; Carroll, "On the Lineage of the Walther Legend" (1953); and Surles, *Roots and Branches* (1987), 17–25.

references to Walter, Hagen, and Hildegund occur in a number of other Middle High German works, including *Biterolf and Dietlieb* and *Rabenschlacht*, and in the thirteenth-century Scandinavian *Þiðrekssaga*. This *Þiðrekssaga* is the only other account to include certain details of the story found in the *Waltharius*, namely, the loss of Høgni's (Hagen's) eye (l. 1393), the banquet and lover's plot (ll. 260–321), and the taking of the gold (ll. 265–7). Yet the absence of these details in other versions does not necessarily imply that they were invented by our poet and adopted in the *Þiðrekssaga*, although this is quite possible. Many of the sources for Walter's story are later (and thus much altered) or fragmentary. For example, although the extant fragments of the Anglo-Saxon *Waldere* do not mention Walter stealing Attila's gold, they suggest such a situation through their allusions to Gunther's refusal of gold rings and to Walter having been the champion of Attila. Where else would the treasure have come from? Similarly, the *Waldere* fragments do not include the end, so we cannot tell whether Hagen's wound (and likewise those of Gunther and Walter) were included.

THE AUTHORSHIP AND DATING OF THE *WALTHARIUS*

After Grimm's edition of 1838 and until the early twentieth century scholars generally attributed the poem to a monk of St. Gall, Ekkehard I (d. 973). It was argued that Ekkehard had composed the poem in his youth (see ll. 1453–5) perhaps for his mentor Geraldus as an exercise in classical verse composition. Furthermore, Geraldus was sometimes believed to have prefixed another 256 hexameter lines, including the twenty-two line prologue—appearing in some of the extant manuscripts of the poem—in which he dedicated the work to Bishop Erchembald of Strasbourg. Finally, an eleventh-century monk, Ekkehard IV of St. Gall, was said to have corrected Germanisms and poetic aberrations in the *Waltharius* for Archbishop Aribo of Mainz.[27] This attribution was based on the *Casus Sancti Galli* 80 by Ekkehard IV:

> Scripsit [Ekkehardus I] et in scolis metrice magistro, vacillanter quidem, quia in affectione non in habitu erat puer, vitam Walthari manu fortis, quam Magontiae positi, Aribone archiepiscopo iubente, pro posse et nosse nostro correximus; barbaries enim et idiomata eius Teutonem adhuc affectantem repente latinum fieri non patiuntur. Unde male docere solent discipulos semimagistri dicentes: Videte, quomodo disertissime coram Teutone aliquo proloqui deceat, et eadem serie in latinum verba vertite. Quae deceptio Ekkehardum in opere illo adhuc puerum fefellit; sed postea non sic.[28]

---

[27] See Surles, *Roots and Branches* (1987), 12–13.
[28] The Latin text is from Haefele, *St. Galler Klostergeschichten* (1980), 168.

[Ekkehard I] also wrote in meter for his teacher during his school years—but quite unsteadily since he was a boy in his disposition, though not in his manner—the life of Waltharius "Strong-Hand," which I personally corrected in Mainz at the bidding of Archbishop Aribo as far as my ability and knowledge permitted. For on account of his barbarisms and idiomatic language a German novice may not swiftly attain skill in Latin. Therefore, second-rate teachers often instruct their students poorly when they say: "See how one should speak most eloquently with a German, and then translate these very words in the same order into Latin." This same false idea brought about Ekkehard's failure in that work, while he was yet a boy, but not so afterwards.

In the late 1930s, some scholars began to oppose the majority belief according to which Ekkehard I was the author. Thus, in 1938 Alfred Wolf gave an influential lecture in Berlin wherein he claimed that Ekkehard IV had referred not to our *Waltharius* but rather to a lost poem about Walter of Aquitaine or a similarly named Christian knight, such as the one in the *Chronicon Novaliciense*.[29] He asserted that the *Waltharius* does not appear to have been corrected and is not the sort of saintly *vita* that the young monk Ekkehard I would have written, since we know he later wrote ecclesiastical sequences and antiphonies. All of these are points of opinion, but Wolf did offer another piece of evidence—a library catalog at Toul (from 1085) which mentions two works about a Walter, one among the "books of the divine poets" (*libri divinorum poetarum*) and another among the "books of the lay poets" (*libri gentilium poetarum*). Wolf's conclusion was that our poem was the work of an unidentified writer of the Carolingian era, that is, the ninth century. Several other scholars followed in Wolf's footsteps. Strecker and Schumann included the *Waltharius* in *Monumenta Germaniae Historica, Poetae*, vol. VI/1 (1951), where it was attributed to an anonymous Carolingian author.

Von den Steinen (1952) followed Wolf in rejecting Ekkehard as author, but—unlike Strecker, who did not believe the prologue to be Carolingian—attributed the *Waltharius* to the Gerald of the prologue rather than to an unknown author, since he believed that the wording of the prologue had to stem from the author of the poem, not from a reviser or dedicator, as others have suggested. The "highest priest" Erkambald to whom Gerald addresses his prologue has been variously identified as Bishop Erkambald of Eichstätt (882–912), Bishop Erkambald of Strasbourg (965–991), Chancellor Erkambald (797–812), or Archchancellor Erkambald (856–865). Von den Steinen chooses the last option, dating the poem to the 850s or 860s, although

---

[29] On Wolf's lecture, see Surles, *Roots and Branches* (1987), 13. For his influential arguments against Ekkehard's authorship, see Wolf, "Der mittellateinische *Waltharius*" (1940–41). The *Chronicon Novaliciense* is an eleventh-century Italian chronicle that blends the story of a later monk with that of our *Waltharius*. See Learned, *The Saga of Walther of Aquitaine* (1892), 44–61, for a Latin text of the pertinent passages and Magoun and Smyser, *Walther of Aquitaine* (1950), 38–40, for a translation.

it seems highly unlikely, if not impossible, that a chancellor could be called "highest priest" (*pontifex summus*), as Schaller has rightly noted.[30]

Bate too argued that the poem was written by the Geraldus of the prologue,[31] and he suggested that the Erkambold to whom Gerald dedicates the work was either the bishop of Eichstätt in Bavaria (884–912) or the bishop of Strasbourg (965–991). From the distribution of manuscripts and from place names mentioned in the poem, Bate infers that Strasbourg is the likely center for the spread of the *Waltharius*. Kratz too wanted a Geraldus to be the author of both prologue and poem.[32] However, like Von den Steinen, he placed Gerald in the ninth rather than the tenth century because of the poem's alleged echoes of Theodulf and Rabanus Maurus (necessarily after 820) as well as references to Chalon as the capital of Burgundy and to Metz as metropolis (historically appropriate before 890)—at lines 52 and 582 respectively.

Langosch (1956, 1979, 1983) and Zeydel (1959) were some of the earliest and most energetic opponents of Wolf's hypothesis. They and others still attribute the work to Ekkehard I of St. Gall, regarding the year 930 as its approximate date of composition. According to Zeydel, some of the circumstances which may bolster Wolf's suggestion include:

1) No manuscript of the poem names Ekkehard I as author.
2) No manuscript has ever been connected with St. Gall.
3) Why is the *Waltharius* so different from other writings by Ekkehard I?
4) Why would Archbishop Aribo want a copy?
5) Ekkehard IV does not seem to have been a good enough Latinist to "correct" the Latin of the *Waltharius*, which is mostly adapted from Vergil and other excellent Latin authors.
6) The phonology of the German names could date from the Carolingian period.
7) Three important manuscripts are connected with a region around Aachen and west of Mainz and Strasbourg, perhaps suggesting an origin there.
8) Leonine rhyme is not as pervasive as one might expect in the tenth century.

---

[30] See Schaller, "Ist der *Waltharius* frühkarolingisch?" (1983), esp. 67–8 n. 24.

[31] See Bate, *Waltharius of Gaeraldus* (1978), 2–5.

[32] See the introduction to his translation and commentary: Kratz, *Waltharius and Ruodlieb* (1984), xii–xv. He says on p. xiv: "I favor a ninth-century date and lean toward accepting Gerald as the author." However, he admits that this is only conjecture, and his notes consistently refer to the author anonymously. His uncertainty is telling since earlier in *Mocking Epic* (1980: 17 n. 2) Kratz had confidently referred to Gerald as the author. D'Angelo, *Waltharius* (1998), also remains uncertain of the author, dating the *Waltharius* between the Carolingian Renaissance (that is, late 8th/early 9th) and 965, the presumed date of the Lorsch manuscript (p. 35), although he inclines toward a date after 840 (p. 14).

On the other hand, Zeydel lists the following points against Wolf:

1) Sievers's metrical analyses show that other works of Ekkehard I correspond in melody and rhythm to the *Waltharius*.[33]
2) The term *vita* in the *Casus Sancti Galli* need not cause suspicion because it is elsewhere used to describe epics.[34]
3) In the *Casus Sancti Galli*, Ekkehard IV uses expressions that indicate a familiarity with the *Waltharius*:
   a. "silvam *latronibus aptam*," cf. "*apta ... statio latronibus*" (*Walt.*, l. 496);
   b. "se duce qui *illorum mores in armis iam nosset*," cf. "namque *ille meos per proelia mores / iam didicit*" (*Walt.*, ll. 568–9);
   c. "Waltharii *manu fortis*," cf. "recidebat *dextera fortis*" (*Walt.*, l. 1381 in the climactic scene where Walter loses his hand, the symbol of his strength).
4) It violates Occam's razor to postulate two lost works, an original Christian *vita* by Ekkehard I and a form emended by Ekkehard IV, while discarding the credible possibility that the *vita* is the extant *Waltharius*.

To the last objection, one might counter that the catalog from Toul does suggest that two works about Walter existed, although they need not have been about the same Walter.

Some scholars have presented evidence to localize the *Waltharius'* composition at the monastery of St. Gall. For example, in response to the striking geographic discourse at lines 1–9, Bernd Schütte shows that geography was studied at St. Gall.[35] According to one library catalog (St. Gallen, *Stiftsbibliothek*, Cod. 728, second half of the ninth century), the monastery owned a copy of Isidore's *Etymologiae*, which divides the world into three parts (at 14.2), just as in *Walt.* 1–3, and a *mappa mundi*, a medieval T-O world map that would have divided the earth clearly into three parts. A long hexameter poem by Walafrid Strabo (abbot of Reichenau near St. Gall), the

---

[33] See Sievers, "Ekkehard oder Geraldus?" (1927). See also the later analyses of Blaschka, "Eine Versuchsreihe zum Waltharius-Problem" (1956) and "Zweite Versuchsreihe zum Waltharius-Problem" (1962). D'Angelo, *Indagini sulla tecnica versificatoria nell' esametro del Waltharius* (1992), provides the fullest and most recent analysis of the poem's metrics, yet he does not think that they solve the issues of date and authorship.

[34] Compare, for example, metrical saints' lives (such as Alcuin's *Vita Sancti Willibrordi* and Candidus's *Vita Aigili Abbatis Monasterii Fuldae*) composed—like the *Waltharius*—in dactylic hexameter, the verse form of classical epic. It should likewise be noted that medieval titles were often not fixed, so that Ekkehard IV might have used whatever phrase happened to come to his mind. According to Strecker and Schumann, *Nachträge* (1950), 24, the manuscripts of the *Waltharius* show the following headings: *Liber Waltharij, Versus [de uualtā], Poesis Geraldi de Gualtario,* and *Hystoria Waltharii Regis.* In the last example, *Regis* was erased in the manuscript. The variety is telling.

[35] See Schütte, "Länder und Völker im *Waltharius*" (1986).

Vita Mammae, begins with a geographical reference. Alf Önnerfors has collected a number of similarities between the style of Walafrid and that of our poet as evidence of an early Carolingian date for the *Waltharius*,[36] although a later poet such as Ekkehard I at the nearby St. Gall might also have used Walafrid's poetry as a model.[37]

In the controversy over dating and authorship, there has been much discussion of parallels between the *Waltharius* and certain Carolingian texts and authors, so I will briefly touch on this topic, although it does more to help us understand the literary qualities of the *Waltharius* than to help us pinpoint its authorship. Sometimes it is suggested that the poem's parallels with Carolingian authors mean that we should date the *Waltharius* to the Carolingian period, but then it is necessary to decide whether the *Waltharius* or the other text came first or whether they might both be independently following another source. As a test case, I here consider the parallels in Walafrid Strabo, which I mentioned above. Some of these are hardly worth considering as evidence for dating or authorship since similar passages exist in earlier sources that might easily serve as a model for the *Waltharius* or Walafrid.[38] Arguably, the most extensive parallel is at line 1098 (*quo me, domne, vocas, quo te sequar?*), which we can compare with Walafrid Strabo's *Vita Mammae* 3.2: *quo Christe vocas, quo te sequar?*[39] The interrogative *quo* is commonly paired with various forms of *sequor* and *voco* in Latin since Plautus, who even shows the same forms we see in the *Waltharius* and in Walafrid, for instance in *Menaechmi*, l. 835 (*quo me vocas*) and in *Curculio*, l. 721 (*quo sequar te*).[40] Within the *Waltharius* itself we could point to a parallel at line 249 (*ad quaecumque vocas, mi domne, sequar studiose*), but this compares even more closely with a passage from the Roman imperial poet Calpurnius (1.13: *quo me cumque vocas, sequar*), as well as with the later *Carmen de Bello Saxonico* 1.50 (*quo nos cunque vocant, sequimur tua iussa*) cited by Strecker and Schumann.[41] Moreover, the combination of the two verbs and the anaphorical *quo* is not

---

[36] See Önnerfors, *Die Verfasserschaft des* Waltharius-*Epos* (1979), 40–1.

[37] For other evidence connecting the *Waltharius* with St. Gall, see Schaller, "Geraldus und St. Gallen (1965).

[38] Examples: for l. 28, *veniens de germine*, cf. Walafrid Strabo, *Vita Mammae* 1.2 (*MGH Poetae* II, 277), but already in Venantius Fortunatus 4.8.11; for l. 392, *decidit in lectum*, cf. Wal. Str., *Visio Wettini* 944 (*MGH Poetae* II, 33), but already in Vulgate, 1 Mc 1:6 and 6:8; for l. 595, *ignoro penitus*, cf. Wal. Str. *Vita Blaithmae* 151 (*MGH Poetae* II, 301), but already a common idiom as the ametrical *penitus ignoro*, e.g. Vulgate 1 Kgs 20:39 and 2 Kgs 15:11; for l. 1431, *cura subintrat*, cf. Wal. Str. *Visio Wettini* 712 (*MGH Poetae* II, 326), but already in the proem to the *epigrammata* of Prosper of Aquitaine.

[39] *MGH Poetae* II, 278.

[40] One could easily cite additional parallels, such as *Aeneid* 9.94 (*quo fata vocas*) and *Aeneid* 9.490 (*quo sequar*).

[41] See Strecker and Schumann, *Nachträge* (1951), 34.

only found in Walafrid and the *Waltharius*; Seneca's *Oedipus*, l. 296 (*quo vocat me patria, quo Phoebus sequar*) provides an earlier model that either could have followed. Clearly there is reason to doubt that the *Waltharius* and Walafrid are directly related here; much less can we easily decide which came first.

I will deal last with two issues of vocabulary. First, there is the rare adjective *ignicremus* from line 322 (*ignicremis ... flammis*), which Walafrid uses in *Vita Mammae* 26.39: *ignicremis flamma fervente caminis*.[42] Whether we judge the *Vita Mammae* or the *Waltharius* to be the first based on subjective evaluations of their poetry—which I believe is impossible to prove—we can hardly say how long there was between the composition of each. We certainly find a parallel in the late tenth-century poet Uffingus, *Vita Liudgeri* 59 (*ignicremos vapores*).[43] Therefore, the parallel in Walafrid would hardly prove a Carolingian date for the *Waltharius*. Finally, there is the rare syncopated form *partus* (for *paratus*) at l. 947 and also in Walafrid 5.2.26: *parti* for *parati*.[44] As with the previous parallel, even if we can agree on whether Walafrid's poem or the *Waltharius* came first, we cannot say how many years passed between their respective dates of composition. Again we find later parallels; this time in the *Gesta Berengarii* 1.171 and 4.28. If these parallels can occur in later texts, then there is no need to date the *Waltharius* to the Carolingian period.

The academic world remains in disagreement over the authorship of the poem. Following Wolf (1940–41), Dronke (1977), Önnerfors (1979, 1988), and Werner (1990) are the main proponents of an early ninth-century Carolingian date.[45] Önnerfors and Werner are the most recent of a line of scholars, including Wilmotte (1918), who argue that the author spoke a Romance language, not Germanic, while not denying the presence of some Germanic features. Others such as Stach (1943), von den Steinen (1952), Hauck (1954), Bate (1978), Kratz (1980, 1984), and Murdoch (1989, 1996) lean toward the later ninth- or early tenth-century date and prefer

---

[42] *MGH Poetae* II, 295.

[43] *MGH Poetae* V, 255.

[44] *MGH Poetae* II, 352. Compare also the Carolingian Ermoldus Nigellus 1.540 (*MGH Poetae* II, 22: *partus*)

[45] Florio, "*Waltharius*, figuras heroicas, restauración literaria, alusiones políticas" (2006), provides an interesting impressionistic discussion of the poem's heroic ethos, which he sees as revealing the revolutionary influence of the Carolingian Renaissance, but he remains uncertain as to the specific date. Albert/Menegaldo/Mora, *Le Chanson de Walther* (2008), 40, note that Werner's claim according to which Ermold wrote the *Waltharius* during the reign of Louis the Pious is undermined by the fact that Ermold's first letter to the king regularly refer to the Vosges as *Wasacus*, although the *Waltharius* always calls it *Vosagus/Vosegus*. However, two early manuscripts—namely, U (fragments first published in 2004) and V—similarly read *Wasagum* at 490, and V again reads *Wasago* at ll. 769 and 946, and *Wasagus* at l. 823. The confusion is probably due to the fact that the most frequently consulted edition, that of Strecker and Schumann, does not regularly cite the spellings of proper names in its apparatus.

Gerald as author, although several different Geralds are suggested. Besides Langosch
(1956) and Zeydel (1959), Ebeling-Koning (1977), Schaller (1983) and Makkay
(1998) incline toward accepting the authorship of Ekkehard I, and Schieffer (1975)
and Schütte (1986) present extensive supporting evidence for the localization at
Ekkehard's St. Gall. Recently Haug (2004)[46] and Albert, Menegaldo, and Mora
(2008)[47] emphasize the continuing lack of any definitive evidence.

In his commentary D'Angelo (1998) remains unsure of the authorship but sets a
firm upper limit of 965 (the presumed date of the Lorsch manuscript, though Bischoff dates it after 965) and a probable lower limit of 840 because of the poem's
three kingdoms (*Francia*, *Burgundia*, and *Aquitania*), which may anachronistically
reflect the tripartite division of the Frankish kingdom after the death of Louis the
Pious. Furthermore, in his earlier exhaustive study of the poem's metrics, D'Angelo
notes many discrepancies between the style of Gerald's prologue and the epic, even
though he does not think that metrical arguments can decisively answer the questions of author and date.[48] Amidst all these competing theories about the *Waltharius'*
origin, Scharrer summarizes the situation with deft alliteration: "Wir wissen nicht
genau, wer wann wo den Waltharius geschrieben hat" ("We do not exactly know by
whom, when, or where the *Waltharius* was written").[49]

Although I find the evidence in favor of Ekkehard I and an early tenth-century
date most convincing, many of the arguments setting the poem in the Carolingian
period are also tempting. Yet corresponding phrases found in the *Waltharius* as
well as in certain Carolingian authors fail clearly to prove or disprove an earlier
date—otherwise we would not continue to see such disagreement over these
issues.[50] We should also note that certain similarities between the prologue and
the poem itself could—though in no way must—indicate that Gerald (whoever he
is) is the author. Throughout the notes, I will remark on points which pertain to

---

[46] See Haug, "Die Zikade im 'Waltharius'" (2004), esp. 43 n. 18.

[47] See Albert/Menegaldo/Mora, *Le Chanson de Walther* (2008), esp. 41.

[48] See D'Angelo, *Indagini sulla tecnica versificatoria nell' esametro del Waltharius* (1992), 166, sets his
findings forth with no definite conclusions, although he tentatively notes: "… i dati emersi da questa
ricerca sembrano aggiungere un altro piccolo sostegno alle argomentazioni di coloro che, del
W[altharius], respingono la datazione protocarolingia e la paternità geraldiana"—"… the information
gained through this research seems to add some additional support to the arguments of those who reject
the early Carolingian dating and Gerald's authorship for the *Waltharius*."

[49] Scharrer, *Waltharii poesis* (2002), 3. See also Murdoch, "Waltharius the Visigoth" (1996), 91, for
his witty overview (reminiscent of Tolkien's comments on *Beowulf*) of the confused state of scholarship
regarding the poem's date and authorship.

[50] The inconclusive philological arguments are examined by Bertini, "Problemi di attribuzione e di
datazione del *Waltharius*" (2000).

the debate about authorship. However, I will always refer to the author anonymously rather than name him Ekkehard or Gerald.

STYLISTIC FEATURES, METER, AND LANGUAGE

The meter of the *Waltharius* is dactylic hexameter. Our poet knew it both from classical models such as Vergil's *Aeneid*, his most common classical model, and from Christian poetry such as Prudentius's Christian epic *Psychomachia* and Alcuin's metrical *Vita Sancti Willibrordi*. The *Psychomachia*, which describes an allegorical battle of the Virtues and Vices, was perhaps the most important model since the *Waltharius* imports its general moral themes as well as specific scenes and lines from Prudentius. Like other classical Latin verse, the dactylic hexameter is quantitative or based on patterns of long and short syllables (long syllables lasting about twice as long as short syllables)—a system often compared to a musical series of half notes and quarter notes. Dactylic hexameter is a non-stanzaic verse form in which each line invariably provides a rhythmic sequence of four feet consisting of either spondees (long long) or dactyls (long short short) with a two-foot dactyl-spondee combination (long short short long long) at line end. The meter is often ungainly in English even once it is changed to an accentual form. Here is a line from Longfellow's *Evangeline*, one of the few successful English examples, with the six feet marked out: "In the A- | cadian | land, on the | shores of the | Basin of | Minas." The verse could be read in a sort of rhythmic chant. It is interesting to note that D'Angelo finds that the *Waltharius'* rhythmic preference for the first four feet (where variation typically occurs) is very similar to the *Aeneid*—this would suggest that our poet had a good ear for normal Vergilian rhythms.[51]

By the time of the *Waltharius*, no one possessed an innate sense of the syllabic quantities in classical Latin; the length of Latin syllables had to be painstakingly memorized and checked against earlier Latin poetry or ancient commentaries. Medieval poets often followed post-Vergilian metrical practices from early or late imperial Latin—for they read these poets too—and so their meter is often unclassical. For example, they were quite comfortable shortening a final long *o* (as in *porrigo* and *persolvo* in ll. 90–1, or *fugiendo* in l. 169), for which they had some classical precedent.[52]

---

[51] See D'Angelo, *Indagini sulla tecnica versificatoria nell' esametro del Waltharius* (1992), 1–8, cf. 113–14. The medieval poem whose scansion in many respects seems most similar to the *Waltharius*, according to D'Angelo's figures (1–28, 96, 152–6, 163 n. 379), is the anonymous *Ecbasis cuiusdam captivi* (from the early 10th to the late 11th century).

[52] For example, there are numerous classical examples of nominative nouns (for instance, *homo*) and first-person verbs (for instance, *scio*) with shortened final *o*. See Stephens, "New Evidence concerning Iambic and Cretic Shortening" (1985).

They were, however, much less selective than their predecessors in their metrical freedoms, but then they had neither the natural ear of the ancient Latin poets nor our modern access to numerous philological compendia and computer databases to reveal the idiosyncratic metrical liberties of individual classical poets. Sometimes medieval poets even introduced metrical innovations that we might call errors.[53] For example, our poet has *spātam* (l. 1367) instead of *spătam*. Yet these deviations from classical scansion sometimes follow examples set by late antique or early medieval predecessors.[54]

There are a number of other stylistic features of the *Waltharius'* verse form that deserve comment.[55] For example, certain common words such as *forte* (as in ll. 23, 35, 39) and *ecce* (ll. 52, 180, 215) are often used for metrical convenience. Furthermore, contemporary Germanic verse forms were based on accentuation and alliteration, and the *Waltharius* shows probable traces of influence from such poetry, for example, *Hunc hominem! pergant primum, qui cuncta requirant* (575) and *frontem festa cum fronde* (209).[56] However, alliteration was not unknown in classical Latin,[57] so one need not always attribute this to Germanic influence. Finally, most of the lines in Gerald's prologue are leonine hexameters, which means that the final syllable of the line rhymes with a word end at the penthemimeral, hepthemimeral, or trithemimeral caesura—compare *genitor ... amator* (prologue, l. 1) and *trinus ... unus* (prologue, l. 3). The body of the poem does not have so many leonine lines, and those examples cited by Althof do not generally show such strong rhymes as one finds in the prologue.[58] This discrepancy is suggestive but need not prove different authors since the same poet may have purposefully used an exceptional style in the prologue.[59]

Christian stylistic elements abound. Verbal and thematic traces of Prudentius's *Psychomachia* often associate Walther and other characters tellingly with Virtues or

---

[53] Althof, *Waltharii Poesis* (1899), 51–2, lists idiosyncratic or erroneous scansions in the poem. See also Strecker and Schumann, *Nachträge* (1950), 16–17, on the poem's metrics.

[54] Althof, *Waltharii Poesis* (1899), 51, lists precedents for some of the poem's metrical oddities.

[55] See Strecker and Schumann, *Nachträge* (1950), 18–19, for the poem's grammatical peculiarities due to archaisms, Germanisms, and medieval usages.

[56] Althof, *Waltharii Poesis* (1899), 54–7, gives various evidence of influence from Germanic alliterative poetry. Following Jacob Grimm, he even notes (54) that some non-alliterative Latin phrases reflect original alliterative Germanic ones. This theory is attractive, and it is probably not coincidental that *Waltharius* of *Aquitania* fighting in in the *Vosges* corresponds to *Walthari* of *Wascôm* in *Wasgenstein* or that "thorny Hagen" (*Hagano spinosus*, l. 1421) is the equivalent of *Hagano haganîn*.

[57] Cf. Vergil, *Aeneid* 1.55: *magno cum murmure montis*, or 1.246: *proruptum et pelago premit*.

[58] See Althof, *Waltharii Poesis* (1899), 53–4.

[59] Compare the section above on "The Authorship and Dating of the Waltharius" for D'Angelo's opinion regarding the metrical differences between the prologue and the poem itself.

Vices; for example, Gunther is strongly modeled after Pride (ll. 514–15). Elsewhere there are adaptations from other Christian poets such as Venantius (l. 384) and frequent borrowings from the Vulgate such as the wounds received by the three final combatants, which allude to Ex 21:24 and Mk 9:42–7, and phrases such as "root of all evils" (*cunctorum fibra malorum*, l. 858; cf. 1 Tm 6:10). Certain actions by the hero remind us that he is Christian, if no less a sinner—for example, his abstinence from intercourse outside of marriage (ll. 426–7), his prayer for fallen foes (ll. 1160–7), and his making the sign of the cross over his wine (l. 225). Finally, Walter's friend Hagen gives a sort of sermon against avarice (ll. 855–75), and this could be seen as a Christian moral for the whole poem.

As Vergil was the poet's chief model, we find many Vergilian phrases and whole or near whole lines (for instance, ll. 182–3, 328, 383) inserted or adapted to fit the occasion. Much of these may be seen as convenience borrowings, but the poet surely knew the context of the original lines, so intentional allusions are always a possibility. I have noted many Vergilian adaptations in the notes to the translation. Heavy use of classical models means that the poem is full of Roman deities, Mars (l. 731) and Orcus (l. 913), for example; but here the poet's practice is typical of post-classical Christian poets who treat pagan gods as personified ideas, a poetic license already well-established in classical times through the poetic device of metonymy.

The language of the *Waltharius* is for the most part classical Latin modeled on Vergil and other ancient Roman poets, but this is peppered with medieval idioms such as *Gratia Vestra* ("Your Grace," l. 306), archaic forms gleaned from grammatical treatises such as *iteri* ("journee," l. 331), select Greek vocabulary such as *sophista* (ll. 104, 605),[60] and Germanic-derived phrases such as *vitam … et artus* ("life and limb," l 603) and *sic sic* (cf. Anglo-Saxon *swa swa*, l. 1404).[61] There are even a handful of Germanic words, *nappa* (l. 308), *wantis* (l. 1426), and *wah* (l. 1429). Although poetry is always loose with verb tenses, it also reasonable to see some of the tense

---

[60] The full list of terms that are Greek or derived from the Greek includes *agon* (l. 1025), *athleta* (962, 1046, 1411), *Bachus* (301), *baratrum* (1101), *bissus* (293, cf. 300), *c(h)alibs* (905, 975), *crateres* (301), *ebdomada* (274), *eulogium* (1263), *gausape* (300), *glaucoma* (537), *girus* (792, 965), *girare* (715, 932, 1169), *heremus* (1137), *heros* (292, 317), *hyronia* (235), *licisca* (404, 1231), *migma* (299), *mysteria* (247), *naulum* (434), *phalanx* (536), *fantasma* (769), *Phoebus* (277), *poesis* (1456), *satrapa* (43, 136, 170), *scandalum* (1256), *sophari* (1266), *sophista* (104, 605), *spata* (1367, cf. 1390), *sp(h)era* (1152), *thalamus* (546, 1363), *trophaeum* (1385), *tyrannus* (177, 408, 886, 1082, 1384), and the name *Eleuthir* (1008). See also the notes on *Ospirin* (123) and *choris* (890). Although some terms—such as *adelphus*, *scandalum*, and *mysteria*—are common enough in medieval Latin, others in the poem are not, and the poet surely used them for their literary and poetic feel, as educated English authors might use French or German.

[61] Althof, *Waltharii Poesis* (1899), compares *vitam … et artus* to *lîp unde leben* and lists other Germanic-derived phrases (49–50, 54).

variation in the *Waltharius* as influenced by Germanisms.[62] The combination of these diverse linguistic features along with the numerous allusions to such a broad array of literary traditions makes it incredibly complex to divine the poet's intention at any one place, yet this very complexity is part of what makes the poem so entertaining and rewarding.

THE TRANSLATION AND COMMENTARY

The previous English translations of the *Waltharius* include Magoun and Smyser, Kratz, and Murdoch.[63] None of these is currently in print. The earliest of these by Magoun and Smyser is a relatively rough prose version with many explanations informally given in the text by means of parentheses. Both Kratz and Murdoch produced annotated verse translations which in many ways improved upon the English interpretation of the text. Kratz turned the Latin dactylic hexameter into a regular twelve-syllable iambic line, a length that usually allows him to translate line for line. Murdoch on the other hand used a much freer iambic verse form with varying line lengths.

In addition to earlier English translations, my translation has been guided by the editions and commentaries of Althof (1899, 1905), Langosch (1956), Bate (1978), Wieland (1986), and D'Angelo (1998), as well as by numerous welcome suggestions gleaned from those scholars cited in the bibliography. My translation and commentary are based upon my original Latin text and *apparatus criticus*, the first since Strecker and Schumann (1951).

As any translator knows, a translation is an interpretation, and any interpretation will privilege some aspects of a text over others. This edition provides a new prose translation. A poetic translation gains most when it stands as a poem on its own merit, whereas the virtue of a prose translation is in its freedom to concentrate on reproducing the exact sense and linguistic texture of the original. Where the poet uses archaic Latin forms, I have intentionally used older English spellings and added notes if the meaning might be obscured.[64] Where he employs *recherché* Greek words in place of

---

[62] See Althof, *Waltharii Poesis* (1899), 50, for a full list of the odd tenses in the poem. For example, the poet uses pluperfect for perfect (for example, *coeperat* and *fuerat*, ll. 84–5, which I have translated as simple past) or present for future (for example, *fraudo*, l. 979, and *venor*, l. 1436, which I have translated as future).

[63] See Magoun and Smyser, *Walther of Aquitaine* (1950); Kratz, *Waltharius and Ruodlieb* (1984); Murdoch, *Walthari* (1989). Additionally, selected passages are translated by Peter Godman, *Poetry of the Carolingian Renaissance* (1985), 72.

[64] For example, "mann" for the archaic *homonem* (l. 578).

the normal Latin, I translate with French and provide a note in order to explain to the reader.[65] These Greek-derived words are typically rare or poetical alternatives to simple Latin words, like *tyrannus* ("tyrant/king") for *rex*, *spatha* ("sword") for *gladius*, etc. Likewise, when I can, I hint at biblical allusions by imitating the well-known King James translation.[66] With allusions to Vergil and Prudentius, I have only been able to mimic a lofty, epic style, not the exact words, since no one translation of these poets would be recognized by my readers. The Latin sometimes sounds odd and even discordant on account of the diverse literary and linguistic influences pouring into the narrative, and I do not hide this in my translation. Often this happens when the poet is making multiple allusions in one place, a technique that has been called a "conflation," "multiple reference," or "window reference" by classical scholars.[67] Such references show off the poet's connection to his tradition and advertise how he reads his predecessors and how they read him; or, in other words, the complex of allusions suggest varying ways in which the author and readers may interpret the text.[68] I smooth out the jarring juxtapositions that result from these complex allusions only when they would unduly confuse the reader; and, if I feel the need to do so, I add a footnote to explain what is going on in the Latin.[69] While some readers may wish that I had smoothed over the strangeness of the language, I strongly believe that this helps one to appreciate the texture or feel of the poem in the original Latin.

No matter how much care a translator takes, there is no way to reproduce all the features of the original text, but I comment on notable linguistic and stylistic details that I fail to indicate in the translation. The notes accompanying this translation are the fullest in any English edition, and my emphasis has been on the literary interpretation of the poem, its language and style, especially regarding the poet's allusions to his Latin poetic models, such as Vergil and Prudentius. In addition, I have made

---

[65] For example, "chien-loup" for *liciscae* (l. 403).

[66] For example, "Root of All Evils" (cf. 1 Tm 6:10) for *cunctorum fibra malorum* (l. 858), and "They do not fear to rush to meet a <u>filthy</u> death in their hope for <u>lucre</u>" (cf. 1 Tm 3:8: "filthy lucre") for *non trepidant mortem pro <u>lucro</u> incurrere <u>turpem</u>* (l. 863).

[67] See Thomas, "Virgil's *Georgics* and the Art of Reference" (1986), at 193–8, and Nelis, *Vergil's Aeneid and the Argonautica of Apollonius Rhodius* (2001), 1–21, esp. 5. Thomas notes that multiple references in Vergil "fuse, subsume, and renovate the traditions which he inherited" and that they have "an added motive of sheer demonstration of virtuousity" (195). Nelis writes that such allusions allow the poet to "look through" one model into another (5).

[68] Consider this passage, which sounds needlessly redundant (ll. 450–1): "and he seemed ready for battle, with all his limbs prepared." As my note on these lines indicates, the poet has combined Vergil with Servius's Vergilian commentary in a way that shows two different ways of stating the same thing—poetic variation mixed with double allusion.

[69] Consider the note at ll. 460–1 for "whenever the steed tossed his high neck and was eager to paw the air with his hooves."

reference to relevant historical details, to issues that bear on the question of authorship and date, and to Germanic analogues whenever this has seemed appropriate to
the understanding of the work and its somewhat ambiguous place in history.

ON THE MANUSCRIPT HISTORY AND THE LATIN TEXT

Unlike many medieval Latin texts, the *Waltharius* has been issued in numerous
good critical editions, starting with that of Grimm and Schmeller (1838). The editions of Peiper (1873) and of Strecker and Schumann (1951) are two that stand out
as particularly important in the tradition, and I have consulted both throughout.
I note in the apparatus whenever I am departing from the edition of the poem by
Strecker and Schumann or from Strecker's edition of the prologue, which was published separately.[70] Both Peiper and Strecker provide detailed descriptions of the
manuscript history and earlier editions to which I direct the reader. None of the
most recent editions of the poem by Vogt-Spira, D'Angelo, Florio, and Albert, Menegaldo, and Mora have supplied a thorough critical text; thus, this new edition is
warranted if only to assess the importance of the several fragments discovered since
the edition of Strecker and Schumann.

Besides meticulously comparing citations from the previous critical editions of
Strecker and Schumann, of Althof, and of Peiper, I have personally collated the manuscript Vienna, *Österreichische Nationalbibliothek*, 289, fols. 103a–130b (V), as well as
several sets of fragments. The first set of fragments is from the *Universitätsbibliothek*
at Munich, oct. cod. ms. 479 (M); these fragments, which were not available to Peiper, were part of the group that Strecker included under the designation I. Whenever
the apparatus refers to a reading that I have personally affirmed, I cite the manuscript
as M instead of I to denote my own reading of these fragments. The second set of
fragments that I have collated were not available to Strecker, since they were only
published in 2004. They were found in the binding of an incunable at the University
of Illinois at Urbana-Champaign, and they too belong to the larger group of fragments
that Strecker together designated as I, since they all derive from the same manuscript.[71]
Again, in cases where the apparatus refers to a reading that I have personally affirmed,
I cite the manuscript as U instead of I. The third and fourth sets that I examined are
the late tenth-century fragments at Hamburg, *Staats- und Universitätsbibliothek*,

---

[70] See Strecker, *Die Ottonenzeit* (1937), 405–08.
[71] On the fragments from Urbana-Champaign, see the original publication by Green, "*Waltharius*
Fragments" (2004), which confirms the identification with I, and the later article by Vollmann, "Marginalglossen zu den *Waltharius*-Fragmenten aus Urbana (2006).

cod. 17 *in scrinio*, frag. 1 (H), which likely represents an early manuscript of the gamma family, and the fragments at Leipzig, *Universitätsbibliothek*, Ms. 1589 (L), which almost certainly derive from V.

There are two major families of manuscripts recognized by both Peiper and Strecker, the gamma family (γ), which includes B, P, and T, and the alpha family (α), which includes K and S. The manuscript V most often shares readings with α but occasionally with γ. The gamma family contains the prologue by Geraldus while K, S, and V do not. The fragmentary manuscript that Strecker designated I (which I cite as I or, when I have affirmed the readings personally, as M or U) also contains the prologue and is important because it is one of the earliest manuscripts and because its readings, even more than with V, tend to show an independence from the alpha and gamma families. Other manuscript evidence includes the fragments at Hamburg (H) and the lost fragments from Engelberg (E). The excerpts of the *Waltharius* cited from the *Chronicon Novaliciense* (N) are from an eleventh-century manuscript, but have dubious authority since its text of the poem was altered to fit the larger story of the chronicle.

The signs α or γ will indicate when all the manuscripts of the appropriate family agree. The sign ω will indicate that all manuscripts agree, while Cet. (*ceteri*) will indicate the reading of all other manuscripts besides those specifically cited. The readings of Strecker (or Strecker and Schumann) and Peiper will be indicated by Str. and Peip. Other scholars will be cited by last name.

Alpha Family (Strecker's Southern Group)

K = Karlsruhe, *Badische Landesbibliothek*, Cod. Rastatt 24 (*olim* Durlach 103), fols. 224r–248v. Early to mid-twelfth century, probably from Hirsau.
S = Stuttgart, *Württembergische Landesbibliothek*, MS. Theol. et Phil. oct. 41, fols. 46r–63v. Thirteenth century, from St. Emmeram, Regensburg.[72]

Gamma Family (Strecker's Northwestern and Western Group)

B = Brussels, *Bibliothèque royale de Belgique*, 5380–84, fols. 92r–116v. Mid-eleventh century, from Gembloux.[73] Like manuscript V, the text of B seems to have been much emended by someone seeking to fix both metrical and linguistic errors, especially in comparison to P and T.

---

[72] See Berschin, "*Waltharius*-Glossen" (2008).
[73] See Babcock, "Sigebert of Gembloux and the *Waltharius*" (1986).

P = Paris, *Bibliothèque nationale de France*, lat. 8488A. Eleventh century, from Fleury.[74]

T = Trier, *Stadtbibliothek*, 2002/92 4°, fols. 108v–129r. Early fifteenth century, from Mettlach.

Other Manuscripts

V = Vienna, *Österreichische Nationalbibliothek*, Cod. 289, fols. 103v–130v. Early twelfth century, from Salzburg. This is one of the older manuscripts. It shares readings with both families but seems more closely related to the alpha family. Although it is early and may be independent of both major families, it contains many conjectures, even entire inserted and omitted lines, which attempt to improve the poem but obscure the original reading.

I = Strecker assigned the designation I to a fragmentary manuscript. For, multiple sets of fragments removed from bindings were found over time starting in 1889, and Strecker was able to prove by paleographic analysis that they all derived from the same manuscript. The extant fragments include MSS. Berlin, *Staatsbibliothek*, fragm. 61 (16 strips); Innsbruck, *Universitätsbibliothek und Landesbibliothek*, fragm. 89 and 90 (22 strips); Munich, *Universitätsbibliothek*, oct. cod. ms. 479 (13 strips); and University of Illinois at Urbana-Champaign, University Library, Pre-1650 MS 0148 (8 strips). The fragments date to the second third of the eleventh century.[75] The Latin text is thus one of the oldest, comprising Latin and Germanic glosses of the twelfth century.[76] Like the gamma family, it contained the prologue by Geraldus. At l. 145 it shares *instigandi*, possibly the original reading, only with P, the oldest manuscript of the gamma family; at l. 319 it agrees with the alpha family and with V in producing the correct reading, where the gamma family errs. Strecker suggests in his apparatus that it probably included l. 661, which is omitted in the alpha family and in V. I believe that it also contained l. 257, which is omitted in the alpha family, E, and V. I infer this from the correlation of ll. 234–39 and 265–70 on the two sides of one fragment described by Green—indicating a 31-line page including line 257.[77] Although this manuscript shows no tendency

---

[74] See Pellegrin, "Membra disiecta Floriacensia" (1959).

[75] See Daniel, *Die lateinischen mittelalterlichen Handschriften* (1989), 185.

[76] On the Old High German glosses in this manuscript, see Bergmann and Stricker, *Katalog der althochdeutschen und altsächsischen Glossenhandschriften* (2005), 201–02 (# 35, 288, 712).

[77] See Green, "*Waltharius* Fragments" (2004), 74 n. 5, for evidence of a 31-line page in this part of the manuscript.

to V's rampant conjectures, it does share a number of readings with V alone (*seria* at l. 147, *ambos* at l. 750, *falsum* at l. 1311), which indicates a close connection to V's source.

M = Munich, *Universitätsbibliothek*, oct. cod. ms. 479. As explained above, this is part of the fragmentary manuscript I. In the apparatus, I use M to distinguish my own reading of the Munich fragments, which I personally examined, from Strecker's collation of I.

U = Urbana-Champaign, University of Illinois at Urbana-Champaign Library, Pre-1650 MS 0148. These fragments, first published in 2004, add about 130 lines or nearly ten percent to the extant portion of the fragmentary manuscript designated as I. In the apparatus, I use U for these fragments, which I have examined from high-quality digital photographs.

N = Turin, *Archivio di Stato*, Arch. Reg. Novalic. Mazzo 2, n. 20 (*Chronicon Novaliciense*). This is a North Italian chronicle that strangely inserts segments of the *Waltharius* into its historiographic narrative about a much later Walter. Although it is one of the earliest textual witnesses, its version of the included portions of the *Waltharius* is highly idiosyncratic because the author was rather creative in altering the text to fit the chronicle. Therefore, it is of ambiguous worth as an independent witness.

H = Hamburg, *Staats- und Universitätsbibliothek*, Cod. 17 in scrinio, 1. Fragment. Last quarter of the tenth century, from Lorsch.[78] Strecker dates this fragmentary manuscript with two pages (ll. 316–39 and 388–411) to the thirteenth century, but it is elsewhere dated to the late tenth century. Strecker includes it in his Northwestern and Western group (the gamma family), but it is not clear whether the original manuscript included the prologue of Geraldus as do B, P, and T. It is from Lorsch, which interestingly puts its origin geographically closer to the manuscripts of the alpha family. However, some shared errors clearly demonstrate that it has a connection with the gamma family: *videres* (l. 319), *uteri* (l. 331), *subreptus* (l. 396). I have personally examined digital reproductions of these fragments.

L = Leipzig, *Universitätsbibliothek*, Ms. 1589. Early thirteenth century. These two folios (with ll. 143–213 and 351–414) apparently come from a late copy of V, as Strecker suggests, since L follows many of V's characteristic revisions (for example at ll. 388 and 391), but introduces careless errors (for instance at ll. 361 and 375). Thus it is not very valuable for establishing the original text of the poem, although it attests to continued interest in the *Waltharius*. I have examined digital reproductions of these fragments.

---

[78] For the tenth-century date and the attribution to Lorsch, see Vollmann, "Waltharius" (2006).

E = The fragmentary Engelberg manuscript contained thirteen leaves dated to the eleventh century by Pertz and the thirteenth by Grimm and Peiper. Its readings show a close relationship to K, S, and V. It has been lost and so is cited from Grimm, but from the often poor quality of its readings I would agree with Peiper that we need not complain about its loss.

Bibliography

Abert, Johann Joseph, *Ekkehard. Oper in fünf Akten. Nach J. V. v. Scheffel's gleichnamigem Roman frei bearbeitet* (first performed, Berlin: Hofoper, 1878).

Albert, Sophie, Silvère Menegaldo, and Francine Mora, *Le Chanson de Walther (Waltharii poesis)* (Grenoble: Ellug, 2008).

Althof, Hermann (ed.), *Waltharii Poesis. Das Waltharilied Ekkehardes I. von St. Gallen*, vol. 1 (Leipzig: Dieterich, 1899); vol. 2 (Leipzig: Dieterich, 1905).

—, *Das Waltharilied, ein Heldensang aus dem zehnten Jahrhundert*, 2nd ed. (Leipzig: Göschen, 1907; reprinted, Berlin and Leipzig: de Gruyter, 1925).

Anderson, Earl R., "Flyting in *The Battle of Maldon*," *Neuphilologische Mitteilungen* 71.2 (1970): 197–202.

Autenrieth, Johanne, and Franz Brunhölzl (ed.), *Festschrift Bernhard Bischoff zu seinem 65. Geburtstag* (Stuttgart: Hiersemann, 1971).

Babcock, Robert, "Sigebert of Gembloux and the *Waltharius*," *Mittellateinisches Jahrbuch* 21 (1986): 101–05.

Bachrach, Bernard S., *Early Carolingian Warfare: Prelude to Empire* (Philadelphia: University of Pennsylvania Press, 2001).

Barwick, Karl, and Friedmar Kühnert (ed.), *Flavii Sosipatri Charisii Artis grammaticae libri V* (Leipzig: Teubner, 1964).

Bate, A. Keith, *Waltharius of Gaeraldus* (Reading: University of Reading Press, 1978).

Baumbach, Manuel, and Silvio Bär (ed.), *Brill's Companion to Greek and Latin Epyllion and Its Reception* (Boston: Brill, 2012).

Behr, Francesca D'Alessandro, "A Narratological Repraisal of Apostrophe in Virgil's *Aeneid*," *Arethusa* 38.2 (2005): 189–221.

Bennett, Matthew, Jim Bradbury, Kelly DeVries, Iain Dickie, and Phyllis Jestice (ed.), *Fighting Techniques of the Medieval World, AD 500–AD 1500: Equipment, Combat Skills, and Tactics* (New York: St. Martin's Press, 2006).

Bergmann, Rolf, and Stephanie Stricker, *Katalog der althochdeutschen und altsächsischen Glossenhandschriften*, vol. 1 (Berlin: de Gruyter, 2005).

Berschin, Walter, "*Waltharius*-Glossen," *Journal of Medieval Latin* 18 (2008): 346–56.

Bertini, Ferrucio, "Problemi di attribuzione e di datazione del *Waltharius*," *Filologia Mediolatina* 6–7 (2000): 63–77.

Bisanti, Armando, "Il *Waltharius* fra tradizioni classiche e suggestioni germaniche," *Pan* 20 (2002): 175–204.

Blaschka, Anton, "Eine Versuchsreihe zum Waltharius-Problem," *Wissenschaftliche Zeitschrift der Martin-Luther-Universität Halle-Wittenberg* 5 (1956): 413–19.

—. "Zweite Versuchsreihe zum Waltharius-Problem," *Wissenschaftliche Zeitschrift der Martin-Luther-Universität Halle-Wittenberg* 11 (1962): 1539–42.

Bornholdt, Claudia, "The Bridal-Quest Narratives in *Þiðreks* Saga and the German *Waltharius* Poem as an Extension of the Rhenish Bridal-Quest Tradition," in *Old Norse Myths, Literature and Society, Proceedings of the 11th International Saga Conference, 2–7 July 2000*, ed. Geraldine Barnes and Margaret Clunies Ross (Sydney: Centre for Medieval Studies, University of Sydney, 2000), 44–52.

Brady, Caroline, Review of Walther of Aquitaine, *Materials for the Study of His Legend*, by F. P. Magoun and H. M. Smyser, *Speculum* 26 (1951): 397–401.

Bredow-Goerne, Adele Elisa Gräfin von, *Ekkehard. Nach dem Roman von Josef Victor Scheffel* (Berlin: Kortkampf, 1868).

Brinkmann, Hennig. "Ekkehards *Waltharius* als Kunstwerk," *Zeitschrift für deutsche Bildung* 4 (1928): 625–36.

Brunhölzl, Franz, *Was ist der Waltharius?* (Munich: Wilhelm Fink, 1988).

Carlson, Signe M., "The Monsters of *Beowulf*: Creations of Literary Scholars," *Journal of American Folklore* 80.318 (1967): 357–64.

Carroll, B. H., "An Essay on the Walther Legend," *Florida State University Studies* 5 (1952): 123–79.

—. "On the Lineage of the Walther Legend," *Germanic Review* 28 (1953): 34–41.

Classen, Carl Joachim, "Beobachtungen zum *Waltharius*," *Mittellateinisches Jahrbuch* 21 (1986): 75–8.

Coenen, Frederic E., Werner P. Friederich, George S. Lane, and Ralph P. Rosenberg (ed.), *Middle Ages—Reformation—Volkskunde: Festschrift for John G. Kunstmann* (Chapel Hill, N.C.: University of North Carolina Press, 1959).

Coupland, Simon. "Carolingian Arms and Armor in the Ninth Century," *Viator* 21 (1990): 29–50.

Curtius, Ernst R., *European Literature and the Latin Middle Ages*, trans. Willard R. Trask (New York: Pantheon Books, 1953; reprinted, Princeton: Princeton University Press, 1973).

D'Angelo, Edoardo, *Indagini sulla tecnica versificatoria nell' esametro del Waltharius* (Catania: Centro di studi sull'antico cristianesimo, 1992.

—, *Waltharius: epica e saga tra Virgilio e i Nibelunghi* (Milan: Luni, 1998).

Daniel, Natalia, *Die lateinischen mittelalterlichen Handschriften der Universitätsbibliothek München. Die Handschriften aus der Oktavreihe* (Wiesbaden: Harrassowitz, 1989).

—, "La 'Pharsalia' nell' epica latina medievale," in *Interpretare Lucano. Miscellanea di studi*, ed. Paolo Espositio and Luciano Nicastri (Naples: Arte tipographica, 1999), 389–53.

Dickins, Bruce, *Runic and Heroic Poems of the Old Teutonic Peoples* (Cambridge: Cambridge University Press, 1915).

Drew, Katherine Fischer, *The Laws of the Salian Franks* (Philadelphia: University of Pennsylvania Press, 1991).

Dronke, Peter, "Functions of Borrowing in Medieval Latin Verse," in *Classical Influences on European Culture, AD 500–1500*, ed. Robert Bolgar (Cambridge: Cambridge University Press, 1971), 159–65.

—, and Ursula Dronke, *Barbara et antiquissima carmina* (Barcelona: Universidad Autónoma de Barcelona, 1977).

Dümmler, Ernst (ed.) *Poetae Latini Aevi Carolini*, Monumenta Germaniae Historica, Poetae Latini Medii Aevi 1 (Berlin: Weidmann, 1881).

Dumville, David, "Ekiurid's *Celtica lingua*: An Ethnological Difficulty in *Waltharius*," *Cambridge Medieval Celtic Studies* 6 (1983): 87–93.

Ebeling-Koning, Blanche T., *Style and Structure in Ekkehard's Waltharius* (Ph.D. diss., Columbia University, 1977).

Eis, Gerhard, "Waltharius-Probleme," in *Britannica. Festschrift für Hermann M. Flasdieck*, ed. Wolfgang Iser and Hans Schabram (Heidelberg: Winter, 1960), 96–112.

Ernst, Ursula, "Walther—ein christlicher Held?," *Mittelateinisches Jahrbuch* 21 (1986): 79–83.

Fickermann, Norbert, "Zum Verfasserproblem des *Waltharius*," *Beiträge zur Geschichte der deutschen Sprache und Literatur* 81 (1959): 267–73.

Florio, Ruben, *Waltharius* (Madrid: Bellaterra, Universitat Autònoma de Barcelona, 2002).

—, "*Waltharius*, figuras heroicas, restauración literaria, alusiones políticas," *Maia* 58.2 (2006): 207–29.

—, "Literatura e historia en el *Waltharius*," *Faventia* 31.1/2 (2009): 111–28.

Gäbe, Sabine, "Gefolgschaft und Blutrache im *Waltharius*," *Mittellateinisches Jahrbuch* 21 (1986): 91–4.

Genzmer, Felix, "Wie der *Waltharius* entstanden ist," *Germanisch-Romanische Monatsschrift* 35 (1954): 161–78.

Gillespie, George, "The Significance of Personal Names in German Heroic Poetry," in *Medieval German Studies: Presented to Frederick Norman by His Students, Colleagues and Friends on the Occasion of His Retirement* (London: Institute of Germanic Studies, University of London, 1965), 16–21.

Glauche, Günter, *Schullektüre im Mittelalter. Entstehung und Wandlungen des Lektürekanons bis 1200 nach den Quellen dargestellt* (Munich: Arbeo-Gesellschaft, 1970).

Godman, Peter, *Poetry of the Carolingian Renaissance* (London: Duckworth, 1985).

Gordon, Colin Douglas, *The Age of Attila: Fifth-Century Byzantium and the Barbarians* (Ann Arbor, Mich.: University of Michigan, 1960).

Graus, František, "Troja und trojanische Herkunftssage im Mittelalter," in *Kontinu-ität und Transformation der Antike im Mittelalter*, ed.Willi Erzgraber (Sigmarin-gen: Thorbecke, 1989), 25–43.

Green, Dennis Howard, *Irony in the Medieval Romance* (Cambridge: Cambridge University Press, 1979).

Green, Jonathan, "*Waltharius* Fragments from the University of Illinois at Urbana Champaign," *Zeitschrift für deutsches Altertum und deutsche Literatur* 133.1 (2004): 61–74.

Grégoire, Henri, "La patrie des *Nibelungen*," *Byzantion* 9 (1934): 1–39.

—. "Le *Waltharius* et Strasbourg," *Bulletin de la Faculté des Lettres de Strasbourg* 14 (1936): 201–13.

Grimm, Jacob, *Deutsche Rechtsalterthümer*, 4th ed. (Leipzig: Dieterich, 1899).

—, and Johann Andreas Schmeller, *Lateinische Gedichte des X. und XI. Jahrhunderts* (Göttingen: Dieterich, 1838).

Haefele, Hans, "Vita Waltharii manufortis," in *Festschrift Bernhard Bischoff zu seinem 65. Geburtstag*, ed. Johanne Autenrieth and Franz Brunhölzl (Stuttgart: Hierse-mann, 1971), 260–76.

—, *St. Galler Klostergeschichten* (Darmstadt: Wissenschaftliche Buchgesellschaft, 1980).

—, "Geraldus-Lektüre," *Deutsches Archiv für Erforschung des Mittelalters* 54 (1998): 1–22.

Harms, Wolfgang, *Der Kampf mit Freund oder Verwandten in der deutschen Literatur bis um 1300* (Munich: Fink, 1963).

Hauck, Karl, "Das Walthariusepos des Bruders Gerald von Eichstätt," *Germanisch-Romanische Monatsschrift* 35 (1954): 1–27; reprinted in *Waltharius und Walther-sage. Eine Dokumentation der Forschung*, ed. Emil Ernst Ploss (Hildesheim: Olms, 1969), 135–61.

Haug, Arthur, "Die Zikade im 'Waltharius'—Bemerkungen zum Autor und zum Publikum," *Mittellateinisches Jahrbuch* 39 (2004): 31–43.

Halama, Alta Cools, "Flytes of Fancy: Boasting and Boasters from Beowulf to Gang-sta Rap," *Proceedings of the Illinois Medieval Association* 13 (1996): 81–96.

Heintze, Michael. "Gualter de Hum im Rolandslied," *Mittellateinisches Jahrbuch* 21 (1986): 95–100.

Jones, Charles W., *Medieval Literature in Translation* (New York: McKay, 1959), 192–208.

Jones, George F., "The Ethos of the *Waltharius*," in *Middle Ages—Reformation—Volkskunde. Festschrift for John G. Kunstmann*, ed. Frederic E. Coenen et al. (Chapel Hill, N.C.: University of North Carolina Press, 1959), 1–20.

Katscher, Rosemarie, "*Waltharius*—Dichtung und Dichter," *Mittellateinisches Jahr-buch* 9 (1973): 48–120.

Keil, Heinrich (ed.), *Grammatici latini*, vol. 7: *Scriptores de orthographia* (Leipzig: Teubner, 1880).

—, and Martin Hertz (ed.), *Grammatici latini*, vol. 2: *Prisciani Institutionum Grammaticarum libri I–XII* (Leipzig: Teubner, 1855).

Kershaw, Nora, *Stories and Ballads from the Far Past* (Cambridge: Cambridge University Press, 1921).

Kiefer, Albert, "*Waltharii poesis*, nouvelles recherches: les armes des héros," *L'Outre-Forêt: Revue du Cercle d'Histoire et d'Archéologie de l'Alsace du Nord* 113 (2001): 33–44.

—, "*Waltharii poesis*: les fragments Waldere," *L'Outre-Forêt: Revue du Cercle d'Histoire et d'Archéologie de l'Alsace du Nord* 115 (2001): 57–61.

—, "*Waltharii poesis*: Hagen von Tronje," *L'Outre-Forêt: Revue du Cercle d'Histoire et d'Archéologie de l'Alsace du Nord* 116 (2001): 13–15.

—, "*Waltharii poesis*: débuts d'un sentiment national dans la dépréciation de l'autre," *L'Outre-Forêt: Revue du Cercle d'Histoire et d'Archéologie de l'Alsace du Nord* 116 (2001): 15–16.

Klante, Diethard, *Ekkehard: nach dem Roman von Victor von Scheffel. Ein Film* (Bremen: Radio Bremen, 1990).2

Klopsch, Paul, "Der Waltharius," *Der altsprachliche Unterricht* 6 (1963): 45–62.

Kopecky, Jan (trans.), *Waltharius* (Prague: Arcibiskupské gymnázium, 2005).

Krammer, Hedwig, *Die Verfasserfrage des Waltharius* (Vienna: Verband der wissenschaftlichen Gesellschaften Österreichs, 1973).

Kratz, Dennis M., "*Quid Waltharius Ruodliebque cum Christo?*," in *The Epic in Medieval Society*, ed. Harold Scholler (Tübingen: Niemeyer, 1977), 126–49.

—, *Mocking Epic, Waltharius, Alexandreis, and the Problem of Christian Heroism* (Madrid: José Porrúa Turanzas, 1980).

—, *Waltharius and Ruodlieb* (New York: Garland, 1984).

Kroes, Hendrik Wilhelm, "Die Walthersage," *Beiträge zur Geschichte der deutschen Sprache und Literatur* 77 (1955): 77–88.

Krusch, Bruno (ed.), *Fredegarii et aliorum chronica, vitae sanctorum*, Monumenta Germaniae Historica, Scriptores Rerum Merovingiarum 2 (Hanover: Hahn, 1888).

Langosch, Karl, "Waltharius," in *Die deutsche Literatur des Mittelalters: Verfasserlexikon*, ed. Wolfgang Stammler and Karl Langosch (Berlin: de Gruyter, 1953), 4:776–8.

—, *Waltharius, Ruodlieb, Märchenepen. Lateinische Epik des Mittelalters mit deutschen Versen* (Berlin: Rütten and Loening, 1956).

—, "Die Vorlage des *Waltharius*," in *Festschrift Bernhard Bischoff zu seinem 65. Geburtstag*, ed. Johanne Autenrieth and Franz Brunhölzl (Stuttgart: Hiersemann, 1971), 226–59.

—, *Waltharius. Die Dichtung und die Forschung* (Darmstadt: Wissenschaftliche Buchgesellschaft, 1979).

—, "Zum Waltharius Ekkeharts I. von St. Gallen," *Mittelateinisches Jahrbuch* 18 (1983): 84–99.

Learned, Marion Dexter, *The Saga of Walther of Aquitaine* (Baltimore, Md.: Modern Language Association of America, 1892; reprinted, Westport, Conn.: Greenwood, 1970).

Lincoln, Bruce, "Rewriting the German War God: Georges Dumézil, Politics and Scholarship in the late 1930s," *History of Religions* 37.3 (1998): 187–208.

—, *Theorizing Myth: Narrative, Ideology, and Scholarship* (Chicago: University of Chicago Press, 1999).

Lührs, Maria, "Hiltgunt," *Mittellateinisches Jahrbuch* 21 (1986): 84–7.

Magennis, Hugh, "Waltharius," in *The Literary Encyclopedia*, http://www.litencyc.com/php/sworks.php?rec=true&UID=11998 (first published April 30, 2003, accessed August 4, 2015).

Magoun, Francis Peabody, and H. M. Smyser, *Walther of Aquitaine: Materials for the Study of his Legend* (New London, Conn.: Connecticut College, 1950).

Makkay, János, *Iranian Elements in Early Mediaeval Heroic Poetry: The Arthurian Cycle and the Waltharius* (Budapest: J. Makkay, 1998).

Mänchen-Helfen, Otto, *The World of the Huns: Studies in their History and Culture*, ed. Max Knight (Berkeley: University of California Press, 1973).

Millet, Victor, *Waltharius—Gaiferos. Über den Ursprung der Walthersage und ihre Beziehung zur Romanze von Gaiferos und zur Ballade von Escriveta* (Frankfurt am Main: Lang, 1992).

—, *Épica germánica y tradiciones épicas hispánicas, Waltharius y Gaiferos: la leyenda de Walter de Aquitania y su relación con el romance de Gaiferos*, Biblioteca románica hispánica 410 (Madrid: Gredos, 1998).

Morgan, Gareth, "Walter the Wood-Sprite," *Medium Aevum* 41 (1972): 16–19.

Murdoch, Brian, *Walthari: A Verse Translation of the Medieval Latin Waltharius* (Glasgow: Scottish Papers in Germanic Studies, 1989).

—, "Waltharius the Visigoth and Louis of the West Franks," in the author's *The Germanic Hero: Politics and Pragmatism in Early Medieval Poetry* (London and Rio Grande, Ohio: Humbledon, 1996), 89–117.

Nelis, Damien, *Vergil's Aeneid and the Argonautica of Apollonius Rhodius* (Cambridge: Francis Cairns, 2001).

Nickel, Helmut, "About the Sword of the Huns and the 'Urepos' of the Steppes," *Metropolitan Museum Journal* 7 (1973): 131–42.

Niermeyer, J. F., and C. van de Kieft, *Mediae Latinitatis Lexicon Minus*, rev. J. W. J. Burgers, 2 vols. (Leiden: Brill, 2002).

O'Hara, James, *True Names* (Ann Arbor, Mich.: University of Michigan Press, 1996).

Olsen, Karin E., Antonina Harbus, and Tette Hofstra (ed.), *Germanic Texts and Latin Models: Medieval Reconstructions* (Louvain: Peeters, 2001).

Orchard, Andy, *A Critical Companion to Beowulf* (Rochester, N.Y.: D. S. Brewer, 2003), 136–7.

Önnerfors, Alf, *Die Verfasserschaft des Waltharius-Epos aus sprachlicher Sicht* (Opladen: Westdeutscher Verlag, 1979).

—, *Das Waltharius-Epos. Probleme und Hypothesen* (Stockholm: Alquist & Wiksell International, 1988).

—, "Bemerkungen zum Waltharius-Epos," *Latomus* 51 (1992): 633–51; reprinted with a supplement in the author's *Classica et Mediaevalia. Kleine Schriften zur lateinischen Sprache und Literatur der Antike und des Mittelalters* (Hildesheim: Weidmann, 1998), 86–146.

Panzer, Friedrich, *Der Kampf am Wasichenstein. Waltharius-Studien* (Speyer: Historisches Museum der Pfalz, 1948).

—, "Der *Waltharius* in neuer Beleuchtung," *Forschungen und Fortschritte* 24 (1948): 156–8.

Parkes, Ford B., "Irony in the *Waltharius*," *Modern Language Notes* 89.3 (1974): 459–65.

Peiper, Rudolph (ed.), *Ekkehardi Primi Waltharius* (Berlin: Gustav Schade, 1873).

Pellegrin, Elisabeth, "Membra disiecta Floriacensia," *Bibliothèque de l'École des Chartes* 117 (1959): 25–43.

Pheifer, Joseph Donovan, "*Waldere* I 29–31," *Review of English Studies* (New Series) 11.42 (1960): 183–6.

Pinkster, Harm, "Is the Latin present tense the unmarked, neutral tense in the system?," in *Latin in Use*, ed. Rodie Risselada (Amsterdam: Gieben, 1998), 63–83.

Ploss, Emil Ernst (ed.), *Waltharius und Walthersage. Eine Dokumentation der Forschung* (Hildesheim: Olms, 1969).

Reeh, Rudolf, "Zur Frage nach dem Verfasser des Walthariliedes," *Zeitschrift für deutsche Philologie* 51 (1926): 413–31.

Renoir, Alain, "*Nibelungenlied* and *Waltharii Poesis*: A Note on Tragic Irony," *Philological Quarterly* 43 (1964): 14–19.

Ronge, Herbert, *Walthari, ein deutsches Helden- und Liebeslied der Völkerwanderungszeit* (Munich: Ernst Heimeran, 1934).

Ross, Rebecca Sophia, *The Monk of St. Gall: A Dramatic Adaptation of Scheffel's "Ekkehard"* (London: Trübner, 1879).

Schaller, Dieter, "Geraldus und St. Gallen. Zum Widmungsgedicht des *Waltharius*," *Mittellateinisches Jahrbuch* 2 (1965): 74–84.

—, "Ist der *Waltharius* frühkarolingisch?," *Mittellateinisches Jahrbuch* 19 (1983): 63–83.

—, "Von St. Gallen nach Mainz? Zum Verfasserproblem des *Waltharius*," *Mittel-lateinisches Jahrbuch* 24–5 (1989–90): 423–37.

Shalem, Avinoam, "The Fall of al-Madā'in: Some Literary References concerning Sasanian Spoils of War in Mediaeval Islamic Treasuries," *Iran* 32 (1994): 77–81.

Scharrer, Dirk, "*Waltharii poesis*—Arbeitsmaterial zum *Waltharius*" (2002), accessed August 4, 2015, at http://www.swisseduc.ch/altphilo/latein/lintlekt/poesie.html.

Scheffel, Joseph Victor von, *Ekkehard. Eine Geschichte aus dem zehnten Jahrhundert*, 2 vols. (Frankfurt am Main: Meidinger, 1855; new edition, Lengwil am Boden-see: Libelle, 2000).

—, and Alfred Holder (ed.), *Waltharius, lateinisches Gedicht des zehnten Jahrhunderts, nach der handschriftlichen Überlieferung berichtigt* (Stuttgart: Metzler, 1874).

—, *Ekkehard: A Novel*, trans. Rudolf Tombo (New York: F. Ungar, 1965).

Scherello, Bernd, "Die Darstellung Gunthers im *Waltharius*," *Mittellateinisches Jahr-buch* 21 (1986): 88–90.

Schieffer, Rudolf, "Silius Italicus in Sankt Gallen—ein Hinweis zur Lokalisierung des *Waltharius*," *Mittellateinisches Jahrbuch* 10 (1975): 7–19.

—, "Zu neuen Thesen über den *Waltharius*," *Deutsches Archiv* 36 (1980): 193–201.

Schneider, Hermann, "Das Epos von Walther und Hildegund," *Germanisch-Romanische Monatsschrift* 13 (1925): 14–32, 119–30.

Scholler, Harold, *The Epic in Medieval Society: Aesthetic and Moral Values* (Tübin-gen: Niemeyer, 1977).

Schröder, Edward, "Die deutschen Personennamen in Ekkehards *Waltharius*," in *Deutsche Namenkunde. Gesammelte Aufsätze zur Kunde deutscher Personen- und Ortsnamen*, ed. Edward Schröder and Ludwig Wolff (Göttingen: Vandenhoeck and Ruprecht, 1944), 81–92; reprinted in *Waltharius und Walthersage. Eine Doku-mentation der Forschung*, ed. Emil Ernst Ploss (Hildesheim: Olms, 1969), 356–68.

Schuhmann, Roland, "Dichtersprachliches im *Waltharius*. Zum Verhältnis zwischen den Vorlagen um den Waltharius-Epos anhand der Vergleiche," in *La langue poétique indo-européenne: actes du colloque de travail de la Société des études indo-européennes*, Paris, 22–24 octobre 2003, ed. Georges-Jean Pinault and Daniel Petit (Louvain: Peeters, 2006), 449–57.

Schumann, Otto, "Statius und *Waltharius*," in *Studien zur deutschen Philologie des Mittelalters. Friedrich Panzer zum 80. Geburtstag am 4. September 1950 darge-bracht*, ed. Richard Kienast (Heidelberg: Winter, 1950), 12–19.

—, "Zum Waltharius," *Zeitschrift für deutsches Altertum* 83 (1951): 12–40.

—, "Waltharius-Literatur seit 1926," *Anzeiger für deutsches Altertum und deutsche Literatur* 65 (1951–52): 13–41.

Schütte, Bernd, "Länder und Völker im Waltharius," *Mittelateinisches Jahrbuch* 21 (1986): 70–4.

Schwab, Ute, "Nochmals zum ags. Waldere neben dem Waltharius," *Beiträge zur Geschichte der deutschen Sprache und Literatur* 101 (1979): 229–51, 347–68.

Schwartz, Stephen P., "Gods and Heroes," in his *Poetry and Law in Germanic Myth* (Berkeley: University of California Press, 1973), 39–49.

Segaert, Michiel, "De invloed van Lucanus' *Pharsalia* op het *Waltharius*" (Licentiate thesis, University of Gent, 2008).

Sievers, Eduard, "Ekkehard oder Geraldus?," *Beiträge zur Geschichte der deutschen Sprache und Literatur* 51 (1927): 222–32.

Smyser, H. M., and Francis Peabody Magoun, *Survivals in Old Norwegian of Medieval English, French, and German Literature, together with the Latin Versions of the Heroic Legend of Walter of Aquitaine* (Baltimore, Md.: Waverly, 1941), 111–45.

Stach, Walter, "Geralds Waltharius—das erste Heldenepos der Deutschen," *Historische Zeitschrift* 168 (1943): 57–81.

Stackmann, Karl, "Antike Elemente im Waltharius," *Euphorion* 45 (1950): 231–48.

Stephens, Laurence, "New Evidence concerning Iambic and Cretic Shortening in Classical Latin," *Classical Philology* 80.3 (1985): 239–44.

Stiene, Heinz Erich, *Konkordanz zum Waltharius-Epos* (Frankfurt am Main and Berne: Peter Lang, 1982).

Strecker, Karl, "Ekkehard und Vergil," *Zeitschrift für deutsches Altertum* 42 (1898): 339–65.

—, *Bemerkungen zum Waltharius* (Dortmund: Crüwell, 1899).

— (ed.), *Die Ottonenzeit*, Monumenta Germaniae Historica, Poetae Latini Medii Aevi 5, part 1 (Leipzig: Hiersemann, 1937), 405–08.

—, "Vorbemerkungen zur Ausgabe des Waltharius," *Deutsches Archiv für Geschichte des Mittelalters* 5 (1942): 23–54; reprinted in *Waltharius und Walthersage. Eine Dokumentation der Forschung*, ed. Emil Ernst Ploss (Hildesheim: Olms, 1969), 1–32.

— (ed.) and Peter Vossen (trans.), *Waltharius* (Berlin: Weidmann, 1947).

—, and Otto Schumann, *Nachträge zu den Poetae Aevi Carolini I*, Monumenta Germaniae Historica, Poetae Latini Medii Aevi 6, part 1 (Weimar: Böhlau, 1951), 1–85.

Surles, Robert L., *Roots and Branches: Germanic Epic/Romanic Legend* (New York, Berne, Frankfurt am Main, and Paris: Lang, 1987).

Süß, Gustav Adolf, "Die Probleme der Waltharius-Forschung," *Zeitschift für Geschichte des Oberrheins* 99 (1951): 1–53.

Tavernier, Wilhelm, "*Waltharius, Carmen de prodicione Guenonis* und Rolandepos," *Zeitschrift für französische Sprache und Literatur* 42 (1914): 41–81; reprinted in *Waltharius und Walthersage. Eine Dokumentation der Forschung*, ed. Emil Ernst Ploss (Hildesheim: Olms, 1969), 150–213.

Thomas, Richard F., "Virgil's *Georgics* and the Art of Reference," *Harvard Studies in Classical Philology* 90 (1986): 171–98.

Thompson, Edward Arthur, and P. J. Heather, *The Huns* (Oxford: Blackwell, 1996).

Townsend, David, "Ironic Intertextuality and the Reader's Resistance to Heroic Masculinity in the *Waltharius*," in *Becoming Male in the Middle Ages*, ed. Jeffrey Jerome Cohen and Bonnie Wheeler (New York and London: Garland, 1997), 67–86.

Vogt-Spira, Gregor, *Waltharius, lateinisch/deutsch, mit den Waldere-Bruchstücken* (Stuttgart: Reclam, 1994).

Vollmann, Benedikt, "Waltharius," in *Reallexikon der germanischen Altertumskunde*, ed. Herbert Jankuhn and Johannes Hoops, vol. 33 (Berlin: de Gruyter, 2006), 162.

—, "Marginalglossen zu den *Waltharius*-Fragmenten aus Urbana," *Zeitschrift für deutsches Altertum und deutsche Literatur* 135.3 (2006): 336–9.

von den Steinen, Wolfram, "Der *Waltharius* und sein Dichter," *Zeitschrift für deutsches Altertum* 84 (1952): 1–47.

Vynckier, Henk, "Arms-Talks in the Middle Ages: Hrotsvit, *Waltharius*, and the Heroic *Via*," in *Hrotsvit of Gandersheim: Rara avis in Saxonia? A Collection of Essays*, ed. Katharina M. Wilson (Ann Arbor, Mich.: Medieval and Renaissance Collegium, 1987), 183–200.

Wagner, Hans, *Ekkehard und Vergil. Eine vergleichende Interpretation der Kampfschilderungen im Waltharius* (Heidelberg: Bilabel, 1939).

Wallach, Luitpold, Review of *Nachträge zu den Poetae Aevi Carolini*, by Karl Strecker and Otto Schumann, *Speculum* 28.1 (1953): 212–17.

Ward, John O., "After Rome: Medieval Epic," in *Roman Epic*, ed. Anthony James Boyle (London and New York: Routledge, 1993), 261–93.

Wawrzyniak, Udo, "Der Waltharius im Kloster Lugau. Rezeptionsgeschichtliche Randbemerkung zu einer Raabe-Stelle," *Mittellateinisches Jahrbuch* 18 (1983): 100–04.

Wehrli, Max, "Waltharius—gattungsgeschichtliche Betrachtungen," *Mittellateinisches Jahrbuch* 2 (1965): 63–73.

Werner, Karl Ferdinand, "*Gouverner l'empire chrétien*," in *Charlemagne's Heir: New Perspectives on the Reign of Louis the Pious (814–840)*, ed. Peter Godman and Roger Collins (Oxford: Clarendon Press, 1990), 1–123.

Westra, Haijo Jan, "A Reinterpretation of *Waltharius* 215–259." *Mittellateinisches Jahrbuch* 15 (1980): 51–6.

Wieland, Gernot R., *Waltharius* (Bryn Mawr, Pa.: Bryn Mawr College, 1986).

Wilmotte, Maurice, "La patrie du *Waltharius*," *Revue historique* 127 (1918): 1–30; reprinted in *Waltharius und Walthersage. Eine Dokumentation der Forschung*, ed. Emil Ernst Ploss (Hildesheim: Olms, 1969), 214–43.

Wolf, Alfred, "Der mittellateinische Waltharius und Ekkehard I. von St. Gallen," *Studia Neophilogica* 13 (1940–41): 80–102.

—, "Zum *Waltharius christianus,*" *Zeitschrift für deutsches Altertum* 85 (1954–55): 291–3.

Wolf, Alois, "Volkssprachliche Heldensagen und lateinische Mönchskultur. Grundsätzliche Überlegungen zum Waltharius," in *Geistesleben um den Bodensee im frühen Mittelalter. Vorträge eines Mediävistischen Symposions*, ed. Achim Masser and Alois Wolf (Freiburg im Breisgau: Schillinger, 1989), 157–83.

Wunderlich, Werner, "Medieval Images: Joseph Viktor von Scheffel's Novel *Ekkehard* and St. Gall," in *Medievalism in the Modern World: Essays in Honor of Leslie J. Workman*, ed. Richard Utz and Tom Shippey (Turnhout: Brepols, 1998), 193–225.

Zeydel, Edwin H., "Prolegomena to an English Translation of Waltharius," in *Middle Ages— Reformation—Volkskunde: Festschrift for John G. Kunstmann*, ed. Frederic E. Coenen et al. (Chapel Hill, N.C.: University of North Carolina, 1959), 21–38.

Ziolkowski, Jan M., Review of *Mocking Epic: Waltharius, Alexandreis and the Problem of Christian Heroism*, by Dennis M. Kratz, *Classical Journal* 78.3 (1983): 266–8.

—, "Fighting Words: Wordplay and Swordplay in the *Waltharius*," in *Germanic Texts and Latin Models: Medieval Reconstructions*, ed. Karin E. Olsen, Antonina Harbus, and Tette Hofstra (Louvain: Peeters, 2001), 29–51.

—, "Blood, Sweat, and Tears in the *Waltharius*," in *Insignis Sophiae Arcator: Essays in Honour of Michael W. Herren on his 65th Birthday*, ed. Gernot R. Wieland, Carin Ruff, and Ross G. Arthur (Turnhout: Brepols, 2006), 149–64.

—, "Of Arms and the (Ger)man: Literary and Material Culture in the *Waltharius*," in *The Long Morning of Medieval Europe*, ed. Jennifer Davis and Michael McCormick (Aldershot: Ashgate, 2008), 193–208.

Zwierlein, Otto, "Das Waltharius-Epos und seine lateinischen Vorbilder," *Antike und Abendland* 16.2 (1970): 153–84; reprinted in the author's *Lucubrationes Philologae*, ed. Jakobi Rainer, Rebekka Junge, and Christine Schmitz (Berlin: de Guyter, 2004), 2:519–64.

The Text and Translation

Prologus Geraldi[1]

Omnipotens[2] genitor, summae virtutis amator,
iure pari natusque amborum spiritus almus,
Personis trinus,[3] vera deitate sed unus,
Qui vita vivens cuncta et sine fine tenebis,
5 Pontificem summum tu salva nunc et in aevum
Claro Erckambaldum[4] fulgentem nomine dignum,
Crescat ut interius sancto spiramine plenus,
Multis infictum quo sit medicamen in aevum.
Praesul sancte dei, nunc accipe munera servi,
10 Quae tibi decrevit de larga promere cura
Peccator fragilis Geraldus nomine vilis,
Qui tibi nam certus corde estque fidelis alumnus.
Quod precibus dominum iugiter precor omnitonantem,
Ut nanciscaris factis, quae promo loquelis,
15 Det pater ex summis caelum terramque gubernans.

Serve dei summi, ne despice verba libelli,
Non canit alma dei, resonat sed mira tyronis,
Nomine Waltharius, per proelia[5] multa resectus.[6]
Ludendum magis est dominum quam sit rogitandum,
20 Perlectus longaevi stringit inampla diei.

Sis felix sanctus per tempora plura sacerdos,
Sit tibi mente tua Geraldus carus adelphus.

---

[1] Prologus Geraldi] Ring; INCIPIT POESIS GERALDI DE GVALTARIO B; prologue precedes poem in γMU

[2] Omnipotens] red initial's bottom edge visible U

[3] trinus] marks inside letters, apparently remnants of text decoration U

[4] Erckambaldum] P; Erkēmbaldum T; Erchamboldum B; ERcHeNBaLDŪ with marks inside some letters as above in trinus U

[5] proelia] B; abbreviated p̄lia PM

[6] Waltharius … resectus] PTM; Waltharii … resecti (fixing illogical syntax) B; resectus apparently glossed "fatigatus" M

Geraldus's Prologue[1]

[1] Almighty Father, Lover of the highest virtue,[2] and Nourishing Spirit, born of both, with equal right,[3] triple in person, but one in true deity, you who live in life[4] and who will perpetually hold all things—grant salvation for now and forever to the highest priest,[5] glorious Erkambald,[6] worthy of a famous name,[7] so that he may grow within filled with holy inspiration and may be a medicine prepared[8] for many men in time to come. Holy priest[9] of God, now receive the gifts of your servant, which a feeble and trivial sinner by the name of Gerald[10] has decided to produce for you from his generous devotion[11]—for he is sure of heart and your faithful pupil.[12] May the Father, governing the heavens and earth from on high, grant[13] the thing for which I pray continually to the Lord who thunders through all the heavens,[14] namely, that you obtain in action[15] what I set forth in speech.

[16] Servant of the highest God, do not look down upon the words of this little book. It does not sing the nourishing works of God but resounds the wondrous deeds of a young warrior—Walter[16] by name, a man maimed[17] through much fighting. It requires one to play rather than pray to the Lord. When read through, it shortens the undistinguished hours of the long-aged day.[18]

[21] May you, holy priest, be happy through further years, and may Gerald your dear *frère*[19] be in your mind!

Poesis Waltharii[7]

Tertia pars orbis, fratres, Europa vocatur,
Moribus ac linguis varias et nomine gentes
Distinguens cultu, tum religione[8] sequestrans.
Inter quas gens Pannoniae residere probatur,
5   Quam tamen et Hunos plerumque vocare solemus.
Hic populus fortis virtute vigebat et armis,
Non circumpositas solum domitans regiones,
Litoris oceani[9] sed pertransiverat oras,
Foedera[10] supplicibus[11] donans sternensque rebelles.
10 Ultra[12] millenos fertur dominarier annos.

Attila[13] rex quodam tulit illud tempore regnum,
Impiger antiquos sibimet renovare triumphos.
Qui sua castra movens mandavit visere Francos,
Quorum rex Gibicho solio pollebat in alto,
15 Prole recens[14] orta gaudens, quam postea narro:
Namque marem genuit, quem Guntharium[15] vocitavit.

Fama volans pavidi regis transverberat aures,
Dicens hostilem cuneum transire per Ystrum,[16]
Vincentem numero stellas atque amnis arenas.[17]
20 Qui non confidens armis vel robore plebis
Concilium cogit, quae sint facienda, requirit.
Consensere omnes foedus debere precari

---

[7] Poesis Waltharii] Ring, cf. line 1456; Liber Waltharii in red T; heading has been erased, perhaps
versus quidam (Grimm) or versus de waltā (Holder) P; Hystoria Waltarii regis K; no heading SV
[8] religione] VT; relligione Str.
[9] litoris oceani] glossed apparently "wer … schin" U
[10] foedera] fédere wrongly VU
[11] foedera supplicibus] glossed "pace subditis" U
[12] ultra] glossed "mer" U
[13] Attila] Etcilo E
[14] recens] recente V
[15] Guntharium] Cuntharium K
[16] Ystrum] SV; Hystrum BP and Str.
[17] Vincentem … arenas] om. V

Waltharius

Part I: The Hunnish Conquests and Walter's Escape

[1] A third part of the earth is called Europe,[20] brothers,[21] and it divides its races, which differ in customs, languages, and names, by culture and separates them also by religion. Among these races, the Pannonians[22] are known to reside, a race which we generally call the Huns. This nation was once strong and courageous in warfare, not only lording over the surrounding territories but even passing over the lands of the Ocean's shore, granting treaties to suppliant peoples, and subduing all who revolted. It is said that their dominion lasted more than a thousand years.

[11] King Attila once ruled that kingdom, a man who was busy to revive their age-old victories in his own time. He roused his forces and commanded that they go against the Franks, whose king, powerful on his high throne, was Gibicho,[23] who had recently rejoiced at the birth of a child, of whom I shall tell later,[24] for he fathered a son whom he called Gunther.[25]

[17] Rumor flies and soon whips at the fearful king's ears: a hostile host was crossing the Ister,[26] a force outnumbering the stars and the sands of the riverbank. The king, not trusting in warfare or the strength of his people, gathers a council and asks what they should do. Everyone agreed that they ought to ask for a treaty and to join hand in hand, if the Huns would, and to give hostages and pay the tribute that was ordered. They thought this would be better than to lose both their lives and land as well as their sons and wives.

Et dextras, si forte darent, coniungere dextris
Obsidibusque datis censum persolvere iussum;
25 Hoc melius fore quam vitam simul ac regionem
Perdiderint natosque suos pariterque maritas.

Nobilis hoc[18] Hagano fuerat sub tempore tiro
Indolis egregiae, veniens de germine Troiae.
Hunc, quia Guntharius nondum pervenit ad aevum,
30 Ut sine matre queat vitam retinere tenellam,
Cum gaza ingenti decernunt mittere regi.
Nec mora, legati censum iuvenemque ferentes
Deveniunt pacemque rogant ac foedera firmant.

Tempore quo validis steterat Burgundia sceptris,
35 Cuius primatum Herericus[19] forte gerebat.
Filia huic tantum fuit unica nomine Hiltgunt,[20]
Nobilitate quidem pollens ac stemmate formae.
Debuit haec heres aula residere paterna
Atque diu congesta frui, si forte liceret.

40 Namque Avares firma cum Francis pace peracta
Suspendunt[21] a fine quidem regionis eorum.
Attila sed celeres mox huc deflectit habenas,
Nec tardant reliqui satrapae vestigia adire.
Ibant aequati numero, sed et agmine longo.
45 Quadrupedum cursu tellus concussa gemebat,[22]
Scutorum sonitu pavidus superintonat aether.
Ferrea silva micat totos rutilando per agros:
Haud aliter primo quam pulsans aequora mane

---

[18] hoc] V²; ac V¹
[19] Herericus] VU; Heriricus PT and Str.; Henricus BE; Herricus S; Her ricus with erasure after first r K
[20] Filia … Hiltgunt] Hildcund P; Hilcund B; Hildgunt T; unica nata fuit huic tantum nomine Hiltgunt V
[21] suspendunt] discedunt over erasure in new hand V
[22] gemebat] tremebat V

[27] Now, noble Hagen[27] at that time was a young man of outstanding bloodline, descending from the race of Troy.[28] Since Gunther had not yet reached the age when he could manage his own tender life without his mother, they decided to send Hagen along with a mass of treasure to the Hunnish king. There was no delay. The ambassadors, taking the tribute and the youth, went and asked for peace and affirmed the treaty.

[34] At this time Burgundy was under mighty kingship. Hereric then held its chief office. He had only a single daughter, Hildegund by name,[29] excellent for her nobility as well as for her beautiful figure. She, as heiress, was supposed to reside at her father's court and, if she had been allowed that, to enjoy the wealth collected there.

[40] For the Avars, after settling a firm peace with the Franks, kept away from their territory; but Attila then quickly turned his reins away to Burgundy, nor were the rest of his vassals slow to follow his footsteps. They marched along well-ordered and in a long line. The earth groaned as she was pounded by their horses racing along. The air above thundered in fright at the clashing of their shields. An iron forest flashed with ruddy light through all the fields not unlike when the beautiful sun strikes the sea, gleaming in the early morn at the edge of the world.[30] And now their host had crossed the deep rivers, the Saône and the Rhône, and the whole army dispersed to ravage the land.

Pulcher in extremis renitet sol partibus orbis.
50 Iamque Ararim Rodanumque amnes transiverat altos
Atque ad praedandum cuneus dispergitur omnis.

Forte[23] Cabillonis[24] sedit Herericus,[25] et ecce
Attollens oculos speculator vociferatur:
"Quaenam condenso consurgit pulvere nubes?
55 Vis inimica venit, portas iam claudite cunctas!"
Iam tum, quid Franci fecissent, ipse sciebat
Princeps et cunctos compellat sic seniores:
"Si gens tam fortis, cui nos similare nequimus,
Cessit Pannoniae, qua nos virtute putatis
60 Huic conferre manum et patriam defendere dulcem?
Est satius, pactum faciant censumque[26] capessant.[27]
Unica nata mihi, quam tradere pro regione
Non dubito; tantum pergant, qui foedera firment."

Ibant legati totis gladiis spoliati,
65 Hostibus insinuant, quod[28] regis iussio mandat,
Ut cessent vastare, rogant. quos Attila ductor,
Ut solitus fuerat, blande suscepit et inquit:
"Foedera plus cupio quam proelia mittere vulgo.
Pace quidem Huni[29] malunt regnare, sed armis
70 Inviti feriunt, quos cernunt esse rebelles.
Rex ad nos veniens[30] dextram[31] det atque resumat."

---

23 Forte] missing decorative initial V
24 Cabillonis] Cavillonis αV
25 Herericus] V; Heriricus PT and Str.; Henricus B; Herricus S; Her ricus with erasure after first r K
26 censumque] censum M
27 capessant] glossed "arce[ssant]" (Ring), not "accip[iant]" (Str.) M
28 quod] quid B
29 Huni malunt] malunt Huni suggested by corrector to fix hiatus V
30 veniens] [veni]at M
31 dextram det atque] PTEM; det dextras atque B; pacem det atque α; pacem detque atque V

[52] Hereric[31] by chance was then at Châlon,[32] and behold![33] the watchman, lifting his eyes, exclaimed: "What cloud is this that rises up in a dense mass of dust? An enemy force is coming. Close the gates now!" Already then the prince knew what the Franks had done, and he addressed all the elders[34] in this way: "If such a strong race has left Pannonia—a race which we cannot match—then with what courage do you think we will engage this host and defend our sweet country? It is better that we make a pact with them, and they receive a tribute. I have a single daughter whom I do not hesitate to hand over on behalf of our kingdom; only let them be quick to affirm a treaty."

[64] The ambassadors go and, relieved of their weapons, enter the enemy camp. They ask what the king had ordered, that the Huns stop their ravaging. Attila the leader receives them, as usual in a charming manner, and says: "I would rather make treaties than conduct indiscriminate wars. The Huns prefer to rule by peace, but they do, unwillingly, strike their opponents in war, if they see that they are in rebellion. Let your king come to us and give and receive a hand in pledge."

Exivit princeps asportans[32] innumeratos
Thesauros pactumque ferit natamque reliquit.
Pergit in exilium pulcherrima gemma parentum.

75 Postquam complevit pactum statuitque tributum,
Attila in occiduas promoverat agmina partes.
Namque Aquitanorum tunc Alphere regna tenebat,
Quem sobolem sexus narrant habuisse virilis,
Nomine Waltharium, primaevo flore nitentem.
80 Nam iusiurandum Herericus[33] et Alphere reges
Inter se dederant, pueros quod consociarent,
Cum primum tempus nubendi venerit illis.

Hic ubi cognovit gentes has esse domatas,[34]
Coeperat ingenti cordis trepidare pavore,[35]
85 Nec iam spes fuerat saevis defendier armis.
"Quid cessemus,"[36] ait, "si bella movere nequimus?[37]
Exemplum nobis Burgundia, Francia donant.[38]
Non incusamur, si talibus aequiperamur.
Legatos mitto foedusque ferire[39] iubebo
90 Obsidis inque vicem dilectum porrigo natum
Et iam nunc Hunis censum persolvo futurum."

Sed quid plus remorer? dictum compleverat actis.
Tunc Avares[40] gazis onerati denique multis
Obsidibus sumptis Haganone, Hiltgunde[41] puella
95 Nec non Walthario redierunt pectore laeto.

---

[32] asportans] adportans M
[33] Herericus] TVM; Heriricus α; Henricus B
[34] Hic … domatas] Hic postquam domitas gentes has comperit esse V; … it gentes has domatas [esse?] M
[35] pavore] tumultu B
[36] cessemus] cessamus B
[37] decorative scrolling beneath this line M
[38] donant] praebent B
[39] ferire] referre V
[40] Avares] Avari with gloss "Hūnen" U
[41] Hiltgunde] α; Hilgunde B; Hiltgunda V; Hildguntque T

[72] The prince[35] of the Burgundians goes out bringing countless treasure, and he strikes a pact and leaves his daughter with Attila. The most beautiful gem of her parents then went into exile.

[75] After completing the pact and establishing tribute, Attila moved his ranks out and into the western regions. Now, the kingship of the Aquitanians was then in the hands of Alphere,[36] who they say had offspring of the male sex named Walter, who shone with the blossom of youth. Furthermore, Hereric and Alphere had sworn an oath between them to bind together their children as soon as they came to a marriageable age.

[83] When Alphere had seen that these two races had been conquered, he then began to quiver with great fear in his heart, nor did he retain any hope of defense from savage arms. "What should we cede," he said, "if we cannot raise a war? Burgundy and Frankland have provided us with an example. We are not shamed if we should be compared to such as them. I shall send ambassadors, and I shall tell them to establish a treaty and shall offer my beloved son as a hostage and shall promptly pay the Huns the tribute which they assign."[37]

[92] Why should I linger? He fulfilled his words with deeds. Then at last the Avars, burdened with much treasure, took the hostages—Hagen, the girl Hildegund,[38] and lastly Walter—and returned with happy hearts.[39]

Attila Pannonias ingressus et urbe receptus
Exulibus pueris magnam exhibuit pietatem
Ac veluti proprios nutrire iubebat alumnos.[42]
Virginis et curam reginam mandat habere,[43]
100 Ast adolescentes propriis conspectibus ambos
Semper adesse iubet, sed et artibus imbuit illos
Praesertimque iocis belli sub tempore habendis.

Qui simul ingenio crescentes mentis et aevo
Robore vincebant fortes animoque sophistas,
105 Donec iam cunctos superarent fortiter Hunos.
Militiae primos tunc Attila fecerat illos,
Sed haud[44] immerito, quoniam, si quando moveret[45]
Bella, per insignes isti micuere triumphos;
Idcircoque nimis princeps dilexerat ambos.
110 Virgo etiam captiva deo praestante supremo
Reginae vultum placavit et auxit amorem,
Moribus eximiis operumque industria habundans.
Postremum[46] custos thesauris provida cunctis
Efficitur, modicumque deest, quin regnet et ipsa;
115 Nam quicquid voluit de rebus, fecit et actis.

Interea Gibicho[47] defungitur, ipseque regno
Guntharius[48] successit et ilico Pannoniarum[49]
Foedera[50] dissolvit censumque subire negavit.
Hoc ubi iam primum[51] Hagano cognoverat exul,

---

[42] alumnos] γNE, heredes αV; ac veluti pueros nutrire iubebat heredes (first hand), ac velut heredes pueros nutrire iubebat (second hand) V
[43] Virginis … habere] γN; om. αVE, but added at bottom edge in K
[44] haud] non (fixing scansion) VN
[45] moveret] moverent V
[46] postremum] postremo V
[47] Gibicho] Gibico B; Gybichus N
[48] Guntharius] Cuntharius S; Cundharius N
[49] Pannoniarum] Pannoniorum B
[50] foedera] glossed pacem U
[51] primum] primo V

[96] After he entered Pannonia and was received in the city, Attila showed fatherly care[40] for the exiled children and bid that they be raised as his own. And he ordered the queen to care for the maiden, but he bid both the youths to be always in his sight. Moreover, he also instructed them in the arts and particularly in making jests in times of war.[41]

[103] Growing both in intelligence and age, they surpassed the brave in strength and the *sophistes* in wit,[42] until soon they boldly excelled all the Huns. Then Attila made them first men in his army and not undeservedly, since, whenever he made a campaign, these two sparkled amidst triumphal decorations. Therefore, the prince loved them both very much. The maiden, although captive, by the grace of the highest God, relaxed the queen's doubting face and increased her love, for the girl abundantly displayed her outstanding character and the industry of her works. At last she was made the steward to watch over all the king's treasure, and she was but little short of ruling herself, for, whatever she wanted, she actually did.

[116] Meanwhile Gibicho died, and Gunther himself succeeded to the kingship, and immediately he dissolved the treaty with the Huns and refused to endure the tribute. As soon as Hagen had heard this in his exile, at night he undertook flight and hastened to his lord.[43] But Walter went to battle at the head of the Huns, and, wherever he went, prosperous outcomes soon followed.

120 Nocte fugam molitur et ad dominum properavit.[52]
Waltharius tamen ad pugnas praecesserat Hunos,
Et quocumque iret, mox prospera sunt comitata.

Ospirin elapsum Haganonem, regia coniunx,
Attendens domino suggessit talia dicta:[53]
125 "Provideat caveatque, precor, sollertia regis,
Ne vestri imperii labatur forte columna,
Hoc est, Waltharius vester discedat amicus,
In quo magna potestatis vis extitit huius;
Nam vereor, ne fors fugiens Haganonem imitetur.
130 Idcircoque meam perpendite nunc rationem:
Cum primum veniat, haec illi dicite verba:
'Servitio in nostro magnos plerumque labores
Passus eras ideoque scias, quod gratia nostra
Prae cunctis temet nimium dilexit amicis.
135 Quod volo plus factis te quam cognoscere dictis:
Elige de satrapis nuptam tibi Pannoniarum
Et non pauperiem propriam perpendere cures.
Amplificabo quidem valde[54] te rure domique,
Nec quisquam, qui dat sponsam, post facta pudebit.'[55]
140 Quod si completis, illum stabilire potestis."
Complacuit sermo regi, coepitque parari.[56]

Waltharius venit, cui princeps talia pandit,
Uxorem suadens sibi ducere; sed tamen ipse[57]
Iam tum praemeditans, quod post compleverat actis,
145 His[58] instigandi[59] suggestibus obvius infit:
"Vestra quidem pietas est, quod modici famulatus

---

[52] properavit] properatur B
[53] talia dicta] talia fando B
[54] valde] gazis V
[55] quisquam … sponsam] sponsam quisquis dat eum (second hand) V
[56] parari] parare SI; parere V
[57] ipse] glossed "Wal" U
[58] his] mark in intial perhaps remnant of text decoration U
[59] his instigandi] UP; his instiganti TE and Str.; his instigandis B; investiganti his αV

[123] Ospirin[44] the royal wife, noticing Hagen was gone, advised her lord in such words: "Let the king's clever mind be aware and careful lest the pillar of Your[45] empire totter and fall—that is, lest Walter your friend leave, for a great force of power resides in him. Take care since I fear that he may flee in imitation of Hagen. Therefore, consider now my plan. When first he comes, say these words to him, 'As our servant, you were accustomed to endure great toils, and so you should know that Our Grace[46] loved you very much, more than all our friends. This I want to affirm for you by my deeds rather than by my words. Choose yourself a bride from my Hunnish vassals, and do not worry about your poverty. I will enrich you greatly with both land and home. Nor will anyone who gives you his daughter as bride be sorry about it afterwards.' If you do as I say, you can keep him faithful." Her speech pleased the king, and he began preparations.

[142] Walter came, and the prince declared these things to him, persuading him to take a wife, but he, even then thinking ahead to what he later did,[47] answered the king, who had urged him with these suggestions: "You show fatherly care since you take note of the situation of a lowly servant. But because you carry my servile acts in your mind's eye, I could never have earned this. Still I beg that you receive the

Causam conspicitis; sed quod mea seria[60] mentis
Intuitu fertis, numquam meruisse valerem.
Sed precor, ut servi capiatis verba fidelis:
150 Si nuptam accipiam domini praecepta secundum,
Vinciar inprimis curis et amore puellae
Atque a servitio regis plerumque retardor,
Aedificare domos cultumque intendere ruris
Cogor, et hoc oculis senioris adesse moratur
155 Et solitam regno Hunorum impendere curam.
Namque voluptatem quisquis gustaverit, exin
Intolerabilius consuevit ferre labores.
Nil tam dulce mihi, quam semper inesse fideli
Obsequio domini; quare, precor, absque iugali
160 Me vinclo permitte meam iam ducere vitam.
Si sero aut[61] medio noctis mihi tempore mandas,
Ad quaecumque iubes, securus et ibo paratus.
In bellis nullae persuadent cedere curae,
Nec nati aut coniunx retrahentque fugamque movebunt.[62]
165 Testor per propriam temet, pater optime, vitam
Atque per invictam nunc gentem Pannoniarum,[63]
Ut non ulterius me cogas[64] sumere taedas."
His precibus victus suasus rex deserit omnes,
Sperans Waltharium fugiendo recedere numquam.

170 Venerat interea satrapae certissima fama
Quandam, quae nuper superata, resistere gentem
Ac bellum Hunis confestim inferre paratam.

Tunc ad Waltharium convertitur actio rerum.
Qui mox militiam percensuit ordine totam

---

[60] seria] VUL; sergia α; senia PT but with superlinear mark in P; segnia B
[61] aut] an VL
[62] retrahentque … movebunt] retrahent without -que PT; retrahunt(que) fugamque precantur, the first
-que in erasure V; retrahunt fugē precantur L
[63] Pannoniarum] Pannoniorum VL
[64] me cogas] cogas me V

words of a faithful slave. If I receive a wife in accordance with my lord's commands, I shall be bound in utmost care and love to a girl and be generally retarded from my service to the king. I shall be driven to build homes and attend to the cultivation of my fields, and this will delay me from being in my lord's presence and from rendering the usual devotion to the kingship of the Huns. For, whoever has tasted pleasure, straightaway he is accustomed to bear toils with less tolerance. Nothing is so sweet to me as to be faithfully obedient to my lord. Therefore, I beg. Allow me now to conduct my life without the conjugal bond. If in the late or middle part of the night you give me your command, I shall go free of other concerns and prepared for whatever mission you order. In wars no anxieties will persuade me to yield—not sons nor wife will draw me back and urge me to flee. I beg you, best father, by your life and by the yet unconquered race of the Huns that you stop compelling me to take up the marriage torch." Conquered by these entreaties, the king deserted all his persuasion, expecting that Walter would never run away.

[170] Meanwhile, a very well-confirmed rumor had come to the satrap[48] that a certain race which had recently been conquered was now in revolt, already prepared, and hurrying to bring war against the Huns.

[173] Then the management of the affair was turned over to Walter, who soon reviewed the whole army in order and encouraged the hearts of his warriors, exhorting

175   Et bellatorum confortat[65] corda suorum,
       Hortans praeteritos semper memorare triumphos
       Promittensque istos solita virtute tyrannos
       Sternere et externis terrorem imponere terris.

       Nec mora, consurgit[66] sequiturque exercitus omnis.
180   Ecce locum pugnae conspexerat et numeratam[67]
       Per latos aciem campos digessit et agros.
       Iamque infra iactum teli congressus uterque
       Constiterat[68] cuneus: tunc undique clamor[69] ad auras
       Tollitur, horrendam confundunt classica vocem,
185   Continuoque hastae volitant hinc indeque[70] densae.
       Fraxinus et cornus ludum miscebat[71] in unum,
       Fulminis inque modum cuspis vibrata micabat.
       Ac veluti boreae sub tempore nix glomerata
       Spargitur, haud aliter saevas iecere sagittas.
190   Postremum[72] cunctis utroque ex agmine pilis
       Absumptis manus ad mucronem vertitur omnis.
       Fulmineos promunt enses clipeosque revolvunt,
       Concurrunt acies demum pugnamque restaurant.
       Pectoribus partim rumpuntur pectora equorum,
195   Sternitur et quaedam pars duro umbone virorum.

       Waltharius tamen in[73] medio furit agmine bello,[74]
       Obvia quaeque metens armis ac limite pergens.
       Hunc ubi conspiciunt hostes tantas dare strages,
       Ac si praesentem metuebant cernere mortem,

---

[65] et … confortat] ut bellatorum confortet L
[66] consurgit] consurgens VL
[67] numeratam] numerose L
[68] iamque … constiterat] cf. *Aen.* 11.608
[69] tunc … clamor] cf. *Aen.* 11.622
[70] hinc indeque] huc undique VL
[71] miscebat] miscentur V, cf. *Aen.* 12.714
[72] postremum] postremo BVL
[73] tamen in] tunc in L
[74] bello] belli L

them always to remember past triumphs and promising that he would lay these *tyrans*[49] low with his usual virtue[50] and subject the foreign lands to their terror.

[179] There was no delay. All the army rose and followed. Behold! He has seen the place for battle and has arranged his numbered battle-line through the wide meadows and fields. And now each host has come together and stopped within a spear's throw. Then on all sides the clamor rises up to the air; the military trumpets confound their horrific cries, and suddenly the spears fly dense from this side and that. Ash and cornel-wood mix in the game,[51] and the swinging spear flashes like a lightning bolt. And, as a dense cloud of snow at winter-time scatters, not otherwise do they shoot their savage arrows.[52] At last, when all the spears from both sides are spent, every hand turns to the sword. They whip out lightning blades and whirl their shields around; the ranks finally meet and renew battle. Horses fall after ramming each other chest to chest; men fall as they clash shield to shield.

[196] Walter raged with war in the middle of his line—reaping with his sword whatever was in his way and continuing along his path. When the enemy saw him wreaking such havoc, they feared his sight as present death itself.[53] And wherever Walter headed, whether on the right or left, they all then turned tail and tossed their

200 Et quemcunque locum, seu dextram sive sinistram,[75]
     Waltharius peteret, cuncti mox terga dederunt
     Et versis scutis laxisque feruntur habenis.
     Tunc[76] imitata ducem gens maxima Pannoniarum[77]
     Saevior insurgit caedemque audacior auget,[78]
205 Deicit obstantes, fugientes proterit usque,
     Dum caperet plenum belli[79] sub sorte triumphum.
     Tum super occisos ruit et spoliaverat omnes.
     Et tandem ductor recavo[80] vocat agmina cornu
     Ac primus frontem festa cum fronde revinxit,
210 Victrici lauro cingens sua timpora[81] vulgo,[82]
     Post hunc signiferi, sequitur quos cetera pubes.
     Iamque triumphali redierunt stemmate compti
     Et patriam ingressi propria se quisque locavit
     Sede, sed ad solium mox Waltharius properavit.

215 Ecce palatini[83] decurrunt arce ministri
     Illius aspectu hilares equitemque tenebant,
     Donec vir sella descenderet inclitus alta.
     Si bene res vergant, tum demum forte requirunt.
     Ille aliquid modicum narrans[84] intraverat aulam
220 (Lassus enim fuerat), regisque cubile petebat.

     Illic Hiltgundem[85] solam offendit residentem.
     Cui[86] post amplexus atque oscula dulcia dixit:
     "Ocius huc potum ferto, quia fessus anhelo."

---

[75] seu dextram sive sinistram] seu dextra sive sinistra αV
[76] tunc] hunc VL, cf. hunc in 198
[77] Pannoniarum] Pannoniorum VL
[78] saevior … auget] om. αVLE; … audet B
[79] dum … belli] donec perciperet belli VL
[80] ductor recavo] recavo ductor VL
[81] timpora] αPV; tempora BTL
[82] vulgo] lauro L
[83] palatini] paulatim B
[84] modicum narrans] narrans modicum B
[85] Hiltgundem] α; Hiltgundam V; Hilgundem BN
[86] cui] qui BV

shields and slackened their reins to run. The mighty race of the Huns, imitating their leader, rose up more fiercely, and more boldly they increased the slaughter, chasing those who fled, until they had attained a full triumph in the lot of war. Then they rushed over the slain and despoiled them all. And at last the leader called his ranks with a curved horn and first bound his forehead with a festal frond,[54] girding his temples all around with victorious laurel.[55] After him went the standard bearers, who were followed by the rest of the youth. Now decorated in triumphal garb, they returned and, entering their homeland, each placed himself in his own seat, but Walter hurried then to the throne.

[215] Behold! The palace servants run down from the citadel. Rejoicing at seeing him, they take hold of his steed[56] so that the famous man might dismount from his high seat. They ask then if things are well. Giving them some brief response—for he was tired—he enters the court and seeks the king's chamber.

[221] There he met Hildegund sitting alone, to whom, after an embrace and sweet kisses, he spoke:[57] "Swiftly bring me drink here! I am tired and out of breath." She then filled a precious goblet[58] with unmixed wine and offered it to the man, who received it while making the sign of the Cross, and gripped the maiden's hand

Illa mero tallum complevit mox pretiosum
225 Porrexitque viro, qui signans accipiebat
Virgineamque manum propria constrinxit. at illa
Astitit et vultum reticens intendit[87] herilem,
Walthariusque bibens vacuum vas porrigit[88] olli[89]
—Ambo etenim norant de se sponsalia facta—
230 Provocat et tali caram sermone puellam:
"Exilium pariter patimur[90] iam tempore tanto,[91]
Non ignorantes,[92] quid nostri forte parentes
Inter se nostra de re fecere futura.
Quamne[93] diu tacito premimus haec ipsa palato?"

235 Virgo per hyroniam[94] meditans hoc[95] dicere sponsum
Paulum conticuit, sed postea talia reddit:[96]
"Quid lingua simulas, quod ab imo pectore damnas,
Oreque persuades,[97] toto quod corde refutas,
Sit veluti talem pudor ingens ducere nuptam?"

240 Vir sapiens contra respondit et intulit ista:
"Absit quod memoras, dextrorsum porrige sensum!
Noris me nihilum simulata mente locutum,
Nec quicquam nebulae[98] vel falsi interfore crede!
Nullus adest nobis exceptis namque duobus.
245 Si nossem temet mihi promptam impendere mentem
Atque fidem votis servare per omnia cautis,
Pandere cuncta tibi cordis mysteria vellem."

---

87 intendit] conspexit V
88 porrigit] PTαV; reddidit BN
89 olli] illi TVN
90 pariter patimur] patimur pariter TVE
91 tempore tanto] tempore longo VE
92 non ignorantes] haut ignorantes V
93 quamne] quodne V; -ne glossed perhaps "an" U
94 hyroniam] yroniam V; glossed "spot" U
95 hoc] γ; haec αVU
96 reddit] dixit V
97 oreque persuades] oreque quid suades U
98 nebulae] nubili V

in his own.[59] But she stood by and quietly but intently watched his lordly expression, and Walter, drinking the cup dry, held it out to her; and, indeed, they both knew that pledges of betrothal had been made for them.[60] Then with this speech he challenged the dear girl: "We have both endured exile so long—being not unaware of what our parents arranged concerning our future mutual estate. How long will we suppress these very things with a silent palate?"[61]

[235] The maiden, thinking that her betrothed had spoken in *ironie*,[62] was silent a while but then said these words: "Why do you pretend with your tongue what you condemn from the depths of your soul and persuade with your mouth what you reject with all your heart, as if it were a great shame to marry a betrothed one such as this?"

[240] The wise man answered in reply and spoke these words: "Away with these words you say! Set straight your sentiment! You know I spoke nothing from a dissembling mind,[63] and don't think there was anything nebulous or false in what I said, for no one is here but the two of us. If I knew you would lend me a ready mind and keep your pledge through everything with careful vows, I would be willing to show you all the mysteries of my heart."

Tandem virgo viri genibus curvata profatur:
"Ad quaecumque vocas, mi domne, sequar studiose
250 Nec quicquam placitis malim praeponere iussis."

Ille dehinc: "piget exilii me denique nostri
Et patriae fines reminiscor saepe relictos
Idcircoque fugam cupio celerare[99] latentem.
Quod iam prae multis potuissem forte diebus,
255 Si non Hiltgundem[100] solam remanere dolerem."

Addidit has imo virguncula corde loquelas:
"Vestrum velle meum, solis his aestuo rebus.[101]
Praecipiat dominus, seu prospera sive sinistra
Eius amore pati toto sum pectore praesto."

260 Waltharius tandem sic virginis inquit in aurem:
"Publica custodem rebus te nempe potestas
Fecerat, idcirco memor haec mea verba notato:
Inprimis galeam regis tunicamque trilicem
Assero loricam fabrorum insigne ferentem,
265 Diripe, bina dehinc mediocria scrinia tolle.
His armillarum tantum da Pannonicarum,[102]
Donec vix unum releves[103] ad pectoris imum.
Inde[104] quater binum[105] mihi fac de more coturnum,[106]
Tantundemque tibi patrans[107] imponito vasis:
270 Sic fors ad summum complentur scrinia labrum.[108]

---

[99] celerare] accelerare MT
[100] Hiltgundem] Hiltgundam V
[101] Vestrum ... rebus] γ; om. αVE
[102] Pannonicarum] Pannoniorum changed to -arum by first hand U; Pannoniarum T; Pannoniarum with "c" above second "a" in first hand P
[103] releves] glossed "eleves" U
[104] inde] deinde V
[105] quater binum] quater denum but glossed "octo" V
[106] coturnum] marginal gloss at lines 267–71: "Ovidius / grande sonant tragici / tragicos decet ire coturnis / grossis calceis / [versi Kommediis]" U, cf. Ov. *Rem.* 375
[107] patrans] patrato V
[108] labrum] Germanic gloss "part" U

[248] Finally, the maiden, bowing at the man's knees, said: "My lord, I will eagerly follow wherever you call me, nor would I prefer to place anything above your pleasing commands."

[251] After this he replied: "In short, I am ashamed of our exile, and I often recall the territory of our homeland that I left behind, and so I desire a swift and secret flight. This I could already have done, many days earlier if I were not grieved that Hildegund would remain alone."

[256] The dear maiden added these words from the depths of her heart: "Your will is mine; I am seething within for this thing alone. Let my lord order, whether prosperous or ill-omened, I am ready with all my heart to suffer."

[260] Walter at last spoke thus in the maiden's ear: "Truly public authority has made you guardian over the treasury; therefore, carefully note these words of mine. First, the king's helmet and shirt, the triple-ply hauberk[64] bearing the maker's mark,[65] steal these; then take two medium-sized coffers. Fill these with so many of the Huns' bracelets that you can scarcely lift it to the bottom of your chest.[66] Then see that you make me eight boots according to custom and, getting the same number for yourself, put them in the containers. Thus the coffers will be filled to the top. Also secretly request some bent hooks from the smiths. Let our traveling fare be fish as well as birds. I must be a fisherman as well as a bird-hunter.[67] Do all these things cautiously and gradually *dans la semaine*.[68] You have heard what a traveler must have.

Insuper a fabris hamos clam posce retortos:
Nostra viatica sint pisces simul atque volucres,
Ipse ego piscator, sed et auceps esse coartor.
Haec intra ebdomadam caute per singula comple.
275 Audisti, quid[109] habere vianti forte necesse est.

Nunc quo more fugam valeamus inire, recludo:
Postquam septenos Phoebus remeaverit orbes,
Regi ac reginae satrapis ducibus famulisque[110]
Sumptu permagno convivia laeta parabo
280 Atque omni ingenio potu sepelire studebo,
Donec nullus erit, qui sentiat hoc, quod agendum est.
Tu tamen interea mediocriter utere vino
Atque sitim vix ad mensam restinguere cura.
Cum reliqui surgant, ad opuscula nota recurre.
285 Ast ubi iam cunctos superat violentia potus,
Tum simul occiduas properemus quaerere partes."

Virgo memor praecepta viri complevit. et ecce
Praefinita dies epularum venit, et ipse
Waltharius magnis instruxit sumptibus escas.
290 Luxuria in media residebat[111] denique mensa,
Ingrediturque aulam velis rex undique septam.
Heros magnanimus solito quem more[112] salutans
Duxerat ad solium, quod[113] bissus compsit[114] et ostrum.
Consedit laterique[115] duces hinc indeque binos
295 Assedisse iubet; reliquos locat ipse[116] minister.

---

109 quid] quod BNV
110 regi … parabo] regi ac reginae satrapis convivia laeta parabo (unmetrical conflation of 278 and 279)
V; 279 before 278 N
111 Luxuria … residebat] Luxurians media resedebat B
112 more] γIEN; corde αV
113 quod] BIV; quem PTαNE
114 bissus compsit] γIEN; compsit bissus αV
115 laterique] lateri U
116 ipse] ille U

[276] "Now I shall disclose how we can make our flight. After Phoebus[69] has completed seven circuits, I shall prepare a merry party for the king and queen, their vassals, dukes, and attendants. And I shall be quick with all my wit to bury them in drink until no one is left to realize what I shall do. But you, meanwhile, drink your wine moderately and take care scarcely to slake your thirst at the table. When the rest get up, return to your well-known task. But when the violence of drink has overcome everyone, then together let us hasten to seek the western lands."

[287] The maiden mindfully completed the man's commands. Behold! The appointed day for the feast arrives, and Walter himself has arranged the food at great expense.[70] At last there is Luxury in the midst of the table,[71] and the king enters the hall closed off by curtains on every side. The great-spirited hero, greeting him in the accustomed way, leads him to a throne which is clothed in purple and fine linen.[72] He bids two dukes to sit on either side; acting as a servant, he seats the rest. The king's companions[73] took one hundred seats at once. The guests each taste a different dish and begin to sweat. When these dishes are taken away, others are brought in to eat. Exquisite *vin mêlé*[74] steams in gold—only gold goblets stand on the fine

Centenos[117] simul accubitus iniere sodales,
Diversasque dapes libans conviva resudat.[118]
His et sublatis[119] aliae referuntur edendae,
Atque exquisitum fervebat migma[120] per aurum[121]
300   —Aurea bissina[122] tantum stant gausape vasa—
Et pigmentatus crateres[123] Bachus[124] adornat.
Illicit ad haustum species dulcedoque potus.
Waltharius cunctos ad vinum hortatur et escam.[125]

Postquam epulis depulsa fames sublataque mensa,[126]
305   Heros iam dictus dominum laetanter adorsus
Inquit: "in hoc, rogito, clarescat gratia vestra,
Ut vos inprimis, reliquos tunc[127] laetificetis."
Et simul in verbo nappam dedit arte peractam
Ordine sculpturae referentem gesta priorum.
310   Quam rex accipiens haustu vacuaverat uno
Confestimque iubet reliquos imitarier omnes.

Ocius accurrunt[128] pincernae moxque recurrunt,
Pocula plena dabant et inania suscipiebant.
Hospitis ac regis certant hortatibus omnes.
315   Ebrietas fervens tota dominatur in aula;
Balbutit madido facundia fusa palato.
Heroas validos plantis titubare videres.

---

[117] centenos] centeni U
[118] Diversasque … edendae] floral decoration in margin U
[119] sublatis] ablatis U
[120] migma] glossed "mecu" (Green) or "merum" (Vollman) U
[121] aurum] auram B
[122] bissina] P; byssina B ; bis sena T; bissino αV
[123] crateres] crateras BV
[124] Bachus] Bacchus B
[125] escam] escas αV
[126] postquam … mensa] postq' epulis (-as V) absumpta (ass- V) quies mensaeque remotae αV, cf. *Aen.*
1.216 (fames) and 1.723 (quies)
[127] tunc] nunc αV
[128] accurrunt] occurrunt V

linge de table.[75] And painted Bacchus adorns the *boules.*[76] The sight and sweetness of the drink entices them to drink. Walter exhorts them all to wine and food.

[304] After hunger was driven away by feasting, and the table was removed,[77] the aforementioned hero addressed his lord and said: "I beg that Your Grace be conspicuous in this, namely, that you first make yourself and then the others merry." And as he spoke he gave him a *hnapf*[78] crafted with skill and displaying in ordered relief the deeds of earlier men.[79] This the king took and drained in one draught, and immediately ordered the rest to do likewise.

[312] Swiftly the servers run back and forth; they give full cups and take back empty. At the exhortations of their host and king they all compete in drinking. Hot Drunkenness is lord throughout the hall.[80] Their sagacious speech, spilled out of their sopping mouths, stutters.[81] You would have seen, were you there, strong heroes totter about on their feet.

Taliter in seram produxit bachica[129] noctem
Munera Waltharius retrahitque redire[130] volentes,[131]
320 Donec vi potus pressi somnoque gravati[132]
Passim porticibus sternuntur humotenus[133] omnes.
Et licet ignicremis vellet[134] dare moenia flammis,
Nullus qui causam potuisset scire remansit.

Tandem dilectam vocat ad semet mulierem,[135]
325 Praecipiens causas citius[136] deferre paratas.
Ipseque de stabulis victorem duxit equorum,
Ob virtutem quem[137] vocitaverat ille Leonem.
Stat sonipes ac frena ferox spumantia mandit.[138]
Hunc postquam faleris solito circumdedit, ecce
330 Scrinia plena gazae lateri suspendit utrique
Atque iteri[139] longo modicella cibaria ponit
Loraque virgineae mandat fluitantia dextrae.

Ipseque lorica vestitus more gigantis
Imposuit capiti rubras cum casside cristas
335 Ingentesque ocreis suras complectitur aureis
Et laevum femur[140] ancipiti praecinxerat ense
Atque alio dextrum pro ritu Pannoniarum;
Is tamen ex una tantum dat vulnera parte.
Tunc hastam dextra rapiens clipeumque sinistra
340 Coeperat invisa trepidus decedere terra.

---

129 bachica] bacchica B; bachina H
130 redire] om. H
131 volentes] αVI; videres BPTH
132 donec … gravati] om. V; only descenders visible U
133 sternuntur humotenus] glossed "ceciderunt" U
134 vellet] glossed "aliquis" U
135 Tandem … mulierem] floral design in right margin U
136 citius] otius V
137 ob … quem] quemque ob virtutem V; quem virtute sua H
138 stat … mandit] cf. *Aen.* 4.135
139 iteri] SV, cf. note on translation; iteneri K; itineri E; itinere N; uteri γH
140 laevum femur] femur laevum B

[318] In such a way Walter kept serving the gifts of Bacchus late into the night, and he detained those who wanted to go home, until, suppressed by the force of the drink and burdened by sleep, they all lay strewn on the ground here and there about the colonnades. Even if he had wanted to commit the walls to burning flame, no one would have remained to know what he had done.[82]

[324] At length, he called his beloved woman to his side and ordered her quickly to bring out the things she had prepared. And he himself led the champion of the horses from the stable, the one whom he had named Lion on account of his courage. The hoof-tapper stood and wildly chomped on its foaming bit. After he had covered the horse with its accustomed gear, he promptly hung the coffers full of treasure from each side, packed modest provisions for a long *journee*,[83] and entrusted the flowing reins to the maiden's hand.

[333] And he himself, clothed in a hauberk like a giant,[84] places a red-crested helm on his head, surrounds his calves in golden greaves, and girds his left thigh with a double-edged sword and his right with another in the manner of the Huns—but he dealt blows only from one side.[85] Then, taking his spear in his right hand and his shield in his left, he anxiously starts to leave the hated land.

Femina duxit equum nonnulla talenta[141] gerentem,
In manibusque simul virgam tenet ipsa[142] colurnam,
In qua piscator hamum transponit in undam,
Ut[143] cupiens pastum piscis degluttiat[144] hamum.[145]
345 Namque gravatus erat vir maximus undique telis
Suspectamque habuit cuncto sibi tempore pugnam.

Omni nocte quidem properabant currere, sed cum
Prima rubens terris ostendit lumina Phoebus,
In silvis latitare student et opaca requirunt,
350 Sollicitatque metus vel per loca tuta fatigans.
In tantumque timor muliebria pectora pulsat,
Horreat ut cunctos aurae ventique susurros,
Formidans volucres collisos sive racemos.
Hinc odium exilii patriaeque amor incubat inde.
355 Vicis[146] diffugiunt,[147] speciosa novalia linquunt,
Montibus[148] intonsis cursus ambage[149] recurvos
Sectantes tremulos variant per devia gressus.

Ast urbis populus somno vinoque solutus[150]
Ad medium lucis siluit recubando sequentis.
360 Sed postquam surgunt, ductorem quique requirunt,
Ut grates faciant ac festa laude salutent.[151]
Attila nempe manu caput amplexatus utraque
Egreditur thalamo rex Walthariumque dolendo
Advocat, ut proprium quereretur forte dolorem.

---

141 nonnulla talenta] nonnulla dona V; nonnullum tale E
142 ipsa] ipse B
143 ut] et V
144 degluttiat] V; deglutiat Str.
145 hamum] uncum αV
146 vicis] glossed "villis" U; vicos TVL
147 diffugiunt] effugiunt VL
148 montibus] motibus U
149 ambage] glossed "c[ir]cuitu" U
150 solutus] sepultus STN²U, cf. Aen. 3.630; faded decorative mark in right margin U
151 salutent] salutant L

[341] The woman led the horse bearing several talents of treasure, and in her hands she held a hazel-wood rod[86] of the sort with which a fisherman put a hook in the water so that the fish, desiring to eat, might swallow the hook. For the mighty man was burdened all over with armor and weapons, and he feared he might need to fight at any time.

[347] While through all the night they hurried to run, yet, when Phoebus reddened showing the first light to the earth, they are eager to hide in the forest and seek the shadowed places. Dread wearing them down troubled them even in the safe places. Fear struck the woman's heart so much that she shuddered at every whisper of the windy breeze, scared by the birds or branches as they dashed against each other. On this side hatred of exile and on that love of their homelands urged them on. They flee the villages and leave behind the beautiful fields, following[87] their winding, curved path through uncut mountains, they turn their nervous steps this way and that through the pathless wild.

[358] But the people of the city, loosed by sleep and wine,[88] lie quiet in slumber until the middle of the following day. But, after they rise, they all seek out the duke[89] to thank him and greet him in festive praise. King Attila, holding his head in his hands, leaves the chamber and calls Walter in pain to complain about his headache.[90] His attendants answer that they cannot find the man, but the prince hopes he is still quietly held in sleep and that he has chosen a hidden place for his slumber.

365 Respondent ipsi se non potuisse ministri
     Invenisse virum, sed princeps sperat eundem
     Hactenus in somno tentum recubare quietum
     Occultumque locum sibi delegisse sopori.

     Ospirin[152] Hiltgundem[153] postquam cognovit abesse
370 Nec iuxta morem vestes deferre suetum,[154]
     Tristior immensis satrapae clamoribus inquit:
     "O detestandas, quas heri sumpsimus, escas!
     O vinum, quod Pannonias[155] destruxerat omnes!
     Quod domino regi iam dudum[156] praescia dixi,
375 Approbat[157] iste dies, quem[158] nos superare nequimus.
     En hodie imperii[159] vestri cecidisse columna
     Noscitur, en robur procul ivit et inclita virtus:
     Waltharius,[160] lux Pannoniae, discesserat inde,
     Hiltgundem quoque[161] mi caram[162] deduxit alumnam."

380 Iam princeps nimia succenditur efferus ira,[163]
     Mutant laetitiam maerentia corda priorem.
     Ex humeris trabeam[164] discindit ad infima totam
     Et nunc huc animum tristem, nunc dividit illuc.[165]
     Ac velut Aeolicis[166] turbatur arena procellis,

---

[152] Ospirin] Ospirn VL (large initial V); spirin (missing initial) P
[153] Hiltgundem] Hiltegundem L
[154] deferre suetum] deferreque svetas VL
[155] Pannonias] Pannonicas L; Pannoniam hanc destruxerat omnem E
[156] quod … dudum] quod dudum iam domino L
[157] approbat] αγU; abstulit VL
[158] quem] quam L
[159] imperii] glossed "regni" U
[160] Waltharius] Waltherius U
[161] Hiltgundem quoque] Hiltgundemque U; Hiltigundemque L
[162] caram] karam L
[163] iam … ira] large floral design in right margin U
[164] trabeam] glossed "vestem" U
[165] et … dividit] cf. *Aen.* 4.285, 8.20
[166] Aeolicis] Eloicis B

[369] Ospirin, after noticing that Hildegund was not there to bring out the queen's clothes as she used to, sadly cried out to the satrap[91] and said: "O you detestable food which we ate yesterday! O wine which has destroyed all the Huns! That day of which I, in my foreknowledge, warned my lord the king some time ago has come, and we can do nothing about it. Behold! Today the pillar of your empire has clearly fallen. Behold! Your strength and famous courage have gone far from here. Walter, light of Pannonia, has departed hence, and my dear child Hildegund too— he took her with him."

[380] Now the prince is fired up, wild with excessive anger;[92] a grieving heart takes the place of his former happiness. From his shoulders he tears off his cloak, rending it down to the hem. And now he shifts his sad mind this way, now that. As the sand is stirred by Aeolian gales, so the king's mind whirls within, his internal concerns all about him;[93] and, imitating his changing heart with changing face, he showed outside whatever he endured within. Anger permitted him no words. In fact, on this day, he disdained food and drink, nor could his worry give calm rest to his

385 Sic intestinis rex fluctuat undique curis,[167]
     Et varium pectus vario simul ore imitatus
     Prodidit exterius, quicquid toleraverat intus,
     Iraque sermonem permisit promere nullum.[168]
     Ipso quippe die potum fastidit et escam,
390 Nec placidam[169] membris potuit dare cura quietem.[170]
     Namque ubi nox rebus iam dempserat atra colores,[171]
     Decidit in lectum, verum nec lumina clausit,
     Nunc latus in dextrum fultus nunc inque sinistrum,
     Et veluti iaculo pectus transfixus acuto
395 Palpitat atque caput huc et mox iactitat illuc,
     Et modo subrectus[172] fulcro[173] consederat amens.
     Nec iuvat hoc, demum surgens discurrit[174] in urbe,[175]
     Atque thorum veniens simul attigit atque reliquit.
     Taliter insomnem consumpserat Attila[176] noctem.
400 At profugi comites per amica silentia euntes
     Suspectam[177] properant post terga relinquere terram.

     Vix tamen[178] erupit cras, rex patribusque vocatis[179]
     Dixerat: "o si quis mihi Waltharium[180] fugientem
     Afferat[181] evinctum ceu nequam forte liciscam![182]

---

167 ac ... procellis] cf. Ven. Fort. 7.14.31
168 sermonem ... nullum] sermonem dare non permiserat ullum VL
169 placidam] placitam H
170 Nec ... quietem] cf. *Aen.* 4.5
171 namque ... dempserat] et cum nox terris depresserat VL
172 subrectus] α; surrectus VL; subreptus γH
173 fulcro] fulchro VL
174 discurrit] decurrit VL
175 urbe] PTHK; urbem corrected to urbe S; urbem BVLN
176 Attila] Attala H
177 Suspectam] Suspectant B
178 tamen] om. L
179 vix ... vocatis] floral design in right margin U
180 Waltharium] Waltherium U
181 afferat] afferret above afferat U; afferret EN; efferat H
182 liciscam] licyscam P; laciscam U; faded gloss "na.." (Green), "tigris" (Vollman), or perhaps "vulpem" (Ring) U

limbs for, when dark night had stolen color from the world,[94] he fell into bed but did not close his eyes. Now propped up on his right side, now on his left, and, like one pierced in the heart by a sharp javelin,[95] he feels about and tosses his head this way and that, and then in madness he sits bolt upright on his mattress. Nor does this please him—at last, he leaps up and runs about the city; and, whenever he returns to his bed, he leaves it as soon as he touches it. In such a way, Attila spent a restless night. But the fugitive companions, going through the friendly silence,[96] hurried to leave the feared land behind their backs.

[402] Scarcely now had the next day broken, when the king called his elders together and said: "O, if only someone would bring me this fugitive Walter, bound like a worthless *chien-loup*![97] Then I would clothe him in oft resmelted gold[98] and

405　Hunc ego mox auro vestirem saepe recocto[183]
　　Et tellure quidem stantem hinc inde onerarem[184]
　　Atque viam penitus clausissem vivo[185] talentis."[186]

　　Sed nullus[187] fuit in tanta regione tyrannus[188]
　　Vel dux sive comes seu miles sive[189] minister,
410　Qui, quamvis cuperet proprias ostendere vires
　　Ac virtute sua laudem captare perennem
　　Ambiretque simul gazam infarcire cruminis,[190]
　　Waltharium tamen[191] iratum praesumpserat[192] armis
　　Insequier strictoque virum mucrone videre.
415　Nota equidem virtus, experti sunt quoque, quantas
　　Incolomis dederit strages sine vulnere victor.
　　Nec potis est ullum rex persuadere virorum,
　　Qui promissa velit hac condicione talenta.

　　Waltharius fugiens, ut dixi, noctibus ivit,[193]
420　Atque die saltus arbustaque densa requirens
　　Arte accersitas pariter capit arte volucres,
　　Nunc fallens visco, nunc fisso denique ligno.
　　Ast ubi pervenit, qua flumina curva fluebant,
　　Immittens hamum rapuit sub gurgite praedam
425　Atque famis pestem pepulit tolerando laborem.
　　Namque fugae toto se tempore virginis usu
　　Continuit vir Waltharius laudabilis heros.

---

[183] recocto] Germanic gloss "gepranten" (Green) U
[184] inde onerarem] inde atque onerarem (fixing scansion) VL; atque in later hand above inde K
[185] vivo] dum above vivo to mark parenthetical verbal form V
[186] vivo talentis] mole talentum U
[187] nullus ... regione] fuit in tanta nullus regione H
[188] tyrannus] tirannus LH
[189] sive] seu L
[190] cruminis] crumenis L
[191] tamen] tunc L
[192] praesumpserat] γV; praesumpserit αN; presumeret L
[193] ivit] ibat M

would weigh him down on this side and that right where he stood—I would shut him up with treasure, as I live."[99]

[408] But there was not a single *tyran*[100] in so large a country—whether duke, count, soldier, or attendant—who, though eager both to show his strength and to win unending praise through his courage, and also ambitious to stuff his purse with treasure,[101] nevertheless undertook to pursue Walter, since he was angry and armed. They did not wish to see the man with sword drawn—for his courage was known, and they had even personally experienced what great slaughter he had worked scathelessly and victoriously, without receiving a single wound, and so the king could not persuade any of his men, though they wanted the treasure he promised in exchange.

[419] Walter, as I said, went fleeing by night; and by day, seeking out wooded valleys and dense stands of trees, he skillfully lured and caught birds, now tricking them with bird-lime, now with split wood.[102] But, when he came to where the curved rivers flowed, he would throw in a hook and catch his prey from beneath the swirling waters. Enduring this hard task, he staved off destructive hunger. And always Walter the praiseworthy hero restrained himself from intercourse with the fugitive maiden.[103]

Ecce quater denos sol circumflexerat orbes,
Ex quo Pannonica[194] fuerat digressus ab urbe.
430 Ipso quippe die, numerum qui clauserat istum,
Venerat ad fluvium iam vespere tum mediante,
Scilicet ad Rhenum, qua cursus tendit ad urbem[195]
Nomine Wormatiam regali sede nitentem.
Illic pro naulo pisces dedit antea captos
435 Et mox transpositus graditur properanter anhelus.

Orta dies postquam tenebras discusserat[196] atras,
Portitor exurgens praefatam venit in urbem
Regalique coco, reliquorum quippe magistro,
Detulerat pisces, quos vir dedit ille viator.[197]
440 Hos dum[198] pigmentis condisset et apposuisset[199]
Regi Gunthario, miratus fatur ab alto:
"Istius ergo modi pisces mihi Francia numquam
Ostendit: reor externis a finibus illos.
Dic[200] mihi quantocius: cuias homo detulit illos?"[201]
445 Ipseque respondens narrat, quod nauta dedisset.

Accersire hominem princeps praecepit eundem;
Et, cum venisset, de re quaesitus eadem
Talia dicta dedit causamque ex ordine pandit:
"Vespere praeterito residebam litore Rheni
450 Conspexique viatorem propere venientem
Et[202] veluti pugnae certum per membra[203] paratum:

---

194 Pannonica] Pannoca though possibly missing superlinear abbreviation mark U
195 Rhenum qua … ad urbem] Renum … in urbem U; Rhenum quo V
196 discusserat] ᵉˣcusserat V
197 viator] venator B
198 dum] γNE; cum αV
199 hos … apposuisset] is cum coxisset studiosus et adposuisset V
200 dic … illos] om. B; transposed after 445 P
201 cuias … illos] homo quis tibi dederit istos V
202 et] ac V
203 membra] menbra V

Part II: Crossing the Rhine and the Battle of the Vosges

[428] Behold! The sun had finished four times ten circuits[104] since he had left the Pannonian city. On that very day, which completed this count, he came now in mid-evening to a river, to the Rhine, where it bent its course toward the city named Worms, glorious for its royal seat.[105] There for his passage he gave the ferryman fish he had caught before; and soon, after crossing, he stepped out in breathless haste.[106]

[436] After day had risen and banished the dark shades, the ferryman got up and went to the aforementioned city and brought the chief royal cook the fish which the traveler had given him. When the cook had prepared them with herbs and served them to King Gunther, the king was amazed and spoke from his high seat: "Frankland has never shown me this sort of fish. I think they are from a foreign land. Tell me swiftly. *Of whilce kin*[107] was the man who brought them?" The cook responded and told him that the boatman had given them to him.

[446] The prince ordered the man summoned; and, when he arrived and was questioned concerning the matter, he said the following, explaining the matter in sequence: "Last evening, I was sitting by the bank of the Rhine when I saw a traveler quickly approaching, and he seemed ready for battle, with all his limbs prepared.[108] Indeed, my famous king, he was entirely clothed in bronze; and, as he walked, he carried a shield and a flashing spear—he was quite the brave man, and, though he carried a large load, still his step had a fierce vigor. An attractive and even

Aere[204] etenim penitus fuerat, rex inclite, cinctus
Gesserat et scutum gradiens hastamque coruscam.
Namque viro forti similis fuit, et licet ingens
455   Asportaret onus, gressum tamen extulit acrem.
Hunc incredibili[205] formae decorata nitore[206]
Assequitur calcemque terit iam calce puella.[207]
Ipsaque robustum rexit per lora caballum
Scrinia bina quidem dorso non parva ferentem,[208]
460   Quae, dum cervicem sonipes discusserit altam
Atque superba cupit glomerare volumina crurum,
Dant[209] sonitum, ceu quis[210] gemmis[211] illiserit[212] aurum.
Hic mihi praesentes dederat pro munere pisces.”

His Hagano auditis—ad mensam quippe resedit—
465   Laetior in medium prompsit de pectore verbum:
“Congaudete[213] mihi, quaeso, quia talia novi!
Waltharius collega meus remeavit ab Hunis.”
Guntharius princeps ex hac ratione superbus[214]
Vociferatur, et omnis ei mox aula reclamat:
470   “Congaudete mihi iubeo, quia talia vixi![215]
Gazam, quam Gibicho regi transmisit eoo,
Nunc mihi[216] cunctipotens[217] huc in mea regna remisit.”

---

[204] aere] vere (Str.) or here (Ring) V
[205] incredibili] incredibilis B
[206] nitore] puella S; decore V
[207] puella] natore S
[208] ferentem] gerentem
[209] dant] gloss supplies “scrinia” U
[210] quis] glossed “aliquis” U
[211] gemmis] geminis S; geminis with “scriniis” supplied above U
[212] illiserit] glossed “absconderet” U
[213] congaudete] glossed perhaps “ait” to mark quotation U
[214] Guntharius … reclamat] 468 precedes 469 γIN; 469 precedes 468 αVE
[215] vixi] ITα; novi BPV, cf. 466
[216] nunc mihi] γEI; h[an]c n[un]c S; hanc mihi N; hanc deus V
[217] cunctipotens] omnipotens V

unbelievably beautiful girl[109] followed him and her step kept close to his. By the reins she guided a stout horse, which bore two good-sized coffers on its back; and, whenever the hoof-tapper tossed his high neck and was eager to paw the air with his hooves,[110] the coffers made a sound like someone striking gold with gems. This man gave me the fish here as his fare."[111]

[464] When he heard this, Hagen—who happened to be seated at the table— happily spoke a word from his heart: "Rejoice with me, I beg you, since I have recognized what this means! My comrade Walter has returned from the Huns." Prince Gunther, then, haughtily[112] exclaimed—and soon all the hall shouted back to him: "Rejoice with me, I bid you, since I have lived to see this![113] The treasure which Gibicho sent to the eastern king has now been returned to me here in my kingdom by the Almighty."

Haec ait et mensam pede perculit exiliensque
Ducere equum iubet et sella componere sculpta
475 Atque omni de plebe viros secum duodenos
Viribus insignes, animis plerumque probatos[218]
Legerat. inter quos simul ire Haganona[219] iubebat.
Qui memor antiquae fidei sociique prioris
Nititur a coeptis[220] dominum transvertere rebus.
480 Rex tamen econtra nihilominus instat et infit:
"Ne tardate, viri, praecingite[221] corpora ferro
Fortia, squamosus thorax iam terga recondat.
Hic tantum gazae Francis deducat ab oris?"

Instructi telis, nam iussio regis adurget,
485 Exibant portis, te Waltharium cupientes
Cernere[222] et imbellem lucris fraudare putantes.
Sed tamen omnimodis Hagano prohibere studebat,
At rex infelix coeptis resipiscere non vult.

Interea vir magnanimus de flumine pergens
490 Venerat in saltum iam tum[223] Vosagum[224] vocitatum.
Nam nemus est ingens, spatiosum, lustra ferarum
Plurima habens, suetum canibus resonare tubisque.
Sunt in secessu[225] bini montesque propinqui,
Inter quos licet angustum specus extat amoenum,
495 Non tellure cava factum, sed vertice rupum:
Apta quidem statio latronibus illa cruentis.
Angulus hic virides ac vescas gesserat herbas.

---

[218] probatos] robustos V
[219] ire] et B
[220] a coeptis] inceptis V
[221] praecingite] BTαN; praecingere PVE
[222] cernere] sternere BV
[223] tum] tunc KTVU
[224] Vosagum] Wasagum VU
[225] in successu] glossed "in secreto" U

[473] This he said; and, striking the table with his foot and leaping up, he bid them to bring his horse and to ready his carved saddle. He chose twelve[114] men out of the crowd with him, men remarkable for their strength and generally proven in their courage. Among these he bid Hagen come too. But he, remembering his old pledge and his former ally, strove to change his lord from the quest he had begun. The king, however, insisted in opposition and began: "Be not slow, men! Gird your brave bodies in iron. Let the scaly hauberk cover your backs. Should this man take away so much treasure from Frankish lands?"

[484] All equipped with their weapons, they issued out the gate—for the king's order was urgent. Each of them was wishing to see you, Walter,[115] and was thinking they would cheat[116] an unwarlike man for their gain. Still Hagen was busy trying to hinder them however he could, but the unlucky[117] king did not wish to reconsider wisely what he had begun.

[489] Meanwhile, the great-spirited man continued on from the river and came then into the forested valley called Vosges[118]—it is a huge, broad wood which holds countless haunts of wild beasts and is frequently home to the noise of the hounds and horns of the hunt.[119] There were two mountains close by in a secluded recess, and between these there stood a cave quite pleasant in spite of its cramped chamber. It was not dug out of hollowed earth, but formed by an outcropping of rocky crags. Indeed, it was a fitting refuge for bloody bandits.[120] This little retreat produced edible green vegetation.

"Huc,"[226] mox ut vidit iuvenis, "huc," inquit, "eamus,
His iuvat in castris fessum componere corpus."
500   Nam postquam fugiens Avarum discesserat oris,[227]
Non aliter somni requiem gustaverat idem[228]
Quam super innixus clipeo; vix clauserat orbes.
Bellica tum demum deponens pondera dixit
Virginis in gremium fusus: "circumspice caute,
505   Hiltgunt, et nebulam si tolli videris atram,
Attactu[229] blando me surgere commonitato,
Et licet ingentem conspexeris ire catervam,
Ne excutias somno subito,[230] mi cara,[231] caveto,
Nam procul hinc acies potis es transmittere puras.[232]
510   Instanter cunctam circa explora regionem."
Haec ait atque oculos concluserat ipse nitentes
Iamque diu satis optata fruitur requiete.[233]

Ast ubi Guntharius vestigia pulvere vidit,
Cornipedem rapidum saevis calcaribus urget,
515   Exultansque animis frustra sic fatur ad auras:
"Accelerate, viri, iam nunc capietis euntem,[234]
Numquam hodie effugiet, furata[235] talenta relinquet."
Inclitus at Hagano contra mox reddidit[236] ista:
"Unum dico tibi, regum fortissime,[237] tantum:
520   Si totiens tu Waltharium[238] pugnasse videres
Atque nova totiens, quotiens ego, caede furentem,

---

[226] huc] γ, cf. later in line; hunc IαV
[227] oris] IV; horis BS; arvis N
[228] idem] ipse V
[229] attactu] adtactuV
[230] ne … subito] ne subito excutias somno αV
[231] cara] kara PV; chara T
[232] puras] curas V
[233] iamque … requiete] sic tandem optata fessus fruiturque quiete V
[234] euntem] γ; eundem αVN; eun perhaps with final letters erased and with –tem/-tpm added above line U
[235] furata] at furata B
[236] reddidit] glossed "relocabat," not "respondit" (Green) U
[237] fortissime] superlinear "o" to mark vocative U
[238] Waltharium] Waltherium U

[498] As soon as the young man saw it, he said: "Here, here let us go. I want to rest my tired body at this camp." For, since he had fled the land of the Avars, he had never yet tasted rest other than what he got propped up against his shield. He had scarcely closed his eyes. Then finally, putting aside his burdens of war, he spoke, collapsing into the maiden's lap:[121] "Keep a careful watch, Hildegund, and, if you see a dark cloud[122] rising, wake me up with your charming touch. And, though you should see a huge host coming, please, my dear girl, take care not to disturb me from my sleep right away; for from here you can see clearly far away. Look sharply all around the area!" This he said and closed his shining eyes, now at last enjoying the rest he had so long desired.

[513] But, when Gunther had sighted his tracks in the dust,[123] he urged on his swift steed with sharp spurs[124] and, exulting in his spirit, vainly spoke thus to the air: "Quick now, men! Soon you will catch him going along.[125] Never will he escape us today! He will leave behind the stolen treasure."[126] But famous Hagen soon responded this in turn: "One thing only I tell you, bravest of kings: If you had seen Walter fighting and raging in fresh slaughter as often as I, you would never think he would be so easy to despoil. I have seen the Pannonian ranks, when they stirred war against the northern and southern regions. There Walter, flashing in his own courage, went out to battle—hated by his enemies and admired by his allies. Whoever met him, soon saw Tartarus. O king and companions, trust me since I know how

Numquam tam facile spoliandum forte[239] putares.
Vidi Pannonias acies, cum bella cierent[240]
Contra Aquilonares sive Australes regiones.
525 Illic Waltharius propria virtute coruscus
Hostibus invisus, sociis mirandus obibat.
Quisquis ei congressus erat, mox Tartara vidit.
O rex et comites, experto credite, quantus
In clipeum surgat, quo turbine[241] torqueat hastam."[242]
530 Sed dum Guntharius[243] male sana mente gravatus
Nequaquam flecti posset, castris propiabant.[244]

At procul aspiciens Hiltgunt de vertice montis
Pulvere sublato venientes sensit et ipsum
Waltharium placido tactu vigilare monebat.[245]
535 Qui caput attollens[246] scrutatur, si quis adiret.
Eminus illa refert quandam volitare phalangem.
Ipse oculos tersos somni glaucomate purgans
Paulatim rigidos ferro vestiverat artus
Atque gravem rursus parmam collegit et hastam
540 Et saliens vacuas ferro transverberat auras
Et celer ad pugnam telis prolusit[247] amaram.

Comminus[248] ecce coruscantes mulier videt hastas
Ac stupefacta nimis: "Hunos hic," inquit, "habemus,"
In terramque cadens effatur talia tristis:
545 "Obsecro, mi senior, gladio mea colla secentur,[249]

---

239 forte] credo V
240 cierent] coirent IV; moverent K; egerent N
241 quo turbine] BM; qua turbine PTN; quanta vi αV
242 experto ... hastam] cf. *Aen.* 11.283
243 Guntharius] Guntherius V
244 propiabant] propiabat M
245 monebat] iubebat KV
246 attollens] adtollens V
247 prolusit] p[rae]lusit V
248 comminus] cominus αT; cōminus VU; glossed "prope" U
249 secentur] secede αV

well he wields a shield[127] and with what force he can whirl a spear." But, while Gunther, burdened by a crazed mind,[128] refused to be dissuaded, they were approaching the camp.[129]

[532] Yet Hildegund, looking far away from the top of the mountain, knew they were coming by the dust in the air and with a soothing touch warned Walter to wake up. He lifted his head and asked if anyone was coming. She replied that a *troupe*[130] was flying toward them from afar. He wiped his eyes clearing them of the *glaucoma*[131] of sleep, and bit by bit he clothed his stiff[132] limbs in iron and picked back up his heavy shield and spear. He leapt up and whipped through the empty air with his blade—playing swiftly with his weapons in preparation for bitter battle.

[542] Behold! The woman saw the flashing spears close at hand; and, quite awestricken, she said: "These are the Huns," and, sadly falling to the ground, she continued: "I beg, my lord, that my neck be cut by your sword so that I, who did not get to join myself to you in the arranged marriage bed, shall not suffer carnal intercourse with any other."

Ut, quae non merui pacto thalamo sociari,
Nullius ulterius patiar consortia carnis.»

Tum iuvenis: "cruor innocuus me tinxerit?" inquit
Et:[250] "quo forte modo gladius potis est inimicos
550   Sternere, tam fidae si nunc non parcit amicae?
Absit quod rogitas; mentis depone pavorem.
Qui me de variis eduxit saepe periclis,
Hic valet hic hostes, credo, confundere nostros."
Haec ait atque oculos tollens effatur ad ipsam:
555   "Non assunt Avares hic, sed Franci nebulones,[251]
Cultores regionis," et en galeam Haganonis
Aspicit et noscens iniunxit[252] talia ridens:
"Et meus hic socius Hagano collega veternus."[253]
Hoc heros dicto introitum stationis adibat,
560   Inferius[254] stanti praedicens sic mulieri:
"Hac coram porta verbum modo[255] iacto superbum:
Hinc nullus rediens[256] uxori dicere Francus
Praesumet se impune gazae quid tollere tantae."

Necdum sermonem complevit, humotenus ecce
565   Corruit et veniam petiit, quia talia dixit.
Postquam surrexit, contemplans cautius omnes:
"Horum, quos video, nullum Haganone remoto
Suspicio: namque ille meos per proelia mores
Iam didicit, tenet hic etiam sat callidus artem.
570   Quam si forte volente deo intercepero solam,[257]
Tunc,"[258] ait, "ex pugna tibi, Hiltgunt sponsa, reservor."

---

[250] et] γI; aut αV
[251] Franci nebulones] Franci nivilones N; gloss in right margin "Frazescen h[un]" M
[252] iniunxit] inquit ac V
[253] et … veternus] foral design in right margin M
[254] inferius] interius V
[255] modo] nunc V
[256] nullus rediens] rediens nullus IV (corrected in V)
[257] quam … solam] quem … solum NV
[258] tunc] hac V

[548] Then the young man said: "Shall your innocent blood stain me? How can my sword strike down my enemies, if it does not now spare so faithful a friend? Away with this request of yours! Toss fear out of your mind! The one[133] who has often led me out of various dangers can confound our enemies." These things he said and, lifting his eyes, told her: "These are not the Avars, but the nebulous[134] Franks who dwell here!" Behold! He saw the helm of Hagen; and, recognizing it, he smiled and spoke: "And this is my ally Hagen, my old comrade." After saying this, the hero went toward the entrance to the refuge and spoke thus to the woman standing down inside: "Now before this entryway I speak a haughty boast—not one of the Franks who returns from here will presume to tell his wife that he has taken any of our great treasure without paying for it!"[135]

[564] He had not yet finished speaking, when suddenly he collapsed to the earth and begged forgiveness, since he had said such things.[136] Afterwards he got up, looking at them all more warily. "Of these men, whom I see, I fear none except Hagen, for he has long known my methods of battle; and he too is clever and talented at the art of war. If only, God willing, I can deal with his skillful tactics, then I shall escape the battle alive for you, Hildegund, my betrothed."

Ast ubi Waltharium tali statione receptum
Conspexit Hagano, satrapae mox ista superbo
Suggerit: "o senior, desiste lacessere bello
575   Hunc hominem! pergant primum, qui cuncta requirant,
Et genus et patriam nomenque locumque relictum,
Vel si forte petat[259] pacem sine sanguine praebens
Thesaurum. per responsum cognoscere homonem
Possumus, et si Waltharius remoratur ibidem
580   —Est sapiens—forsan vestro concedet honori."[260]

Praecipit ire virum[261] cognomine rex Camalonem,[262]
Inclita Mettensi[263] quem Francia miserat urbi
Praefectum, qui dona ferens devenerat illo
Anteriore die quam princeps noverit[264] ista.
585   Qui dans frena volat rapidoque simillimus euro
Transcurrit spatium campi iuvenique propinquat
Ac sic obstantem compellat: "dic, homo, quisnam
Sis aut unde venis, quo pergere tendis?"[265]

Heros magnanimus respondit talia dicens:
590   "Sponte tua venias an huc te miserit[266] ullus,
Scire velim." Camalo[267] tunc reddidit ore superbo:
"Noris Guntharium regem tellure potentem
Me misisse tuas quaesitum pergere causas."
His auscultatis suggesserat hoc adolescens:
595   "Ignoro penitus, quid opus sit forte viantis
Scrutari causas, sed promere non trepidamus.
Waltharius vocor, ex Aquitanis sum generatus.

[259] petat] petit V
[260] forsan … concedet] vestro concedet forsan V
[261] virum] hominem with virum above M
[262] Camalonem] Camelonem VM
[263] Mettensi] Metensi V
[264] noverit] PTK; nov[er]at with i above a S; noverat BV
[265] quo … tendis] PαV; quo tandem tendere pergis B; aut tu quo pergere tendis T
[266] miserit] miserat V
[267] Camalo] Camelo V

[572] Yet, when Hagen saw Walter situated in such a place, he then advised the haughty king: "My lord, do not provoke this man to fight! Let someone first follow him and inquire, questioning him quite fully:[137] his family, his homeland, his name, and whence he's come; and let him ask him too if perhaps he would choose to turn over the treasure and receive peace with no bloodshed. By his answer we can discover the *mann*[138] and, if Walter is staying there—he is wise—perhaps, he will concede to your honor."

[581] The king ordered a man named Camalo to go—a man whom famous Frankland had sent to the city Metz as prefect. This man had arrived at court bringing gifts on the day before the prince had received this report.[139] Camalo slackened his reins and flew off, racing very much like the East Wind[140] across the length of the field and, approaching the youth, addressed him thus where he stood blocking the way: "Tell me, fellow. Who are you? Where are you from? Where are you heading?"

[589] The great-spirited hero answered speaking thus: "Do you come on your own, or did someone send you here? I would like to know." Camalo then answered with a haughty voice: "Know then that king Gunther who rules this land sent me to ask your circumstances." When he had heard this, the young man answered thus: "I have absolutely no idea[141] why you need to examine the circumstances of a passer-by, but I am not afraid of telling. I am called Walter, born of Aquitanian parents. I was given hostage-like[142] by my father to the Huns, when I was a little boy. I lived with them and now have returned, eager to see my country again and my dear people." The king's agent replied to this: "The hero[143] whom I just named bids you

A genitore meo modicus puer obsidis ergo[268]
Sum datus ad Hunos, ibi vixi nuncque recessi
600 Concupiens patriam dulcemque revisere gentem."
Missus ad haec: "tibi iam dictus per me iubet heros,
Ut cum scriniolis equitem des atque puellam:
Quod si promptus agis, vitam concedet et artus."

Waltharius contra fidenter protulit ista:
605 "Stultius effatum me non audisse sophistam
Arbitror. en memoras, quod princeps[269] nescio vel quis
Promittat, quod non retinet nec fors retinebit.
An deus est, ut iure mihi concedere possit[270]
Vitam?[271] num manibus tetigit? num carcere trusit
610 Vel post terga meas torsit per vincula palmas?
At tamen ausculta: si me certamine laxat
—Aspicio, ferratus adest. ad proelia venit—
Armillas centum de rubro quippe metallo
Factas transmittam, quo nomen regis honorem."
615 Tali[272] responso discesserat ille recepto,
Principibus narrat, quod protulit atque resumpsit.

Tunc Hagano ad regem: "porrectam[273] suscipe gazam,
Hac potis es decorare, pater, tecum comitantes,[274]
Et modo de pugna palmam revocare memento!
620 Ignotus tibi Waltharius et maxima virtus.
Ut mihi praeterita portendit visio nocte,
Non, si conserimus, nos prospera cuncta sequentur.
Visum quippe mihi te colluctarier[275] urso,

---

[268] a ... ergo] obsidis inque loco parvus genitore coacto V
[269] quod princeps] princeps quod V
[270] possit] M; vitam αV
[271] vitam] possit αV
[272] tali] large initial V
[273] porrectam] sic dixit V
[274] tecum comitantes] BI; te concomitantes PT; c[on]comitantes te S; te cōmitantes K; temet comitantes V
[275] colluctarier] conluctarier V

through me to hand over the horse, the treasure coffers, and the girl too. If you do this promptly, he will grant you your life and limb."[144]

[604] Walter in return boldly declared this: "I think that I have never heard a *sophiste* speak more stupidly.[145] Behold, do you recall what your prince—or whoever he is—promises? It is something that is not in his hands and perhaps never will be. Or is he God that he can rightfully grant me my life? Surely he has not got *this* in his hands? He has not thrust me into a prison cell or twisted my hands behind my back and bound them in chains, has he? Well then, listen! If he lets me go without a fight—for I see he has come in armor ready for battle—I shall send him a hundred bracelets of red gold to honor the king's name."[146] Receiving this response, Camalo left and told the princes what he had spoken, and the answers he had heard.

[617] Then Hagen said to the king: "Take the treasure he's offered. You can decorate your companions with it, Father. Just be sure to recall your fingers from the fight.[147] Walter and his mighty courage are yet unknown to you. As a vision last night showed me, if we join battle, it will not all turn out favorable for us, for it seemed to me that you were wrestling a bear who after a long struggle bit you and tore off one leg up to the knee, all of it below the thigh. Then, as I came to your aid with weapons in hand, he attacked me and cut out one of my eyes as well as some of my teeth."[148]

Qui post conflictus longos tibi mordicus unum
625 Crus cum poplite ad usque femur decerpserat omne
Et mox auxilio subeuntem ac tela ferentem[276]
Me petit atque oculum cum dentibus eruit unum."

His animadversis clamat rex ille superbus:
"Ut video, genitorem imitaris Hagathien ipse.[277]
630 Hic quoque perpavidam gelido sub pectore mentem
Gesserat et multis fastidit proelia verbis."
Tunc heros magnam iuste conceperat iram,
Si tamen in dominum licitum est irascier ullum.
"En,"[278] ait, "in vestris consistant omnia telis.
635 Est[279] in conspectu, quem vultis. dimicet omnis.
Comminus astatis nec iam timor impedit ullum;
Eventum videam nec consors sim[280] spoliorum."
Dixerat et collem petiit mox ipse propinquum
Descendensque ab equo consedit et aspicit illo.[281]

640 Post haec Guntharius Camaloni[282] praecipit aiens:
"Perge et thesaurum reddi mihi praecipe totum.
Quodsi cunctetur—scio tu vir fortis et audax—
Congredere et bello devictum mox spoliato."

Ibat Mettensis Camalo metropolitanus,
645 Vertice fulva micat cassis, de pectore thorax,
Et procul acclamans: "heus! audi," dixit, "amice!
Regi Francorum totum transmitte metallum,
Si vis ulterius vitam vel habere salutem!"
Conticuit paulum[283] verbo fortissimus heros,

---

[276] auxilio … ferentem] cf. *Aen.* 2.216
[277] genitorem … ipse] patrem modo tu ipse agathine imitaris V
[278] en] haec KV; hoc S
[279] est] en V
[280] sim] sum V and M (first hand)
[281] descendensque … aspicit] […] descendens ab equo nam res[picit] (first word possibly sedit) M
[282] Camaloni] Cameloni V
[283] paulum] paulo V

[628] Noting this, that haughty king shouts: "You seem to me to be imitating your father Hagathie. He too held an over-fearful mind in his frigid breast[149] and avoided battles through much talk."[150] Then the great-spirited hero grew justly angry, if it is ever permitted to be angry with a lord, and said: "Behold! Let everything rest upon your skill at arms. The man you want is within sight. Let every man fight! You stand close now, nor does fear still hinder any of you. Let me simply watch the outcome and not take part in the spoils." He finished speaking, then rode to a nearby hill, dismounted from his horse, took a seat and watched from there.

[640] After this, Gunther spoke and ordered Camalo: "Go and order him to give me back all the treasure. But if he should hesitate, since I know you're a brave and daring man, engage with him and, when you've conquered him in combat, take the spoils."[151]

[644] Camalo, metropolitan[152] of Metz, made his way, his helmet glittering over his blond hair and his hauberk about his chest. And from far off he said: "Hello, listen, friend, hand over all the treasure to the king of the Franks, if you want to keep your life and health any longer!" The bravest of heroes kept quiet awhile, waiting for the savage enemy to come nearer. The king's agent rushed onward and called out the same message again.[153] Then the young man, undisturbed, produced this reply: "What are you seeking? What do you compel me to return? Can it be that

650 Opperiens propius hostem adventare ferocem.
Advolitans missus vocem repetiverat istam:
["Regi Francorum totum transmitte metallum!"]²⁸⁴
Tum iuvenis constans responsum protulit istud:
"Quid quaeris? vel quid reddi, importune, coartas?
655 Numquid Gunthario furabar talia regi?
Aut mihi pro lucro quicquam donaverat ille,
Ut merito usuram me cogat solvere tantam?
Num pergens ego damna²⁸⁵ tuli vestrae regioni,
Ut vel hinc iuste videar spoliarier a te?
660 Si²⁸⁶ tantam invidiam cunctis gens exhibet ista,
Ut calcare solum nulli concedat eunti,²⁸⁷
Ecce viam mercor,²⁸⁸ regi transmitto ducentas
Armillas. pacem donet modo bella remittens."²⁸⁹

Haec postquam Camalo²⁹⁰ percepit corde ferino,
665 "Amplificabis," ait, "donum, dum scrinia pandis.
Consummare etenim sermones nunc volo cunctos:²⁹¹
Aut quaesita dabis aut vitam sanguine fundes."
Sic ait et triplicem clipeum collegit in ulnam
Et crispans hastile micans vi nititur omni
670 Ac iacit. at iuvenis devitat cautior ictum.
Hasta volans casso tellurem vulnere mordit.²⁹²

Waltharius tandem: "si sic placet," inquit, "agamus!"
Et simul in dictis hastam transmisit. at illa
Per laevum latus umbonis transivit, et ecce

---

²⁸⁴ regi … metallum] om. ω; added by later hand in margin with sign to insert after 651 S
²⁸⁵ damna] TB; dampna V
²⁸⁶ si] et V
²⁸⁷ ut … eunti] om. αV
²⁸⁸ mercor] merear V
²⁸⁹ remittens] remittat V
²⁹⁰ Camalo] Camelo V
²⁹¹ volo cunctos] cunctos volo (faulty scansion) M
²⁹² mordit] αBP; mordet TV

I was stealing these things from King Gunther? [154] Or had he loaned me something in return for profit so that he rightfully compels me to pay such great interest? Can it be that, while passing through, I have done damage to your territory so that for this reason it seems just for you to despoil me? If this nation shows so much jealousy toward everyone that it does not even grant a wayfarer the right to trod the ground, then, behold, I shall pay for my passage, give the king two-hundred bracelets. Only let him give up battle and grant peace."

[664] After Camalo had received this response in his beastly heart, he said: "You *will* open the coffers and increase your gift. And now I want to put an end to all this talk. Either you will give up what is requested or you will pour out your life-blood." So he spoke and drew his triple-layered shield up on his arm; and, brandishing his flashing spear, he strove to throw it with all his strength, but the youth carefully dodged the blow. The spear flew through air and *bitt*[155] the earth—a pointless wound.

[672] Finally, Walter said: "If this is your wish, let us do so!" With these words he cast his spear at once. It traveled through the left side of Camalo's shield. And behold! His hand, just as he had begun to draw his blade, was pinned to his leg by

675 Palmam, qua Camalo[293] mucronem educere coepit,
Confixit[294] femori transpungens terga caballi.
Nec[295] mora, dum vulnus sentit sonipes, furit atque
Excutiens dorsum sessorem sternere temptat;
Et forsan faceret, ni lancea fixa teneret.
680 Interea parmam Camalo[296] dimisit et, hastam
Complexus laeva, satagit divellere dextram.
Quod mox perspiciens currit celeberrimus heros
Et pede compresso capulo tenus ingerit ensem;
Quem simul educens hastam de vulnere traxit.
685 Tunc equus et dominus hora cecidere sub una.

Et dum forte nepos conspexerat hoc Camalonis,[297]
Filius ipsius Kimo[298] cognomine fratris,
Quem referunt quidam Scaramundum nomine dictum,
Ingemit et lacrimis compellat tristior omnes:
690 "Haec[299] me prae cunctis heu respicit actio rerum.
Nunc aut commoriar vel[300] carum ulciscar amicum."
Namque angusta loci solum concurrere soli
Cogebant, nec quisquam alii succurrere quivit.

Advolat infelix Scaramundus iam[301] moriturus,
695 Bina manu lato[302] crispans hastilia ferro.[303]
Qui dum Waltharium nullo terrore videret
Permotum fixumque loco consistere in ipso,
Sic ait infrendens et equinam vertice caudam

---

[293] Camalo] Camelo V
[294] confixit] affixit V
[295] nec] mid line dash before nec V
[296] Camalo] Camelo V
[297] Camalonis] Camelonis V
[298] Kimo] Chimo B; Timo perhaps rightly V
[299] haec] heu V
[300] vel] aut V
[301] iam] mox M
[302] lato] M; laxo V
[303] bina … ferro] cf. *Aen.* 1.313, 12.165

the spear which drove on through the horse. There was no delay. As the hoof-tapper sensed the blow, he began to rage and shake his back trying to dislodge his rider and perhaps would have if the piercing shaft did not hold him on.

[680] Meanwhile Camalo cast aside his shield and, taking the spear in his left hand, tried to draw it out of his right. As soon as the most celebrated hero noticed this, he ran up, grabbed Camalo's foot, and drove his sword in up to the hilt. As he drew this out, he also removed the spear from the wound. Then at the same time fell both the horse and his lord.

[686] When Camalo's nephew[156]—his brother's son named Kimo, who some say was called Scaramund[157]—saw this, he groaned and sadly addressed all the party in tears: "Alas, this event means more to me than to the rest of you. Now I shall either die or avenge my dear friend!" Indeed, the cramped space forced them to meet one on one, nor could anyone run to the aid of another.

[694] Unlucky Scaramund, soon to die, flew off, brandishing two spears with wide blades in his hand. When he saw Walter entirely undisturbed by fear and standing fixed in the same place, he gnashed his teeth and spoke thus as the horse-haired crest on his helm shook: "In what do you trust? What is your source of hope? I am not seeking treasure now nor any of your things, but I am asking for the life of my slain relative." Walter then said: "If you convince me that I made first trial of com-

Concutiens: "in quo fidis? vel quae tua spes est?
700 Non ego iam gazam nec rerum[304] quidque[305] tuarum[306]
Appeto, sed vitam cognati quaero perempti."
Ille dehinc:[307] "si convincar,[308] quo[309] proelia primus
Temptarim seu quid merui, quod talia possim
Iure pati, absque mora tua me transverberet hasta."

705 Necdum[310] sermonem concluserat, en Scaramundus
Unum de binis hastile retorsit in illum
Confestimque aliud. quorum celeberrimus heros
Unum devitat,[311] quatit ex umbone secundum.
Tunc aciem gladii promens Scaramundus acuti
710 Proruit in iuvenem cupiens praescindere frontem,
Effrenique in equo propius devectus ad illum
Non valuit capiti libratum infindere vulnus,
Sed capulum galeae impegit: dedit illa resultans
Tinnitus ignemque simul transfudit[312] ad auras.
715 Sed non cornipedem potuit girare superbum,
Donec Waltharius sub mentum cuspidis ictum
Fixerat et sella moribundum sustulit alta.
Qui caput orantis proprio mucrone recidens
Fecit cognatum pariter fluitare cruorem.

720 Hunc ubi Guntharius conspexit obisse[313] superbus,
Hortatur socios pugnam renovare furentes:
"Aggrediamur eum nec respirare sinamus,

---

[304] nec rerum] γ; vel rerum Cet. and Peip.
[305] quidque] quicque K; quidquam I
[306] iam … quidque] nunc gazam quicquam rerumque tuarum V
[307] ille dehinc] glossed "Wal. ait" I
[308] convincar] convincas V
[309] quo] PT; quod BSV; quod changed to quot K
[310] necdum] non dum V
[311] devitat] devitit V
[312] transfudit] transfundit V
[313] obisse] obire αV

bat, or if for some reason I rightfully deserve to suffer these things, then without delay let your spear bore through me!"

[705] He had not yet finished speaking when suddenly Scaramund hurled one of his two spears at him and then immediately the other. The most celebrated hero dodged one of these and shook the second from his shield. Then Scaramund, unsheathing his sharp-edged sword, rushed at the youth, intending to split his forehead open. Galloping on the back of his horse and nearing Walter, he could not plant a balanced wound upon his head but slammed his hilt against Walter's helm—it sprang away with a ringing sound as it shot fire into the air. But he could not turn his haughty steed before Walter had fixed a spear-blow under his chin and lifted him off his high seat and cut off his head with his own sword[158] even as he tried to talk—making kindred blood flow together.[159]

[720] When haughty Gunther saw this man die, he began to encourage his raging comrades to renew the fight: "Let's attack him and give him no chance to rest, until he grows tired and fails. Then, beaten, he will return the treasure and will pay the penalty for bloodshed."

Donec deficiens lassescat; et inde revinctus
Thesauros reddet luet[314] et pro sanguine poenas."

725 Tertius en Ewarhardus[315] abit bellumque lacessit,
Quamlibet ex longa generatus stirpe nepotum,
O vir clare, tuus cognatus et artis amator,
Pandare, qui quondam iussus confundere foedus
In medios telum torsisti primus Achivos.[316]
730 Hic spernens hastam pharetram gestavit et arcum,
Eminus emissis[317] haud aequo Marte sagittis
Waltharium turbans.[318] contra tamen ille virilis
Constitit opponens[319] clipei septemplicis orbem,
Saepius eludens[320] venientes providus ictus.
735 Nam modo dissiluit, parmam modo vergit in austrum
Telaque discussit, nullum tamen attigit illum.
Postquam Pandarides se consumpsisse sagittas
Incassum videt, iratus mox exerit ensem
Et demum advolitans has iactitat ore loquelas:
740 "O si ventosos lusisti callide iactus,
Forsan vibrantis dextrae iam percipis ictum."

Olli[321] Waltharius ridenti pectore adorsus:
"Iamque diu satis expecto certamina iusto
Pondere agi. festina, in me mora non erit ulla."[322]
745 Dixerat et toto conixus corpore ferrum
Conicit. hasta volans[323] pectus reseravit equinum:

---

[314] luet] luit V
[315] Ewarhardus] V; Ewurhardus Peip.; Wurhardus K; Wrhardus or Verhardus S; Wirmhardus P; Wrimhardus B; Warmardus T
[316] Pandare ... Achivos] cf. *Aen.* 5.496–7
[317] eminus emissis] cf. Sall. *Iug.* 101.4, *Carmen de bello Saxonico* 1.103
[318] turbans] turbat V
[319] opponens] obponens V
[320] eludens] elusit V
[321] olli] γV; lli missing initial K; Illi S
[322] ulla] illa corrected to ulla by later hand V
[323] dixerat ... volans] cf. *Aen.* 9.410–11

[725] Behold! Third, Evarhard goes and provokes battle—a man born from as long a line of descendants as any—your kinsman and lover of your skill,[160] O famous man, Pandarus, you who once, when ordered to disrupt the treaty, sent your arrow spinning into the midst of the Achaeans![161] This man spurned the spear and carried a bow and quiver, troubling Walter from afar with arrows shot in unfair warfare. Still that manly youth stood facing him, holding the circle of his seven-layered shield before him and continually evading the oncoming shots through his foresight, for now he would jump aside, now turn his shield into the wind[162] and strike away the arrows—none of them touched him. After Pandarides[163] saw he had spent his arrows in vain, soon in anger he brought out his sword and finally, flying forward, cast these words from his mouth: "Well, clever fellow, if you mocked my air-borne shots, perhaps you will now receive a blow from my whirling sword hand."

[742] To *hym*[164] as he smiled Walter began: "Now for a long time I have been waiting to engage in combat on fair footing.[165] Hurry up! For my part there will be no delay!" He had spoken and with all his body he strove and hurled the iron. The spear flying through the air unlocked the horse's breast—the steed rose up and whipped the air with its hooves; and, unseating the rider, collapsed over top of him. The youth[166] ran up and snatched his sword from him by force. Knocking off his

Tollit se arrectum quadrupes et calcibus auras[324]
Verberat effundensque equitem cecidit super[325] illum.
Accurrit iuvenis et ei vi diripit ensem.
750 Casside discussa crines complectitur albos[326]
Multiplicesque preces nectenti dixerat heros:
"Talia non dudum iactabas dicta per auras."
Haec ait et truncum secta cervice reliquit.

Sed non dementem tria visa cadavera terrent
755 Guntharium: iubet ad mortem properare vicissim.
En[327] a Saxonicis oris Ekerich[328] generatus
Quartus temptavit bellum, qui pro nece facta
Cuiusdam primatis eo diffugerat[329] exul.
Quem spadix gestabat equus maculis variatus.
760 Hic ubi Waltharium promptum videt esse duello,
"Dic,"[330] ait, "an corpus vegetet[331] tractabile temet
Sive per aerias fallas,[332] maledicte,[333] figuras.[334]
Saltibus assuetus faunus mihi quippe videris."

Illeque sublato dedit haec responsa cachinno:
765 "Celtica lingua probat te ex illa gente creatum,
Cui natura dedit reliquas ludendo praeire.
At si te propius venientem dextera nostra
Attingat,[335] post Saxonibus memorare valebis,
Te nunc in Vosago[336] fauni fantasma videre."

---

[324] auras] arvum V
[325] tollit … super] cf. *Aen.* 10.892–3
[326] albos] ambos MV
[327] en] large capital V
[328] Ekerich] V; Ekevrid α; Ekivrid BP; Erefrid T
[329] diffugerat] defugerat V
[330] dic] sic V
[331] vegetet] vegetat V
[332] fallas] fallis V
[333] maledicte] "o" above marks vocative V
[334] figuras.] so punctuated in Str.; question mark at line end V
[335] attingat] attingit V
[336] Vosago] Wasago V

helm, the hero seized his blonde hair and addressed him as he was making one prayer after another: [167] "A little while ago you were not casting such words into the air." This he said and left a torso severed from its head.[168]

[754] But the three corpses seen there did not frighten Gunther in his insanity. He bade another to hurry to death in turn. Behold! Fourth, Ekerich, born of the Saxon lands,[169] made trial of battle—he who on account of killing some nobleman had fled from home as an exile. A painted chestnut horse carried this man. When he saw Walter ready for war, he said: "Tell me whether a material body gives you vigor,[170] or if you are a deception made by airy shapes, you cursed fellow! To me at least you seem to be a faun, an inhabitant of the woods."

[764] And Walter laughed and gave this response: "The Celtic tongue[171] proves you were born of that race to whom nature granted to surpass all others at sport. But if you come nearer and my hand touches you, you will be able to tell the Saxons later that today you saw the *fantasme*[172] of a faun in the Vosges." "Well, I will try to discover what you are," said Ekerich, and then he forcefully cast his iron-tipped cornel-wood. It flashed out of his throwing strap,[173] but the stout shield shattered it. Walter in turn replied as he threw his spear: "A sylvan faun sends you this gift.

770 "Attemptabo quidem, quid sis," Ekerich[337] ait, ac mox
Ferratam cornum[338] graviter iacit. illa retorto
Emicat amento; quam durus fregerat umbo.
Waltharius contra respondit cuspide missa:
"Haec tibi silvanus transponit[339] munera faunus.
775 Aspice, num mage sit telum penetrabile nostrum."
Lancea taurino contextum tergore lignum[340]
Diffidit[341] ac tunicam scindens pulmone resedit.
Volvitur infelix Ekerich[342] rivumque cruoris
Evomit: en[343] mortem fugiens incurrit eandem.
780 Cuius equum iuvenis post tergum in gramen abegit.

Tunc a Gunthario clipeum sibi postulat ipsum
Quintus ab inflato Hadawardus[344] pectore lusus.
Qui pergens hastam sociis dimisit habendam,
Audax in solum confisus inaniter ensem.
785 Et dum conspiceret deiecta cadavera totam
Conclusisse viam nec equum transire valere,
Dissiliens parat ire pedes. stetit[345] acer in armis
Waltharius laudatque virum, qui praebuit aequam
Pugnandi sortem. Hadawart tum[346] dixit ad illum:
790 "O versute dolis ac[347] fraudis conscie serpens
—Occultare artus squamoso[348] tegmine suetus
Ac veluti coluber girum collectus in unum
Tela tot evitas[349] tenui sine vulneris ictu

---

337 Ekerich] cf. 756; Ekirih V; Ekivrid α; Ekvrid B; Erefrid T
338 cornum] pinum V
339 transponit] PTV; transpondit α; transmittit B
340 lignum] scutum V
341 diffidit] dividit M
342 Ekerich] cf. 756; Ek[.]rich M; Ekirih V; Ekevrid α; Ekivrid B; Erefrid T
343 en] et V
344 Hadawardus] Hadewardus V; Hadawartus K; Hadawartus S
345 stetit] petit α
346 Hadawart tum] VB; Hadaward tum P; Hadewart tum U; Hadawartum KS; Hadawardum T
347 ac] et αV
348 squamoso] suamoso αV
349 evitas] evita^n s n added by first hand U

See whether my spear is more penetrating." The shaft split the wood covered with bull hide and ripping his shirt lodged in his lung. Unlucky Ekerich rolled over and coughed up a stream of blood. Behold how, while fleeing death, he met it just the same.[174] The youth drove off his horse onto the grass behind him.

[781] Then, fifth, Hadawart, deceived by his own inflated breast, demanded that Gunther promise him Walter's shield. Soon advancing he threw his spear aside for his comrades to hold and boldly trusted vainly in his sword alone. When he saw that the corpses lying there had blocked the whole path and that the horse could not go that way, he leapt off and prepared to proceed by foot. Walter stood there fierce in arms and praised the man since he offered a chance to fight fairly. Then Hadawart told him: "You wily trickster and snake guilty of deception! You always hide your limbs in scaly covering and, like an adder coiled up into a *cercle*,[175] escape so many weapons without even a scratch for a wound! And you strangely evade poisoned arrows! Do you think you will cleverly avoid this blow that my right hand now sends with sure aim as I stand nearby? No such man is the author of this weapon or wound. Hear my advice; put down your painted shield! My lot seeks this, and the king's pledge promises it too. But I don't want you to hurt it since it pleases my eyes. Otherwise, though you take the nourishing light from me,[176] more of my

Atque venenatas ludis sine more sagittas—
795 Numquid et iste putas astu vitabitur ictus,[350]
Quem propius stantis certo libramine mittit
Dextra manus? neque[351] enim is teli seu vulneris auctor.[352]
Audi consilium, parmam deponito pictam:
Hanc mea sors quaerit, regis quoque sponsio praestat;
800 Nolo quidem laedas, oculis quia complacet istis.
Sin alias, licet et lucem mihi dempseris[353] almam,[354]
Assunt hic plures socii carnisque propinqui,
Qui, quamvis volucrem simules[355] pennasque capessas,
Te tamen immunem numquam patientur[356] abire."

805 Belliger at contra nil territus intulit ista:
"De reliquis taceo, clipeum defendere curo.
Pro meritis, mihi crede, bonis sum debitor illi.
Hostibus iste[357] meis se opponere saepe solebat
Et pro vulneribus suscepit vulnera nostris.
810 Quam sit oportunus hodie mihi, cernis[358] et ipse;
Non cum Walthario loquereris forsan, abesset.
Viribus o summis hostem depellere cures,
Dextera, ne rapiat tibi propugnacula muri!
Tu clavum umbonis studeas retinere, sinistra,
815 Atque ebori digitos circumfer glutine fixos!
Istic ne ponas[359] pondus, quod tanta viarum,
Portasti[360] spatia, ex Avarum nam[361] sedibus altis!"

---

[350] ictus] arcus, cf ictu in 793 V
[351] neque] nec SV
[352] neque ... auctor] nec enim telum sine vulnere transit V
[353] dempseris] presseris apparently preceded by erased de M
[354] almam] istam V
[355] volucrem simules] volucri similes V
[356] patientur] paciuntur V, paciantur α
[357] iste] ipse SV; ipsi K
[358] cernis ... ipse] no punctuation after cernis BPK; punctuation following cernis rather than at line end TVS
[359] ne ponas] deponas αV
[360] portasti] portavi with question mark at line end V
[361] nam] iam V

comrades and my blood-kin are here who, even if you play the bird and take to wing,[177] will never let you get away unharmed."

[805] But the warrior, not at all frightened, spoke this in return: "As for the rest, I say nothing, but as for the shield I am anxious to protect it. For its good service I am its debtor—believe me. It has often put itself in the way of my enemies and received wounds itself in place of me. And you yourself see how useful it has been to me today, since you would, perhaps, not be speaking with Walter if it were not here. O, right hand, take care to strike down my enemy with the utmost strength so that he may not snatch away the towers of my wall![178] O, left hand, earnestly grip the handle of my shield and keep your fingers fixed like glue around the ivory. Do not lose the burden which you have carried over so many long paths from the lofty seats of the Avars!"[179]

Ille dehinc: "invitus[362] agis, si sponte recusas.
Nec solum[363] parmam, sed equum cum virgine et auro
820 Reddes: tum demum scelerum cruciamina[364] pendes."[365]
Haec ait et notum vagina diripit[366] ensem.

Inter se variis terrarum partibus orti
Concurrunt. stupuit Vosegus[367] haec fulmina et ictus.[368]
Olli[369] sublimes animis ac grandibus armis,
825 Hic[370] gladio fidens, hic[371] acer et arduus hasta,[372]
Inter se multa et[373] valida vi proelia miscent.
Non sic nigra sonat percussa securibus ilex,
Ut dant tinnitus galeae clipeique resultant.
Mirantur Franci, quod non lassesceret heros
830 Waltharius, cui nulla quies spatiumve dabatur.

Emicat hic impune putans iam Wormatiensis
Alte et sublato consurgit fervidus ense,
Hoc ictu memorans semet finire duellum.
Providus at iuvenis ferientem cuspide adacta
835 Intercepit et ignarum[374] dimittere ferrum
Cogebat. procul in dumis resplenduit ensis.
Hic ubi se gladio spoliatum vidit amico,
Accelerare fugam fruticesque volebat adire.
Alpharides fretus pedibus[375] viridique iuventa

---

362 invitus] glossed "ait" U
363 solum] solam V
364 cruciamina] with Germanic gloss "cholvnge" U
365 pendes] with Germanic gloss "dv gearnest" U
366 diripit] apparently with Germanic gloss "zuchte" U
367 Vosegus] Wasagus V
368 ictus] ecce αV
369 olli] γI; ambo V
370 hic] glossed "unus" I
371 hic] glossed "alter" I
372 hasta] glossed "fidens" I
373 et] om. V
374 ignarum] ignavum V
375 pedibus] in pedibus V

[818] After this the other said: "You act against your will if you willingly refuse. Not only will you give up the shield but also your horse along with the girl and the gold. Then finally will you pay the penalty of torture for your crimes." This he said and stripped his well-known sword from its sheath.

[822] Rising from different regions of the earth[180] they ran together. The Vosges were dumbstruck at the lightening strikes of their blows. They were lofty in spirit and grand arms—this one trusting a sword,[181] this one fierce and tall with his spear. They mixed much in battle with forceful strength. Not so does the black holm-oak resound when struck by the ax as did their helms clatter and their shields rebound. The Franks looked on in wonder because the hero Walter was not yet worn out, though no rest or space of time was given him.

[831] This fellow from Worms, now thinking he could get away with it, leapt up in a boiling rage and raised his sword, calling out that he would end the war with this blow. But the foresightful youth intercepted him in mid-swing with a whack of his spear and made him drop the blade in surprise. From a distance the sword could be seen gleaming in the bushes. When he saw he had been despoiled of his friendly sword, he wanted to flee quickly and enter the thicket. Alpharides,[182] relying on his feet and fresh youth, followed saying: "Where are you fleeing to? Come get my shield!"[183] So he spoke and swiftly lifted his spear in both hands and struck. The man fell, his great shield clanging about him. Nor was the youth slow. He stepped

840 Insequitur dicens: "quonam fugis? accipe scutum!"
    Sic ait atque hastam manibus levat ocius ambis
    Et ferit. Ille cadit, clipeus superintonat ingens.
    Nec tardat iuvenis: pede collum pressit et hasta[376]
    Divellens[377] parmam telluri infixerat illum.
845 Ipse oculos vertens animam sufflavit in auram.[378]

    Sextus erat Patavrid.[379] soror hunc germana Haganonis[380]
    Protulit ad lucem. quem dum[381] procedere vidit,
    Vocibus et precibus conatur avunculus inde
    Flectere proclamans: "quonam ruis? aspice mortem,
850 Qualiter arridet! desiste! en ultima Parcae[382]
    Fila legunt.[383] o care nepos, te mens tua fallit.
    Desine! Waltharii tu denique viribus impar."
    Infelix tamen ille means haec omnia sprevit;
    Arsit[384] enim venis[385] laudem captare cupiscens.

855 Tristatusque[386] Hagano suspiria pectore longa
    Traxit et has imo fudit[387] de corde loquelas:
    "O vortex mundi, fames insatiatus habendi,[388]
    Gurges avaritiae, cunctorum fibra malorum!
    O utinam solum gluttires dira metallum
860 Divitiasque alias, homines[389] impune remittens!

---

376 hasta] hastam U
377 divellens] et vellens, apparently corrected to evellens V
378 auram] auras SU
379 Patavrid] α; Patarid BT; Paterih V; P...h, P..ch (Green) and Patavrith (Vollman) U
380 Haganonis] Hag[a]nis probably missing abbreviation mark U
381 dum] tum V
382 Parcae] with Germanic gloss "die schephen"
383 legunt] ligant I
384 arsit] ardet M
385 venis] ferus V
386 tristatusque] tristatus V
387 fudit] fundit V
388 insatiatus habendi] insaciata tenendi (fixing gender) V
389 homines] vecors V

on the man's neck and, prying away the shield, stabbed through him into the earth. The man rolled back his eyes and breathed his spirit out into the air.

[846] The sixth was Patavrid. Hagen's sister had brought him into the light, and, when he saw him going forth, his uncle called to him shouting, begging, and trying to turn him away from this pursuit: "Where are you rushing off to? Look at Death! How he grins! Stop! Behold! The Fates are gathering your last threads. Oh, my dear nephew, your mind deceives you. Quit this! In short, you are no match for Walter's strength." Still the unlucky fellow went on his way spurning all this advice, for he burned in his veins, lusting to seize glory.

[855] Sadly Hagen drew a long sigh from his breast and poured these words into the air:[184] "O Maelstrom of the World, Insatiate Hunger to Have,[185] Whirlpool of Greed,[186] Root of All Evils![187] Oh, how I wish, you dreadful creature, that you would swallow only precious metals and all other riches but return men without harm! But now you inflame men, blowing through them with your perverse spirit. To no man do his own goods suffice! Behold! They do not fear to rush to meet a

Sed tu nunc homines perverso[390] numine perflans
Incendis, nullique suum iam sufficit. ecce
Non trepidant mortem pro lucro incurrere turpem.
Quanto plus retinent, tanto sitis ardet habendi.
865 Externis modo vi modo furtive potiuntur
Et, quod plus renovat gemitus lacrimasque ciebit,[391]
Caeligenas animas Erebi fornace retrudunt.[392]
Ecce ego dilectum nequeo revocare nepotem;
Instimulatus enim de te est, o saeva cupido.
870 En caecus[393] mortem properat gustare nefandam
Et vili pro laude cupit descendere ad umbras.
Heu, mihi care nepos, matri quid,[394] perdite, mandas?
Quis nuper ductam refovebit, care, maritam,
Cui nec, rapte spei,[395] pueri ludicra dedisti?
875 Quis tibi nam[396] furor est? unde haec dementia venit?"
Sic ait et gremium lacrimis conspersit[397] obortis,
Et longum "formose,[398] vale" singultibus edit.[399]

Waltharius, licet alonge, socium fore maestum
Attendit, clamorque simul pervenit ad aures.
880 Unde incursantem sic est affatus equestrem:
"Accipe consilium, iuvenis clarissime,[400] nostrum
Et te conservans melioribus utere fatis.
Desine, nam tua te fervens fiducia fallit!
Heroum tot cerne neces et cede duello,
885 Ne suprema videns hostes facias mihi plures."

---

390 perverso] diverso V
391 ciebis] γ
392 retrudunt] retrudit V
393 caecus] ceus K; cupiens U; citius V
394 matri quid] TαV; quid matri BPU and Str.
395 rapte spei] PTS; raptae spei K; rapta spei B; rapta spe U; spe rapta V
396 nam] iam V
397 gremium … conspersit] gemitum … compressit V
398 formose] famoso K; formose I
399 et … vale] magnis atque vale longum V
400 clarissime] γI; fortissime αV

filthy death in their hope for lucre.[188] The more they have, the more the thirst to have burns them. They take possession of other men's goods, sometimes by force and sometimes by deceit; and, what causes more fresh groans and stirs new tears, they thrust their heaven-born souls into the furnace of Erebus.[189] Behold! I cannot call my beloved nephew back, for he is urged on by you, Savage Desire![190] Behold how blindly he hastens to taste an unspeakable death and wants to descend to the shades but for cheap glory.[191] Alas, my dear nephew, what, Lost One, are you giving your mother? Who, my dear, shall take care of your newly wedded wife to whom you, stolen from hope, did not give a child to cheer? What madness is this of yours? Where does this insanity come from?" So he spoke and spattered his lap with welling tears. And at last between sobs he proclaimed: "Farewell, my handsome boy!"[192]

[878] Walter, though far off, noticed his comrade's grim sadness, and his voice too reached his ears. Therefore, he addressed the approaching horseman thus: "Take my advice, most illustrious youth; and save yourself to await a better fate! Stop! Your rash confidence deceives you! Look at all these slaughtered heroes, and abandon battle so that you do not see your last hour and make me more enemies."[193]

"Quid de morte mea curas," ait ille, "tyranne?
Est modo pugnandum tibimet, non sermocinandum."
Dixit et in verbo nodosam destinat hastam,
Cuspide quam propria divertens transtulit heros.
890 Quae subvecta choris[401] ac viribus acta furentis
In castrum venit atque pedes stetit ante puellae.
Ipsa metu perculsa[402] sonum prompsit muliebrem.
At postquam tenuis redit in praecordia sanguis,[403]
Paulum[404] suspiciens spectat, num viveret heros.

895 Tum quoque vir fortis Francum discedere bello
Iussit. at ille furens gladium nudavit et ipsum
Incurrens petiit vulnusque a vertice librat.
Alpharides parmam demum concusserat aptam
Et spumantis apri frendens de more tacebat.
900 Ille ferire volens se pronior omnis ad ictum
Exposuit, sed Waltharius sub tegmine flexus
Delituit corpusque suum contraxit, et ecce
Vulnere delusus iuvenis recidebat ineptus.[405]
Finis erat, nisi quod genibus tellure refixis
905 Belliger accubuit calibemque[406] sub orbe cavebat.
Hic dum[407] consurgit, pariter se subrigit ille
Ac citius scutum trepidus sibi praetulit atque
Frustra certamen renovare parabat. at illum
Alpharides fixa gladio petit ocius hasta
910 Et mediam clipei dempsit vasto impete[408] partem,
Hamatam[409] resecans loricam atque ilia nudans.

---

401 subvecta choris] subiecta totis V
402 perculsa] percussa V
403 sanguis] γI; virtus αV
404 paulum] paulo V
405 iuvenis … ineptus] iuvenem decepit ineptum V
406 calibemque] galeaeque with calibemque above V
407 dum] tum V
408 dempsit … impete] depresserat impetu V
409 hamatam] BT; amatam K; armatam S; armaticam V; dilectam I

[886] "Why do you care if I die, you *tyran*?"[194] said the other, "Now you must fight, not talk!" He had spoken and aimed his knotty spear as he talked. But the hero knocked it aside with his own and turned it elsewhere. As it was carried down in a whirling, windy dance[195] and driven by Walter's raging strength, it entered the camp and fixed itself before the girl's feet. Stricken with fear, she exclaimed a womanly cry. But, after a weak pulse returned to her heart, briefly peeking up from below, she looked to see whether the hero was alive.

[895] Then again the brave man[196] ordered the Frank to depart from battle, but he bared his sword in rage and ran to attack Walter and brandished his wound by his head.[197] But Alpharides[198] swung his shield just at the right time and wordlessly gnashed his teeth like a boar foaming at the mouth. In his desire to strike, Patavrid exposed himself all the more openly to a blow, while Walter ducked and hid under his shield, contracting his body. And behold! Cheated of the wound,[199] the youth fell clumsily. It would have been the end, had not the warrior been lying there with his knees bent to the ground, fending off the *acier*[200] under the circle of his shield. While he was getting up, the other also lifted himself and quickly in alarm brought the shield before him and vainly began to renew the contest. But Alpharides[201] also swiftly planted his spear in the ground and attacked him with his sword—taking off half of his shield with a massive swing, cutting through his linked hauberk, and laying bare his loins. Unlucky Patavrid, seeing his own guts, collapsed giving his body to the sylvan beast and his soul to Orcus.[202]

Labitur infelix Patavrid[410] sua viscera cernens
Silvestrique ferae[411] corpus, animam dedit Orco.

Hunc sese ulturum spondens Gerwitus[412] adivit,
915   Qui forti subvectus equo supra volat[413] omnem
Stragem, quae angustam[414] concluserat obvia callem.
Et dum bellipotens recidisset[415] colla iacentis,
Venit et ancipitem vibravit in ora bipennem.
(Istius ergo modi Francis tunc arma fuere.)
920   Vir celer obiecit peltam frustravit et ictum,
Ac retro saliens hastam rapiebat amicam
Sanguineumque ulva viridi dimiserat ensem.

Hic vero[416] metuenda virum[417] tum bella videres.[418]
Sermo quidem nullus fuit inter Martia tela:[419]
925   Sic erat adverso mens horum intenta duello.
Is furit, ut caesos mundet vindicta sodales,
Ille studet vitam toto defendere nisu
Et, si fors[420] dederit, palmam retinere triumphi.
Hic ferit, ille cavet; petit ille, reflectitur iste:
930   Ad studium fors[421] et virtus miscentur in unum.
Longa tamen cuspis breviori depulit hostem
Armatum telo, girat sed et ille caballum[422]
Atque fatigatum cupiebat fallere homonem.
Iam magis atque magis irarum mole gravatus

---

[410] Patavrid] αB; Patafrid T; Paterih V
[411] silvestrique ferae] silvanisque feris V
[412] Gerwitus] αT; Gerwidus V; Gerwintus B
[413] supra volat] super evolat V
[414] angustam] angustum (normalizing gender) V
[415] recidisset] (faulty scansion) γ; resecaret (good scansion) αV
[416] vero] vere V
[417] virum] with orum above to mark genitive plural V
[418] videres] "si fuisses" in left margin marks this clause as part of an understood condition V
[419] tela] bella, cf. 923 V
[420] fors] sors V
[421] fors] sors V
[422] caballum] caballo V, cavallo α

[914] Gerwit came then, promising to avenge this companion. He, borne on a strong horse, flew over all the strewn corpses, which had closed off the narrow pathway. He came and flourished his double-headed axe in Walter's face—at that time the Franks used this sort of weapon[203]—just as the powerful warrior had cut off the dead man's head. Swiftly the man[204] threw his shield in the way, frustrated the blow, jumped back, snatched up his trusty spear, and tossed his bloody sword in the green rushes.

[923] And here then you would have seen fearful wars of men! Indeed, there was no talk to interrupt their martial warfare, so intent were their minds on adverse *warre*.[205] The other raged to honor his slain comrades with revenge, but Walter tried zealously to protect his life with all his effort and, if chance so granted, to retain his victory palm. This one strikes, the other guards; this one attacks, the other leans away. Luck and courage are eagerly mixed together.[206] Still the long spear knocked aside the enemy's shorter weapon, but he circled on his horse, wanting to trick the wearied *mann*.[207] Now more and more burdened by a mass of wrath, Walter lifted the bottom of Gerwit's shield and passed his iron through his groin and penetrated his thigh. Falling backward he brought forth a gloomy shout and a grievous death.[208] He kicked the field with his heels. And even now Walter hacked through the man's neck and left a headless torso, which had once been a count of the lands of Worms.[209]

935   Waltharius clipeum Gerwiti[423] sustulit imum,
      Transmissoque femur[424] penetraverat inguine[425] ferrum.
      Qui post terga ruens clamorem prodidit[426] atrum
      Exitiumque[427] dolens;[428] pulsabat calcibus arvum.
      Hunc etiam truncum caesa cervice reliquit.
940   Idem[429] Wormatiae campis comes extitit ante.

      Tunc[430] primum Franci coeperunt forte morari
      Et magnis precibus dominum decedere pugna
      Deposcunt. furit ille miser caecusque profatur:[431]
      "Quaeso, viri fortes et[432] pectora saepe probata,
945   Ne fors[433] haec cuicumque metum, sed conferat iram.
      Quid mihi, si Vosago[434] sic sic[435] inglorius ibo?
      Mentem quisque meam sibi vindicet. en ego partus[436]
      Ante mori sum, Wormatiam quam talibus actis
      Ingrediar. Petat hic patriam sine sanguine victor?[437]
950   Hactenus[438] arsistis hominem spoliare metallis,
      Nunc ardete, viri, fusum mundare cruorem,
      Ut mors abstergat mortem, sanguis quoque sanguem,[439]
      Soleturque necem sociorum plaga necantis."

---

[423] Gerwiti] αT; Gerwidi V; Kerwiti BP; Kermunti I
[424] transmissoque femur] transmissumque citum (removing strange transferred epithet) V; transmissumque femur S
[425] inguine] inguina (see above) V
[426] prodidit] protulit V
[427] exitiumque] exivitque γ
[428] dolens;] followed by medial punctuation V; no punctuation Str.
[429] idem] idem in V
[430] tum] SB; tunc PKV; cum T; apparently cum corrected to tum I
[431] deposcunt … profatur] om. S
[432] et] o above to mark vocative phrase V
[433] fors] sors V
[434] si Vosago] sivos ago P
[435] Vosago … sic] Wasago si sic V; si sic I
[436] en … partus] e … paratus with a few letters erased V
[437] victor] fuso V
[438] hactenus] actenus PV
[439] sanguem] ω; perhaps sanguen (neuter) Ring

[941] Then by chance the Franks first began to delay and to beseech their lord with great prayers that he depart from battle. He, miserable fellow, grew enraged and blindly spoke: "I ask, brave men and hearts so often tested, that this fortune not bring each man fear but anger instead. What shall I do, if I leave the Vosges as ingloriously as this?[210] Let each adopt my sentiment for himself. Behold! I am ready to die before I enter Worms under such circumstances.[211] Should this fellow seek his homeland victoriously with no blood fine? Till now you burned to despoil the man of his treasures.[212] Burn again, men, burn to honor the blood that has been spilled so that death may wipe away the stain of death, and blood that of blood. Let your murderous blow console your murdered comrades!"

His animum dictis demens incendit et omnes
955   Fecerat immemores vitae simul atque salutis.
Ac velut[440] in ludis alium praecurrere quisque
Ad mortem studuit, sed semita, ut antea dixi,
Cogebat binos bello decernere[441] solos.
Vir tamen illustris dum cunctari videt[442] illos,
960   Vertice distractas suspendit in arbore cristas
Et ventum captans sudorem tersit anhelus.

Ecce repentino Randolf[443] athleta caballo
Praevertens[444] reliquos hunc importunus adivit
Ac mox ferrato petiit sub pectore conto.
965   Et nisi duratis Wielandia[445] fabrica giris
Obstaret,[446] spisso penetraverit ilia ligno.
Ille tamen subito stupefactus corda[447] pavore
Munimen clipei obiecit mentemque recepit;
Nec tamen et galeam fuerat[448] sumpsisse facultas.
970   Francus at emissa gladium nudaverat hasta
Et feriens binos Aquitani vertice crines
Abrasit, sed forte cutem praestringere summam
Non licuit, rursumque alium vibraverat ictum
Et praeceps animi directo obstamine scuti
975   Impegit calibem, nec[449] quivit viribus ullis
Elicere. Alpharides retro,[450] se fulminis instar
Excutiens, Francum valida vi fudit[451] ad arvum

---

[440]   velut] veluti V
[441]   decernere] γ; decedere α; deducere V
[442]   dum … videt] cum … vidit (unmetrical) V
[443]   Randolf] Rantolf E
[444]   praevertens] praeveniens V
[445]   Wielandia] Wielandia BP; Welandia αV; Walandia T
[446]   obstaret] obsisteret (unmetrical) V
[447]   corda] corde VE; corde corrected to corda by first hand B
[448]   fuerat] om. V
[449]   nec] neque V
[450]   retro] retrorsum V
[451]   fudit] fundit V

[954] Saying this, he fired spirits up and made them all forgetful of both their lives and their safety. And, as in some game, each was eager to outrun the other in the race for death.[213] But the path, as I said before, forced only two men to contend in war. Yet the illustrious man, as he saw them delaying, removed his helm and hung it in the tree and, catching his breath, wiped away the sweat as he panted.

[962] Behold! The *athlète*[214] Randolf on his quick horse passed the rest and menacingly raced toward Walter and then aimed under his chest with his iron-tipped pike.[215] And if the Work of Weland[216] with its hardened *cercles*[217] were not in the way, he would have pierced his loins with the thick wood. Still Walter, though stunned in his heart with sudden alarm, threw his protecting shield in the way and recovered his wits. Not yet had there been a chance to grab his helm. But the Frank tossed his spear, stripped his sword, and struck, shaving two locks of hair off the Aquitanian's head. Still he could not—it chanced—scrape the surface of the skin, so he drew back again and struck another blow, but in haste he planted his *acier*[218] directly in the obstructing shield, nor could he withdraw it, no matter how hard he tried. Alpharides[219] in turn, shaking himself free as quick as lightning, threw the Frank to the ground with his powerful strength. Standing over him, he stepped on his chest and said: "Behold! For shaving my head, I shall cheat you of yours, lest this be your boast over me to your betrothed."[220] Scarcely had he said this, when he chopped the man's neck, even as he prayed.[221]

Et super assistens pectus conculcat et inquit:
"En pro calvitio capitis te vertice fraudo,
980   Ne fiat ista tuae de me iactantia sponsae."
Vix effatus haec[452] truncavit colla precantis.

At[453] nonus pugnae Helmnod[454] successit, et ipse[455]
Insertum triplici gestabat fune tridentem,[456]
Quem post terga quidem socii stantes tenuerunt,[457]
985   Consiliumque fuit, dum cuspis missa sederet
In clipeo, cuncti pariter traxisse studerent,
Ut vel sic hominem deiecissent furibundum;
Atque sub hac certum sibi spe posuere triumphum.
Nec mora, dux totas fundens in brachia vires
990   Misit in adversum magna cum voce tridentem[458]
Edicens: "ferro tibi finis, calve, sub isto!"[459]
Qui[460] ventos penetrans[461] iaculorum more coruscat,[462]
Quod genus aspidis ex alta sese arbore tanto
Turbine demittit,[463] quo cuncta obstantia vincat.

995   Quid moror? umbonem sciderat peltaque[464] resedit.
Clamorem Franci tollunt saltusque resultat,[465]
Obnixique trahunt restim simul atque vicissim,
Nec dubitat princeps tali se aptare labori.
Manarunt cunctis sudoris flumina membris.

---

[452] vix … haec] vix haec affatus V
[453] at] et KV; initial a missing P
[454] Helmnod] SB; Heimnod K; Helmon but cf. 1008 V; Helmod T; Helnal but cf. 1008 E
[455] ipse] ipsi V
[456] insertum … tridentem] om. V
[457] tenuerunt] monuerunt V
[458] misit … tridentem] om. V
[459] edicens … finis] est dixit ferro tibi finis o calve sub isto V
[460] qui] quod V
[461] penetrans] penetrat V
[462] coruscat] coruscans V; coruscas α
[463] demittit] γ; dimittit KV
[464] peltaque] petraque V
[465] resedit … resultat] resedit…saltusque om. K; clamorem…resultat om. E

[982] Yet the ninth, Helmnod,[222] succeeded to the fight, and he wielded a trident tied to a three-strand rope, which his comrades standing behind him held. The plan was, when he threw the weapon, and it stuck in the shield, they would all eagerly pull together so that they might cast down even so raging a man. Because of this hope they considered their triumph certain. There was no delay; the duke, pouring all his strength into his arms, threw the trident at his adversary, calling out loudly: "Under this iron, bald man,[223] you will find your end!" It pierced the wind, flashing like javelins,[224] those kind of snakes that shoot down from high trees with such force that they pierce all obstacles.

[995] Why do I linger? It split the shield-boss and settled in the shield; the Franks sent up a shout and leapt backwards. Striving all together and in turn they pulled the rope, nor did the prince hesitate to apply himself to such work. Rivers of sweat seeped down all their limbs, but still the hero stood in this contest, like an ash tree, which seeks the stars with its leafage no more than it seeks Tartarus with its roots— unmoved and holding all the roaring winds in contempt. The enemies contended

1000   Sed tamen haec[466] inter velut aesculus[467] astitit heros,
        Quae non plus petit astra comis quam Tartara fibris,
        Contempnens omnes ventorum immota fragores.
        Certabant hostes hortabanturque viritim,[468]
        Ut, si non quirent ipsum detrudere ad arvum
1005   Munimen clipei saltem[469] extorquere studerent,
        Quo dempto vivus facile caperetur ab ipsis.

        Nomina quae restant edicam iamque trahentum:[470]
        Nonus Eleuthir[471] erat, Helmnod[472] cognomine dictus,
        Argentina quidem decimum dant oppida Trogunt,[473]
1010   Extulit undecimum pollens urbs[474] Spira Tanastum,
        Absque Haganone locum rex supplevit[475] duodenum.
        Quattuor hi adversum summis conatibus unum
        Contendunt pariter multo varioque tumultu.

        Interea Alpharidi vanus labor incutit iram,
1015   Et qui iam pridem nudarat casside frontem,
        In framea tunicaque simul confisus aena[476]
        Omisit parmam primumque invasit Eleuthrin.[477]
        Huic galeam findens cerebrum diffudit et ipsam[478]
        Cervicem resecans[479] pectus patefecit, at[480] aegrum
1020   Cor pulsans animam liquit mox[481] atque calorem.

---

[466] haec] BPV; hic αT; hos E
[467] aesculus] [a]eculus BTV; escilus α
[468] viritim] vicissim V
[469] saltem] saltim ITV
[470] restant … trahentum] restim edicam iam forte trahebant V
[471] Eleuthir] PTV; Heleutir B; Eleuter α
[472] Helmnod] SB; Heimnod K; Helnold here, cf. 982 V; Helmod T; Helnod here, cf. 982 E
[473] Trogunt] α, cf. 1021; Trogum Str. and Cet.
[474] urbs] et V
[475] rex supplevit] γVE; supplevit rex α
[476] aena] enea V; ahena T
[477] Eleuthrin] BT; Eleutrhin P; Eleutrim K; Eleutrī S; Eleuthin V
[478] ipsam] ipsum followed by medial punctuation V
[479] resecans] -que secans V
[480] at] ac V; ad I
[481] liquit mox] γV ; mox liquerat K; liquerat mox IS

with him and encouraged each other, saying that, if they could not drag him out into the open field, they should at least be eager to wrench away his protecting shield so that, with this removed, they might easily take him alive.

[1007] I shall tell the names of those pulling, those who remained. Ninth was Eleuthir,[225] called also by the name Helmnod; the Argentine town[226] provided the tenth, Trogus;[227] the powerful city Speyer produced the eleventh, Tanastus; the king filled the twelfth place, leaving out Hagen. Together these four contended with the utmost effort against one in a great and indecisive struggle.

[1014] Meanwhile the vain toil goaded Alpharides[228] to anger; and, just as he had long now had his head bare of helm, so, relying on his brand[229] and bronze[230] shirt, he cast aside his shield and first attacked Eleuthir. Rending his helm,[231] he split the man's brain in two and, cutting through the neck itself, opened up his chest. The heart beating sickly soon gave up its warm breath.

Inde petit Trogunt[482] haerentem in[483] fune nefando.
Qui subito attonitus recidentis morte sodalis
Horribilique hostis conspectu coeperat acrem
Nequiquam temptare fugam voluitque relicta
1025 Arma recolligere, ut rursum repararet agonem.
(Nam cuncti funem tracturi deposuerunt
Hastas[484] cum clipeis.) sed quanto maximus heros
Fortior extiterat, tanto fuit ocior, olli[485]
Et cursu capto suras mucrone recidit
1030 Ac sic tardatum praevenit et abstulit eius
Scutum. sed Trogus,[486] quamvis de vulnere lassus,[487]
Mente tamen fervens saxum circumspicit ingens,
Quod rapiens subito obnixum contorsit in hostem
Et proprium a summo clipeum fidit usque deorsum.
1035 Sed retinet fractum pellis superaddita lignum.
Moxque genu posito viridem vacuaverat aedem[488]
Atque ardens animis vibratu[489] terruit auras,
Et si non quivit virtutem ostendere factis,
Corde tamen habitum patefecit et ore virilem.
1040 Nec[490] manes ridere videns audaciter infit:
"O mihi si clipeus vel sic modo[491] adesset amicus!
Fors tibi victoriam de me, non inclita virtus
Contulit. ad scutum mucronem hic[492] tollito nostrum!"

Tum quoque subridens "venio iam" dixerat heros
1045 Et cursu advolitans dextram ferientis ademit.

---

482 Trogunt] IK; Trogont corrected to Trogunt S; Trogum (scansion requiring hiatus) γV and Str.
483 in] om. V; sub B
484 hastas] hastam V
485 olli] illi T; ollis E; illis V
486 Trogus] ω; perhaps Trogunt, cf. 1009 and 1021
487 lassus] l[a]esus αVI
488 aedem] ensem K; ulvam V
489 vibratu] uibratvs with v by later hand V; vibravit E
490 nec] om. V
491 sic modo] γ; si modo αVIB²
492 hic] PVIE; hunc T; om. αB

[1021] Then he attacked Trogus, while he was still hanging on to the damnable rope. Trogus, astonished by the sudden death of his falling comrade, at the horrific sight of his enemy began in vain to attempt bitter flight and wanted to recover the weapons he had laid aside so that he might renew the *compétition*[232]—for they had all put aside their spears and shields to pull the rope. But, just as the mighty hero excelled in bravery, so he did also in speed. As he caught up with Trogus in a run, he sliced the man's calves with his sword point, thus slowing him down, and passed him to steal his shield.[233] But Trogus, though weakened by the wound, nevertheless, seething in his mind, saw a huge stone, which he snatched up and suddenly hurled at his enemy, as he strove onward, and split his own shield from top to bottom. But the hide stretched over the frame held the broken wood together. And soon, though on bended knee, Trogus emptied the green house[234] and, burning with emotion, terrified the air with his swings. Though he could not display his manliness[235] through deeds, still he showed his manly manner in heart and voice. And, failing to see the ghosts smiling, he boldly began: "O, if only I had my trusty shield! Luck has given you victory over me, not famed manliness. Here take my sword to match my shield!"[236]

[1044] Then the hero, grinning too,[237] said: "I am coming!" And, flying at Trogus in a run, detached his right hand in mid-swing.[238] But, when the *athlète*[239] was

Sed cum athleta[493] ictum libraret ab aure secundum
Pergentique animae valvas aperire studeret,
Ecce Tanastus[494] adest telis cum rege resumptis
Et socium obiecta protexit vulnere pelta.[495]
1050   Hinc indignatus iram convertit in ipsum[496]
Waltharius humerumque eius de cardine vellit
Perque latus ducto suffudit viscera ferro.
"Ave!"[497] procumbens submurmurat ore Tanastus.[498]
Quo recidente preces contempsit promere Trogus[499]
1055   Conviciisque sui victorem incendit amaris,
Seu virtute animi, seu desperaverat. exin[500]
Alpharides: "morere," inquit, "et haec sub Tartara transfer
Enarrans[501] sociis, quod tu sis ultus eosdem."
His dictis torquem collo circumdedit aureum.[502]
1060   Ecce simul caesi volvuntur pulvere amici,
Crebris foedatum ferientes calcibus arvum.

His rex infelix visis suspirat et omni
Aufugiens studio falerati terga caballi
Scandit et ad maestum citius Haganona volavit
1065   Omnimodisque illum precibus flexisse sategit,
Ut secum pergens pugnam repararet. at ille:
"Me genus infandum prohibet bellare parentum,
Et gelidus sanguis mentem mihi ademit[503] in armis.
Tabescebat enim genitor, dum tela videret,

---

[493] athleta] γV; atleta α; ad letha I
[494] Tanastus] Thanastus A
[495] pelta] belta V
[496] in ipsum] ad ipsum αV
[497] ave] awe T; salve K; ahah V
[498] Tanastus] Thanastus K
[499] Trogus] ω, cf. 1009 and 1021
[500] desperaverat exin] Str.; no punctuation before exin PαVI
[501] enarrans] enarra V
[502] his ... aureum] om. T
[503] ademit] dempsit αV

balancing a second blow by his ear and was eager to open the doors for his spirit to leave, suddenly Tanastus along with the king—they had recovered their weapons—appeared, threw his shield in the way, and warded off the wound from his comrade.

[1050] Then indignantly Walter turned his anger toward this man and tore his shoulder from its joint[240] and sliced through his side with iron, spilling his guts. "Farewell!" Tanastus whispered faintly as he fell forward.[241] As he fell, Trogus disdained to produce prayers[242] but incensed his friend's conqueror with bitter abuse—perhaps through manly spirit, perhaps he was simply desperate. Then Alpharides[243] said: "Die and take this message down to Tartarus.[244] Tell your comrades that you avenged them." This he spoke and put a golden torque about his neck.[245] Behold! The friends lie slain together in the dust, striking the gory earth with twitching heels.[246]

Part III: Hagen's Choice and the Treasure Divided

[1062] The unlucky king, seeing this, drew in his breath and, trying to escape in all eagerness, mounted the back of his finely adorned[247] horse to fly quickly to gloomy Hagen[248] and tried with all kinds of pleas to make him go with him and renew the battle. But Hagen spoke: "The unspeakable race of my parents prevents me from fighting, and cold blood has stolen my wits away in the midst of battle. So I say, for my father melted down whenever he set eyes upon weapons, and fearfully renounced combat with many a word. When you made those taunts, king, among your comrades, our aid to you was shameful indeed."[249]

1070 Et timidus multis renuebat[504] proelia verbis:
      Haec dum iactasses, rex, inter te comitantes,
      Extitit indignum nostri tibi quippe iuvamen.”

      Ille recusanti precibus nihilominus instans
      Talibus aversum satagit revocare loquelis:
1075 “Deprecor[505] ob[506] superos, conceptum pone furorem.
      Iram de nostra contractam decute culpa,
      Quam vita comitante, domum si venero tecum,
      Impensis tibimet benefactis diluo multis.
      Nonne pudet sociis tot cognatisque peremptis
1080 Dissimulare virum? magis, ut mihi quippe videtur,
      Verba valent animum quam facta nefanda movere.
      Iustius in saevum tumuisses mente tyrannum,
      Qui solus hodie caput infamaverat orbis.
      Non modicum patimur damnum de caede virorum;
1085 Dedecus at tantum superabit Francia numquam.
      Antea quis fuimus[507] suspecti,[508] sibila dantes
      ‘Francorum,’ dicent, ‘exercitus omnis ab uno,
      Proh[509] pudor ignotum vel quo,[510] est impune necatus!’”

      Cunctabatur adhuc Haganon et[511] pectore sponsam
1090 Walthario plerumque fidem volvebat et ipsum
      Eventum gestae recolebat in ordine causae.
      Supplicius[512] tamen infelix rex institit illi.
      Cuius subnixe rogitantis acumine motus
      Erubuit domini vultum, replicabat honorem

---

[504] renuebat] rennuebat TV
[505] deprecor] te rogo S; obsecro Peip.
[506] ob] γVE; p with crossed tail for per α
[507] quis fuimus] qui fuerant E
[508] suspecti] PT; suspecte B; praelati V
[509] Proh] Str., cf. Prud. *Psych.* 353; Proch T; pro abbreviated PBV
[510] proh … quo] pro pudor ignoto nunc est inpune V
[511] cunctabatur … et] cunctatur sed adhuc hagano etiam (regularizing the nominative form) V
[512] supplicius] suppliciter E; suppliciis (liciis over erasure, acc. to Str.) with gloss “-cationibus” by first hand V

[1073] The other, nonetheless entreating him yet more as he refused, strove to change him with such words as these: "I beseech you by the gods. Drop this wrath that you have conceived within! Shake off this anger you have for me! If we live and return home together, I shall requite my debt to you with many generous rewards. Do you not feel ashamed to hide away your manhood, when so many of your companions and relatives have died? Words, I think, can move your mind more than awful deeds. You would more justly have grown angry at the cruel *tyran*[250] who alone today dared to defame the Head of the World.[251] We suffer no little loss from the slaughter of men. Yet never will Frankland overcome so great a dishonor.[252] Those who used to fear us will whisper and say: 'All the army of the Franks at the hands of one man—for shame, we do not even know the man—is slain with no retribution.'"

[1089] Still Hagen kept delaying and tossing about in his heart his pledge to Walter and recalling the event in order just as it happened, but the unlucky king pressed upon him, imploring even more, until moved by the vigor of his insistent pleas, he blushed at the face of his lord and thought again of the honor that he had on account of his courage, and how it would perhaps henceforth become vile if he were to spare himself in this situation.

1095   Virtutis propriae, qui fors vilesceret inde,
      Si quocumque modo in rebus sibi parceret istis.

      Erupit tandem et clara sic voce respondit:
      "Quo me, domne, vocas? quo te sequar, inclite princeps?
      Quae nequeunt fieri, spondet fiducia cordi.[513]
1100   Quis tam desipiens quandoque fuisse probatur,
      Qui saltu baratrum sponte attemptarit apertum?
      Nam scio Waltharium per campos sic fore acerbum,
      Ut tali castro nec non statione locatus
      Ingentem cuneum velut unum temnat[514] homullum.
1105   Et licet huc cunctos equites simul atque pedestres
      Francia misisset, sic his ceu fecerat istis.
      Sed quia conspicio te plus doluisse pudore
      Quam caedis damno nec sic discedere velle,
      Compatior, propriusque dolor[515] succumbit honori
1110   Regis: et ecce viam conor reperire salutis,
      Quae tamen aut nusquam[516] ostendit se sive coacte.
      Nam propter carum (fateor tibi, domne) nepotem
      Promissam fidei normam corrumpere nollem.
      Ecce in non[517] dubium pro te,[518] rex, ibo periclum.
1115   Ast hic me[519] penitus conflictu cedere noris.
      Secedamus[520] eique locum praestemus eundi
      Et positi in speculis tondamus prata caballis,
      Donec iam castrum securus deserat artum,
      Nos abiisse[521] ratus. Campos ubi[522] calcet apertos,
1120   Insurgamus et attonitum post terga sequamur:

---

[513] cordi] cordis V
[514] temnat] temptat BE; temptet V
[515] propriusque dolor] -que om I¹; sign for -que added under dolor I²; propius dolor et V
[516] nusquam] numquam αVI
[517] in non] non est (faulty scansion) V
[518] pro te] intervening space for a few characters V
[519] me] non V
[520] secedamus] discedamus V
[521] abiisse] abisse PT; et abisse V
[522] campos ubi] ubi campos K; campos dum V

[1097] At last he burst out and answered thus in a clear voice: "Whither do you call me, lord? Whither shall I follow, famous prince? Confidence promises the heart what cannot happen.[253] Who has ever proved to be so foolish that he has tried to jump into the gaping *abysse*[254] of his own accord? So I say, for I know Walter is so bitter on the field of battle that, situated in such a stronghold and residence, he will despise a huge company as if it were one little man. Even if Frankland had sent all her cavalry and infantry here, still he would have done just the same; but, since I see that you are more grieved by shame than by destructive slaughter, and that you do not want thus to leave, I feel sympathy, and my own grief gives way to my king's honor. And behold! I shall try to find the path of salvation,[255] which shows itself either nowhere or else only under compulsion.[256] So I say, for on my dear nephew's account—I confess, my lord—I would not spoil the oath I pledged.[257] Behold! For you, my king, I shall go into no uncertain danger. But know that I avoid conflict here. Let us depart and give him space to come out, and then place ourselves in a lookout[258] and pasture our horses in the meadow, until, secure at last, he leaves his close-set stronghold, thinking that we have gone. When he steps into the open field, let us rise and attack him from behind while he is surprised. Thus can we try some work of virtue.[259] But this very sure hope I have amongst doubtful things: then, my king, you will be able to fight—if you have a mind for war—for he will never put the two of us to flight, but we must either flee or wage *fiers*[260] war."

Sic aliquod virtutis opus temptare valemus.
Haec mihi in ambiguis spes est certissima rebus.
Tum pugnare[523] potes, belli si, rex, tibi[524] mens est:
Quippe fugam nobis numquam dabit ille duobus,
1125   At nos aut fugere aut acrum[525] bellare necesse est."

Laudat consilium satrapa[526] et complectitur illum
Oscilloque virum demulcet; et ecce recedunt
Insidiisque locum circumspexere sat aptum
Demissique ligant animalia gramine laeto.

1130   Interea occiduas vergebat Phoebus in oras,
Ultima per notam signans vestigia Thilen,
Et cum Scottigenis post terga reliquit Hiberos.
Hic postquam oceanas sensim calefecerat undas,
Hesperos[527] Ausonidis[528] obvertit cornua terris,
1135   Tum secum sapiens coepit tractare satelles,
Utrum sub tuto per densa silentia castro
Sisteret, an vastis heremi committeret arvis.
Aestuat immensis curarum fluctibus, et quid
Iam faceret, sollers arguta indagine quaerit.

1140   Solus enim Hagano fuerat suspectus et illud
Oscillum regis subter complexibus actum.
Ambierat[529] prorsus, quae sit sententia menti
Hostis et an urbem vellent remeare relictam,
Pluribus ut sociis per noctem forte coactis
1145   Primo mane parent bellum[530] recreare[531] nefandum

---

[523] pugnare] bellare αV
[524] belli si rex tibi] BT; belli tibi si rex P; belli rex si tibi αV
[525] acrum] acre V
[526] satrapa] satrapae V
[527] Hesperos] Hesper' B; Hespera et αV
[528] Ausonidis] γVE; Ausoniis α
[529] ambierat] ambigerat αV
[530] parent bellum] bellum parent V
[531] recreare] renovare αV

[1126] His lord praises the advice, embraces him, and comforts him with a kiss. And behold! They leave and search for a place suitable for ambush, and relaxing they tie up their horses on the lush grass.

[1130] Meanwhile, Phoebus tilts toward the western shores, marks his farthest tracks over famous Thule, and leaves the Spaniards along with the Irishmen behind him. After the Sun has gradually warmed the ocean waves, Hesperus[261] turns his horns to the Ausonid[262] lands, and then wisely the warrior begins to think to himself whether to stay in his safe stronghold while all was deeply silent or to entrust himself to the vast fields of a desert. He storms within amidst great waves of worry and searches his wits in a swift hunt.[263]

[1140] So he did, for he feared Hagen alone, and that kiss and embrace of the king. He was totally unsure about the mind of his enemy—would they want to return to the city that they had left to gather more comrades overnight and come back at first light to renew awful war, or would they set an ambush by themselves and lie in wait nearby? In addition to these worries, the forest with its unfamiliar,

An soli insidias facerent propiusque laterent.
Terret ad haec triviis ignoti silva meatus,
Ne loca fortassis incurreret aspera spinis,
Immo quippe feris, sponsamque amitteret illis.[532]

1150 His ita provisis exploratisque profatur:
"En quocumque modo res pergant,[533] hic recubabo,
Donec circuiens lumen spera reddat amatum,[534]
Ne patriae fines[535] dicat rex ille superbus
Evasisse fuga furis de more per umbras."
1155 Dixit et ecce viam vallo praemuniit artam[536]
Undique praecisis spinis simul et paliuris.
Quo facto ad truncos sese convertit amaro
Cum gemitu et cuicumque suum caput applicat atque
Contra orientalem prostratus corpore partem
1160 Ac nudum retinens ensem hac voce[537] precatur:
"Rerum factori, sed et omnia facta regenti,
Nil sine permisso[538] cuius vel denique iussu[539]
Constat, ago grates, quod me defendit iniquis
Hostilis turmae telis nec non quoque probris.
1165 Deprecor at dominum[540] contrita mente benignum,
Ut, qui peccantes non vult sed perdere culpas,
Hos in caelesti praestet mihi sede videri."[541]

Qui postquam orandi finem dedit, ilico surgens
Sex giravit equos et virgis rite retortis

---

[532] immo … illis] caram quippe feris sponsam dimitteret illis (avoiding elision) V
[533] res pergant] respergant BP; res vergant V
[534] amatum] amicum B; amoenum V
[535] fines] ad fines V
[536] artam] arto V
[537] hac voce] KT; sic voce B; hac sic voce E; cum voce (Peip. wrongly "hac cum voce") V; hac cum voce S
[538] permisso] permissu αI[2]
[539] iussu] αVIT; iusso PB and Str.
[540] at dominum] ad dominum BαV
[541] videri] Pα and Str.; videre BTVI

crossing trails made him fear that he might chance upon places rough with thorn-bushes,[264] or even wild beasts, and somehow lose his betrothed.

[1150] After considering all of this, he spoke: "Well, however the affair turns out, I shall rest here until the *sphère*[265] runs its course and returns its beloved light so that that haughty king may not say that I fled the bounds of his country like a thief through the shadows."[266] He spoke and behold! He fortified the tight path with a barricade, placing freshly cut thorns and Christ's thorn[267] together all around. When he had finished, he turned to the maimed corpses with a bitter groan and put the heads beside each of them;[268] and, lying face down toward the East[269] with his bare sword in his hand, he prayed thus: "To the maker of the world who also governs all creation, without whose permission or even command nothing stands, I give thanks that he has defended me from the unjust blows of the hostile band and also from their insults.[270] But I beseech my kind Lord with a repentant mind that he who wants to destroy not sinners but their faults may allow me to see these men in the heavenly home."[271]

[1168] After completing his prayer, straightaway he rises, turns the six horses around, and ties them up with thin twigs twisted in the customary way—only these remained; for two were killed in battle, and King Gunther had driven off three.[272]

1170   Vinciit:[542] hi[543] tantum remanebant, nempe duobus
        Per tela absumptis ternos rex Gunthere[544] abegit.
        His ita compositis procinctum solvit et alte
        Ingenti fumans leviabat pondere corpus.
        Tum maestam laeto solans[545] affamine sponsam
1175   Moxque cibum capiens aegros recreaverat artus,
        Oppido enim lassus fuerat, clipeoque recumbens
        Primi custodem somni iubet esse puellam,
        Ipse matutinam disponens[546] tollere curam,
        Quae fuerat suspecta magis, tandemque quievit.

1180   Ad cuius caput illa[547] sedens solito vigilavit
        Et dormitantes cantu patefecit ocellos.
        Ast ubi vir primum iam expergiscendo soporem
        Ruperat, absque mora surgens dormire puellam
        Iussit et arrepta[548] se fulciit impiger hasta.
1185   Sic reliquum noctis duxit, modo quippe caballos
        Circuit, interdum auscultans vallo propiavit,
        Exoptans orbi species ac lumina reddi.

        Lucifer interea praeco scandebat Olympo
        Dicens: "Taprobane[549] clarum videt insula solem."
1190   Hora fuit, gelidus qua terram irrorat Eous.
        Aggreditur iuvenis caesos spoliarier armis
        Armorumque habitu, tunicas et cetera linquens;
        Armillas tantum, cum bullis baltea[550] et enses,[551]

---

[542] vinciit] αBT; vinxit, cf. revinxit 209 V and Peip.
[543] hi] equi V
[544] Gunthere] SV; Cundhere B; Gunther K; Gunthar. with final e erased T
[545] solans] revocans V
[546] disponens] disponit V
[547] illa] ipsa V
[548] arrepta] arrecta αV
[549] dicens Taprobane] (aprobane B) γ; duci tam probane I; lucens thaprobane (probane V; zaprobane E) αVE
[550] baltea] balthea TV
[551] enses] heriles V

Finishing all of this, he loosens his belt, removes the massive weight, and lightens his steaming body.[273] Then with happy words he consoles his gloomy betrothed. And soon he took food and refreshed his weary limbs, for he was quite exhausted. Then, lying back against his shield, he ordered the girl to keep watch so that he might sleep first. He decided to take the morning watch, which was more suspect, and at last he rested.

[1180] At his head she sat and kept her usual watch and kept her sleepy eyes awake by singing. But when the man first broke his sleep and awoke, he rose without delay, ordered the girl to sleep, and quickly snatched up a spear and propped himself against it. So he continued the rest of the night, for sometimes he would go among the horses, and sometimes he would approach the barricade and listen, wishing that appearances and light would return to the world.

[1188] Meanwhile, Lucifer[274] scaled Olympus as herald, saying: "The isle of Taprobane[275] sees the bright sun." It was the hour when the chilly Eous[276] bedews the land. The youth approached to despoil the slain of their arms and armor. Leaving the shirts and other things, he stripped only the armbands along with the belt bosses, the belts and the swords, and the hauberks too along with their helmets.[277] He loaded four horses with these things, placed the one he called his betrothed on

Loricas quoque cum galeis detraxerat ollis.
1195 Quatuor[552] his oneravit equos sponsamque vocatam
Imposuit quinto, sextum conscenderat ipse
Et primus vallo perrexerat ipse revulso.
At dum constricti penetratur semita callis,
Circumquaque oculis explorans omnia puris
1200 Auribus arrectis ventos captavit et auras,
Si vel mussantes[553] sentiret vel gradientes
Sive superborum crepitantia frena virorum,
Seu saltim ferrata sonum daret ungula equorum.

Postquam cuncta silere videt, praevortit[554] onustas[555]
1205 Quadrupedes, mulierem etiam praecedere iussit.
Scrinia gestantem comprendens ipse caballum
Audet inire viam consueto cinctus amictu.
Mille fere passus transcendit, et ecce puella
—Sexus enim fragilis animo trepidare coegit—
1210 Respiciens post terga videt[556] descendere binos
Quodam colle viros[557] raptim et sine more meantes
Exanguisque virum compellat voce sequentem:
"Dilatus iam finis adest: fuge, domne, propinquant!"

Qui mox conversus visos cognovit et inquit:
1215 "Incassum multos mea dextera fuderat hostes,
Si modo supremis[558] laus desit, dedecus assit.
Est satius pulcram per vulnera quaerere mortem
Quam solum amissis palando[559] evadere rebus.
Verum non adeo sunt desperanda salutis
1220 Commoda cernenti quondam maiora pericla.

---

[552] quatuor] PαV; quattuor B
[553] si vel mussantes] mussantes pariter V
[554] praevortit] T; praevertit BαV
[555] onustas] honustas B; onustos, perhaps rightly IV
[556] videt] viros V
[557] viros] videt V
[558] si … supremis] si nunc in fine (faulty scansion) V
[559] palando] pallendo I; balando V

the fifth, and mounted the sixth himself. Then he went out first, after pulling aside the barricade. Yet, while the path of the confined trail pierced onward, checking everything around him with clear eyes, he caught the airy wind in his ears, pricked to see if he could hear any whispers, footsteps, jangling bridles of haughty men, or even, perhaps, the clatter of an iron-clad horse's hoof.

[1204] After he saw that all was quiet, he moved the burdened horses in front of him and bid the girl too to go ahead. He himself, keeping hold of the horse carrying the coffers, dared to follow the path girt in his usual apparel. He crossed nearly a mile, and behold! The girl—for her fragile sex drove her to fear in her heart—looked back and saw the two men coming down from a hill, going at a fast and unusual pace.[278] Going white, she addressed the man behind her with a cry: "Our delayed end has now come. Flee, my lord! They are closing in!"

[1214] He turned, recognized them at first sight, and said: "In vain did my right hand[279] lay low my enemies, if glory shall abandon me at the last, and dishonor stand at my side. It is better to seek a handsome death in battle than to lose our possessions and escape alone as wanderers.[280] But the rewards of salvation[281] are not so hopeless for one who has seen greater perils. Take the reins of Lion, who carries the gold, go quickly, and hurry into that nearby wood! But I choose rather to stand by on the mountain's slope, waiting for what shall come and greeting them as they arrive." The

Aurum gestantis tute accipe lora Leonis
Et citius pergens luco succede propinquo.
Ast ego in ascensu montis subsistere malo,
Eventum opperiens adventantesque salutans.»
1225 Obsequitur dictis virguncula clara iubentis.
Ille celer scutum collegit et excutit hastam,
Ignoti mores equitis temptando sub armis.

Hunc[560] rex incursans comitante satellite demens
Eminus affatu compellat valde superbo:
1230 "Hostis atrox, nisu deluderis! ecce latebrae
Protinus absistunt, ex quis de more liciscae
Dentibus infrendens rabidis[561] latrare solebas.
En in propatulo, si vis,[562] confligito campo
Experiens, finis si fors queat aequiperari
1235 Principio. scio: Fortunam mercede vocasti
Idcircoque fugam tempnis seu deditionem."

Alpharides contra regi non reddidit ulla,
Sed velut hinc surdus alio[563] convertitur aiens:
"Ad te sermo mihi, Hagano, subsiste parumper!
1240 Quid, rogo, tam fidum subito mutavit amicum,
Ut,[564] discessurus nuper vix posse revelli
Qui nostris visus[565] fuerat complexibus, ultro,
Nullis nempe malis laesus, nos appetat armis?
Sperabam, fateor, de te—sed denique fallor—
1245 Quod, si de exilio redeuntem nosse valeres,
Ipse salutatum mihimet mox obvius ires
Et licet invitum hospitii requiete foveres[566]

---

[560] hunc] unc (missing initial) P; tunc VI; tunc corrected to hunc T¹
[561] rabidis] rabidi V
[562] si vis] mecum V
[563] alio] alias V
[564] ut] et V
[565] visus] visus with i marked perhaps for removal S; usus V
[566] requiete foveres] requie refoveres V

famous young maiden obeys his words as he commands. He quickly grabs his shield and shakes his spear to test the temper of the unfamiliar horse in battle.

[1228] The king races madly at him, with his retainer at his side, and from afar he addresses him in the haughtiest manner: "Savage enemy, you will now be cheated of all your hard work! Behold! Your hidden den is far away, the place from which, like a *chien-loup*[282] bitch, you used rabidly to gnash your teeth and bark. Behold! Fight, if you will, in an open field and find out if luck can get you an end equal to your beginning. I know—you have invited Fortune with a reward,[283] and so you disdain flight or surrender."

[1237] Alpharides[284] gave no reply to the king but, as if deaf, turned from him to the other, saying: "I have words for you, Hagen. Stay a bit! What, I ask, has suddenly changed so faithful a friend such that he who in his recent departure seemed hardly able to be pried away from my embrace will voluntarily seek to attack me, though he is in no way wronged?[285] I admit I had hoped, though wrongly, that, if you were able to discover that I was returning from my exile, you would come then personally to greet me, and would entertain me in restful hospitality, though against my will, and would wish peacefully to take me back to the kingdom of my father. And, thinking this, I was concerned as to where to bring your gifts. Yes, though I went through unfamiliar lands, I said to myself: 'I fear none of the Franks so long as Hagen lives.' I beg you now by our childhood games. Recover your senses. Remember those games, which we with one heart were accustomed to play and share

Pacificeque[567] in regna patris deducere velles;
Sollicitusque fui, quorsum tua munera ferrem.
1250 Namque per ignotas dixi pergens regiones:
'Francorum vereor Haganone superstite nullum.'
Obsecro per ludos, resipiscito iam, pueriles,
Unanimes quibus assueti fuimusque periti
Et quorum cultu primos attrivimus[568] annos.
1255 Inclita quonam migravit concordia nobis
Semper in hoste domique manens nec scandala noscens?
Quippe tui facies patris obliviscier egit,
Tecum degenti mihi patria viluit ampla.
Numquid mente fidem abradis saepissime pactam?
1260 Deprecor, hoc abscide nefas neu bella lacessas,[569]
Sitque inconvulsum nobis per tempora foedus.
Quod si consentis, iam nunc ditatus abibis
Eulogiis, rutilo umbonem complebo metallo."

Contra quae Hagano vultu haec affamina torvo
1265 Edidit atque iram sic insinuavit apertam:[570]
"Vim prius exerces, Walthari, postque sopharis.
Tute fidem abscideras, cum memet adesse videres
Et tot stravisses socios immoque propinquos.
Excusare nequis, quin me tunc affore nosses.
1270 Cuius si facies latuit, tamen arma videbas
Nota satis habituque virum rescire valebas.[571]
Cetera fors tulerim, si vel dolor unus abesset:[572]
Unice[573] enim carum rutilum blandum pretiosum
Carpsisti florem mucronis falce tenellum.
1275 Haec res est, pactum qua irritasti prior almum,

---

567 pacificeque] pacificumque V
568 attrivimus] attriverat γ
569 lacessas] lacesses VT
570 apertam] ne nos incuses mihi vim quia tu prior infers inserted after 1265 (included as Peip. 1266a) V
571 Valebas] valeres αV
572 si ... abesset] ni ... adesset V
573 unice] unicum V

our experience, games in which we spent those earliest years of our lives. Where did that famous harmony we had go? It used always to remain in both war and peace— never knowing a stumbling block.[286] Indeed, it made you forget your father's face, and my great fatherland grew vile as I lived with you. Can it really be true that you have wiped from your mind the oath that we so often affirmed? I beseech you. End this wickedness, do not provoke battle! Let us keep our pact untroubled through the ages. If you agree to this, this very moment you will leave enriched with *éloges*;[287] I shall fill your shield with ruddy metal."[288]

[1264] In reply Hagen produced this address with his face set grim and so expressed his open anger: "You practice force first, Walter, and only later do you play the *sophiste*.[289] You ended our pact when you saw that I was there and yet killed so many of my comrades and even my kinsmen. You cannot deny that you knew then that I was there. Even if my face was hidden, yet you saw my arms, which you know well, and you could recognize the man by his gear. Perhaps I might bear the rest, if this one grief were not with me—uniquely dear, ruddy, charming, and precious was the tender little blossom whom you reaped with your sickle's blade. This is the deed by which you first made void that pact of our youth, and so I want no treasure in return for that pledge. I want to learn in battle whether you have virtue by yourself, and from your hands I seek vengeance for my nephew.[290] Behold! Either I approach my death, or I shall do something memorable."

Iccircoque gazam cupio[574] pro foedere nullam.
Sitne tibi soli virtus, volo discere in armis,
Deque tuis manibus caedem perquiro nepotis.
En aut oppeto sive aliquid[575] memorabile faxo."

1280 Dixit et a tergo saltu se iecit equino,
Hoc et Guntharius nec segnior egerat heros
Waltharius, cuncti pedites bellare parati.
Stabat quisque ac venturo se providus ictu
Praestruxit: trepidant sub peltis Martia membra.

1285 Hora secunda fuit, qua tres hi congrediuntur.
Adversus[576] solum conspirant arma duorum.
Primus maligeram[577] collectis viribus hastam
Direxit Hagano disrupta pace. sed illam
Turbine terribilem tanto et stridore volantem
1290 Alpharides semet cernens tolerare nequire,
Sollers obliqui delusit tegmine scuti:
Nam veniens clipeo sic est ceu marmore levi[578]
Excussa et collem vehementer sauciat usque
Ad clavos infixa solo. tunc pectore magno,
1295 Sed modica vi fraxineum hastile superbus
Iecit Guntharius, volitans quod adhaesit in ima
Waltharii parma, quam mox dum concutit ipse,
Excidit ignavum ligni de[579] vulnere ferrum.

Omine quo maesti confuso pectore Franci
1300 Mox stringunt acies, dolor est conversus ad iras,
Et[580] tecti clipeis Aquitanum invadere certant.

---

574 cupio] BKI; capio PTSV
575 oppeto ... aliquid] succumbo aliquid V
576 adversus] γ; adversum, perhaps rightly αVI
577 maligeram] (a incorrectly long) γI ; maligenam α; malignam (a incorrectly long) V
578 levi] lēvi Str.; laevi Peip.; leni V
579 ligni de] αVI; de ligni BT and Str.
580 et] ac V

[1280] He spoke and, jumping, threw himself from the back of his horse; Gunther too, and the hero Walter did the same no more slowly—all of them ready to make war on foot. Each stood and guarded himself, looking out for the blow to come; their martial limbs shook in anticipation beneath their shields.

[1285] It was the second hour of the day when these three joined. The arms of two conspire against one. First of all, Hagen collects his strength and aims his death-bearing[291] spear, breaking the peace. But as it flies, terrible with a wild whirlwind and shrieking sound, Alpharides,[292] seeing he cannot receive it, cleverly deflects the blow by tilting his shield.[293] As it meets the shield, the spear bounces off as if from polished marble, and it violently stabs the hill, sinking into the ground up to the nails.[294] Then with great heart but little strength haughty Gunther throws his ash shaft, which flies and sticks in the bottom of Walter's shield.[295] But, as soon as he shakes it, the weakling iron falls out of the scratched wood.

[1299] At this sign, the Franks, though gloomy and confused in their hearts, soon strip war from its sheath; their grief turns to anger; and, covering themselves with their shields, they try to attack the Aquitanian. But he vigorously knocked them

Strenuus ille tamen vi cuspidis expulit illos
Atque incursantes vultu terrebat et armis.

Hic rex Guntharius coeptum meditatur ineptum,
1305   Scilicet ut iactam frustra[581] terraeque[582] relapsam
—Ante pedes herois enim divulsa iacebat—
Accedens tacite furtim sustolleret hastam,
Quandoquidem brevibus gladiorum denique telis
Armati nequeunt accedere comminus illi,
1310   Qui tam[583] porrectum torquebat cuspidis ictum.
Innuit ergo oculis vassum[584] praecedere suadens,
Cuius defensu causam supplere valeret.

Nec[585] mora, progreditur Haganon[586] ac provocat hostem,
Rex quoque gemmatum vaginae[587] condidit ensem
1315   Expediens dextram furto actutum faciendo.[588]
Sed quid plura? manum pronus[589] transmisit in hastam
Et iam comprensam sensim subtraxerat illam[590]
Fortunae maiora petens. sed maximus heros,
Utpote qui bello semper sat providus esset
1320   Praeter et unius punctum cautissimus horae,[591]
Hunc inclinari[592] cernens persenserat actum
Nec tulit, obstantem sed mox Haganona[593] revellens,
Denique sublato qui divertebat ab ictu,
Insilit et planta direptum hastile retentat

---

[581] frustra] γ; subito αV
[582] terraeque] missing que in text but mark below final "e" may signal que V
[583] tam] iam V
[584] vassum] falsum IV
[585] nec] initial missing V
[586] haganon] hagano (following usual spelling to produce hiatus) V
[587] vaginae] vagina (ablative) V
[588] expediens … faciendo] extendens dextram furtum tutum faciendo V
[589] pronus] VBT; pronum K; pronam S
[590] illam] ipsam V
[591] praeter … horae] fretus et hunis per punctum cautissimus horae V
[592] inclinari] indignari V
[593] Haganona] Hagano P

away with a sweep of his spear and frightened them with both his countenance and his weapons as they rushed at him.

[1304] Here King Gunther considers a foolish undertaking, thinking how he might quietly and secretly approach to recover his spear, thrown in vain and fallen to the ground—for after being pried free it was lying by the hero's feet. So he thought, since, armed with only their short swords, they could not close hand-to-hand with him, for he kept whirling his outstretched spear around. Therefore, he gave a sign to his vassal with his eyes, encouraging him to edge forward so that with his defense he might complete his plan.

[1313] There was no delay. Hagen went forth and challenged their enemy, and the king, hiding his bejeweled sword in its scabbard, unencumbered his hand for a quick act of theft.[296] But need I say more? He leaned forward, put his hand on the spear, gripped it, and gradually drew it away from Walter—asking too much from Fortune. But the mighty hero, inasmuch as he was always quite alert in war and very observant of all but the briefest moment, saw him leaning down, sensed what he was doing, and did not allow it, but pushed aside Hagen—who stood in the way to deflect his upraised blow—jumped on the spear shaft being snatched away, held it with his foot, and yelled at the king caught in his thievery so that now his knees gave way under the stricken spear. And he would have sent him straight to hungry Orcus if Hagen, the mighty warrior, had not quickly run to his aid, defended his lord with opposing shield, and brought the bare blade of his cruel sword against the face of

1325 Ac regem furto captum sic increpitavit,
      Ut iam perculso sub cuspide genva labarent.
      Quem quoque continuo esurienti porgeret[594] Orco,
      Ni Hagano armipotens citius succurreret atque
      Obiecto dominum scuto muniret et hosti
1330 Nudam aciem saevi mucronis in ora tulisset.
      Sic, dum Waltharius vulnus cavet, ille resurgit
      Atque tremens stupidusque[595] stetit, vix morte reversus.

      Nec[596] mora nec requies: bellum instauratur[597] amarum,
      Incurrunt hominem nunc ambo nuncque vicissim;
1335 Et dum progresso se impenderet acrius uni,
      En de parte alia subit alter et impedit ictum.
      Haud aliter, Numidus[598] quam dum venabitur ursus[599]
      Et canibus circumdatus astat et artubus horret
      Et caput occultans submurmurat ac propiantes
1340 Amplexans Umbros miserum mutire coartat,
      —Tum rabidi[600] circumlatrant hinc inde Molossi
      Comminus ac dirae metuunt accedere belvae—[601]
      Taliter in nonam conflictus fluxerat horam,[602]
      Et[603] triplex cunctis inerat maceratio: leti
1345 Terror, et ipse labor bellandi, solis et ardor.

      Interea herois coepit subrepere menti
      Quiddam, qui tacito premit has sub corde loquelas:
      "Si Fortuna viam non commutaverit, isti[604]

---

[594] porgeret] porrigeret (faulty scansion) V
[595] stupidusque] trepidusque αV
[596] nec] initial n om. V
[597] bellum instauratur] bellumque instaurat V
[598] Numidus] tumidus V
[599] ursus] S ends with line 1337.
[600] rabidi] Str. attributes rabidi to P and rapidi to BTKV (I confirm rapidi for V); Peip. attributes rapidi only to BK and rabidi to TV; Althof similiarly attributes rapidi to BK and rabidi to PTV.
[601] ac … belvae] atque ferae metuunt accedere dirae V
[602] horam] undam P
[603] et] atque V
[604] isti] istis V

his foe. So, while Walter avoided Hagen's blow, Gunther got back up, trembling, and stood there in a stupor, scarcely returned from death.

[1333] There was no delay, no rest. They renewed bitter war. Now the two rush at the man together, now they take turns. And, while he rains fiercer blows on the one who advances, from the other side the second immediately approaches and hinders his swing, not unlike when a Numidian bear[297] is hunted, stands surrounded by dogs, bristles on his limbs,[298] and, covering[299] his head, growls and squeezes the Umbrian[300] hounds that come too close, making them whine miserably; then the rabid Molossians bark from this side and that, and the dreadful beasts fear to come closer.[301] In such a way the conflict flowed on till the ninth hour.[302] And threefold trouble wore on them all—fear of death, the very toil of battle, and the burning heat of the sun.

[1346] Meanwhile, an idea began to creep upon the hero's mind, and he suppressed these words within his heart: "If Fortune does not change her path, they will tire me out and deceive me with their vain sport."[303] Right then he raised his voice and called to Hagen: "O, Christ's thorn,[304] you sprout such foliage that you can

Vana fatigatum memet per ludicra fallent."
1350   Ilico et elata Haganoni voce profatur:
"O paliure, vires foliis, ut pungere possis;
Tu[605] saltando iocans astu me ludere temptas.
Sed iam faxo locum, propius ne accedere tardes:
Ecce tuas—scio,[606] praegrandes—ostendito vires!
1355   Me piget incassum tantos sufferre labores."
Dixit et exiliens contum contorsit in ipsum,[607]
Qui pergens[608] onerat clipeum dirimitque aliquantum
Loricae ac magno modicum de corpore stringit;
Denique praecipuis praecinctus fulserat armis.

1360   At vir Waltharius missa cum cuspide currens
Evaginato regem importunior ense
Impetit et scuto dextra de parte revulso[609]
Ictum praevalidum ac mirandum[610] fecit eique
Crus cum poplite adusque femur decerpserat omne.
1365   Ille super parmam ante pedes mox concidit huius.[611]
Palluit exanguis domino recidente satelles.
Alpharides spatam tollens iterato cruentam
Ardebat lapso postremum infligere[612] vulnus.
Immemor at proprii Hagano vir[613] forte doloris
1370   Aeratum[614] caput inclinans obiecit ad ictum.
Extensam cohibere manum non quiverat heros,
Sed cassis fabrefacta diu meliusque peracta
Excipit assultum mox et scintillat in altum.

---

[605] tu] et V
[606] scio] cito V
[607] ipsum] illum KV
[608] pergens] pungens V
[609] scuto … revulso] scutum … revulsit V
[610] ac mirandum] admirandum V
[611] pedes … concidit] pedes cadit et miser (Str. says -iser and following hui' over erasure) V
[612] postremum infligere] postremo infigere V
[613] at … vir] ac Hagano proprii sit V
[614] aeratum] KV; elatum γ

prick. You jest and dance and try to trick me with your cunning. But now I will make room so that you may not be slow to come closer. Behold! Show me your strength—I know it's very great! I am sick of suffering such great toil in vain."[305] He spoke and, leaping up, whirled his spear at him, and it drove through his shield, weighing it down, and tore through a bit of his hauberk, slicing a tiny piece off his great body. Indeed, he had stood gleaming, girt in marvelous arms.[306]

[1360] But like a man,[307] Walter threw his spear, unsheathed his sword, and ran threateningly to attack the king; he pried Gunther's shield away on the right, made a mighty and amazing blow, and tore off his leg up to the knee, all of it below the thigh.[308] Gunther fell then on top of his shield at Walter's feet. His retainer grew bloodlessly pale at the fall of his lord. Alpharides[309] lifted the bloody *sabre*[310] again, burning to inflict the final wound on the fallen man. But it chanced that, heedless of his own pain, Hagen, like a man,[311] bending his helmeted head, opposed it to the blow. The hero could not check his hand at the end of its swing, but the helm made long ago and finely forged received the attack and sent sparks into the air. Stunned by the helm's hardness, the sword split in two.[312] Oh pain! With a clang it flew apart sparkling in the air and the grass all around.[313]

Cuius duritia stupefactus dissilit ensis,
1375   Proh[615] dolor! et crepitans partim micat aere et[616] herbis.

Belliger[617] ut frameae murcatae[618] fragmina crevit,[619]
Indigne tulit ac nimia furit efferus ira
Impatiensque sui capulum sine pondere ferri,
Quamlibet eximio[620] praestaret et arte metallo,
1380   Protinus abiecit monimentaque tristia sprevit.
Qui dum forte manum iam enormiter exeruisset,[621]
Abstulit hanc Hagano sat laetus vulnere prompto.
In medio iactus[622] recidebat dextera fortis
Gentibus ac populis multis suspecta, tyrannis,
1385   Innumerabilibus quae fulserat ante trophaeis.
Sed vir praecipuus nec laevis[623] cedere gnarus,
Sana mente potens carnis superare dolores,
Non desperavit, neque[624] vultus concidit eius,
Verum vulnigeram clipeo insertaverat ulnam[625]
1390   Incolomique manu mox[626] eripuit semispatam,
Qua dextrum cinxisse latus memoravimus illum,
Ilico vindictam capiens ex hoste severam.
Nam feriens dextrum[627] Haganoni effodit ocellum
Ac timpus resecans pariterque labella revellens
1395   Olli bis ternos discussit[628] ab ore molares.

---

[615] proh] Str.; pro P; proch T; proc V
[616] aere et] acer in V
[617] belliger] initial "b" om. V
[618] murcatae] murratae V
[619] crevit] PT; vidit Str.
[620] eximio] exnimio V
[621] iam ... exeruisset] manum miser exeruisset inermem V
[622] medio iactus] medioque ictu V
[623] laevis] saevis TV
[624] neque] nec V
[625] vulnigeram ... insertaverat] in vulnigeram clipeum mox posuit V
[626] mox] ferus V
[627] nam ... dextrum] ac dextrum feriens V
[628] discussit] excussit V

[1376] The warrior, as he saw the fragments of the broken brand,[314] grew indignant and raged, wild with excessive anger;[315] and, unable to stand his hilt without the burden of its iron, though outstanding for its skillful metal work, he tossed it aside and spurned the sad memorial. While he extended his hand in mighty effort, Hagen quite happily removed it with a prompt swipe. The hand was falling as the mighty swing continued its arc ... the hand once feared by many races, nations, and *tyrans*,[316] the hand which once gleamed before innumerable trophies. But the exceptional man, not knowing how to yield to misfortune, capable in his sound mind of overcoming the pains of the flesh, did not despair, nor did he cast down his face, but stuck the bloody stump in his shield and then snatched up in his unharmed hand the half-sword, with which we have said that he girded his right side,[317] taking severe vengeance from his foe on the spot. He struck Hagen and cut out *hys*[318] right eye, severed *hys* temple, sliced off *hys* lips, and knocked twice three teeth from *hys* mouth.

Tali negotio dirimuntur proelia facto.[629]
Quemque suum vulnus atque aeger anhelitus arma
Ponere[630] persuasit. quisnam hinc[631] immunis abiret,
Qua duo magnanimi heroes tam viribus aequi
1400 Quam[632] fervore animi steterant in fulmine belli!
Postquam finis adest, insignia quemque notabant:
Illic Guntharii regis pes,[633] palma iacebat
Waltharii nec non tremulus[634] Haganonis ocellus.
Sic sic armillas partiti sunt Avarenses![635]
1405 Consedere duo, nam[636] tertius ille iacebat,
Sanguinis undantem tergentes floribus amnem.
Haec inter timidam revocat[637] clamore puellam
Alpharides, veniens quae saucia quaeque ligavit.

His ita compositis sponsus praecepit eidem:
1410 "Iam misceto merum Haganoni et porrige primum;
Est athleta bonus, fidei si iura reservet.[638]
Tum[639] praebeto mihi, reliquis qui plus toleravi.
Postremum volo Guntharius bibat, utpote segnis
Inter magnanimum qui paruit arma virorum
1415 Et qui Martis opus tepide atque enerviter[640] egit."
Obsequitur cunctis Heririci[641] filia verbis.

---

629 tali … facto] Hoc tali facto dirimuntur proelia dura V
630 ponere] linquere V
631 quisnam hinc] quis abhinc V
632 quam] cum V
633 regis pes] γV; pes regis K
634 nec non tremulus] tremulus nec non V
635 sic … Avarenses] om. V
636 nam] sed V
637 revocat] vocat huc V
638 reservet] teneret V
639 tum] post V
640 qui … enerviter] Martis trepidusque timens opus V
641 Hererici] T, cf. 35, 52, 80; Henrici B; Herrici KV; Heririci P and Str.

[1396] The battle was over when this business was done. Each man's wound and harsh panting convinced him to put down his weapons. Who could leave here unharmed, where two great-spirited heroes equal both in strength and in fervor of mind stood in the thunderstorm of war?[319] After it was finished, each of them was marked. There lay King Gunther's foot, there Walter's palm,[320] and here the still quivering eye of Hagen.[321] In just such a way[322] they divided the Avarish bracelets.[323] The two of them sat together—the third was still lying down—and they wiped the torrential river of blood off the flowers. In the meantime, Alpharides[324] called back the fearful girl with a shout, and she came and bandaged each wound.

[1409] When this was done, her betrothed ordered her: "Now mix wine and offer it first to Hagen. He is a good *athlète*,[325] provided that he keeps his pledge. Then hand it to me, since I endured more than the others. Finally, I want Gunther to drink, inasmuch as he appeared sluggish among the arms of great-spirited men, and he did the work of Mars in a lukewarm and weakly manner."[326] Hereric's daughter obeyed his every word, but the Frank, when the wine was offered, though parched within, said: "Give it first to Alpharides[327] your betrothed and lord,[328] maiden, since, I confess, he is braver than me, and not me alone, but he excels all in warfare." Here at last thorny Hagen[329] and the Aquitanian himself, unconquered in mind, though

Francus at oblato licet arens pectore vino[642]
"Defer," ait, "prius Alpharidi sponso ac seniori,
Virgo, tuo, quoniam, fateor, me fortior ille
1420 Nec solum me, sed cunctos supereminet armis."[643]
Hic[644] tandem Hagano spinosus et ipse Aquitanus,[645]
Mentibus invicti, licet omni corpore lassi,
Post varios pugnae strepitus ictusque tremendos
Inter pocula scurrili certamine ludunt.[646]

1425 Francus ait: "iam dehinc cervos agitabis, amice,
Quorum de corio wantis sine fine fruaris:
At dextrum,[647] moneo, tenera lanugine comple,
Ut causae ignaros palmae sub imagine fallas.
Wah![648] sed quid dicis, quod ritum infringere gentis
1430 Ac dextro femori gladium agglomerare[649] videris
Uxorique tuae, si quando[650] ea cura subintrat,
Perverso amplexu circumdabis euge sinistram?[651]
Iam quid demoror? en posthac tibi quicquid agendum est,[652]
Laeva manus faciet." Cui Walthare[653] talia reddit:
1435 "Cur tam[654] prosilias, admiror, lusce Sicamber:
Si venor cervos, carnem vitabis aprinam.
Ex hoc iam famulis tu suspectando iubebis

---

[642] vino] summo V
[643] nec … armis] non solum mihi sed cunctis supereminet ille KV
[644] hic] initial h om. PK; sic T, cf. following note
[645] hic … ipse] Hagano sic tandem spinosus et ille V
[646] inter … scurrili] pocula inter sic scurili (faulty scansion) V
[647] at dextrum] et dextram V
[648] wah] wach VT
[649] agglomerare] glomerare V
[650] si quando] si qua ađo KV
[651] sinistram] sinistra BV; sinistre T
[652] iam … quicquid] quid remoror? certe posthac tibi quidquid V
[653] Walthare] Walthere PT
[654] tam] sic V

exhausted throughout their bodies after the various clamors and fearful blows of the fight, playfully jest[330] with each other while drinking.

[1425] The Frank says: "Henceforth you will chase stags, my friend, so that you may enjoy endless *wantis*[331] made from their hide! But I advise you to stuff your right glove with tender wool so that you can deceive those who do not know with the appearance of a hand. *Wah!*[332] Well, what will you say[333] since you seem to break the custom of your race by fixing a sword at your right thigh? And hey, [334] if ever you feel the desire, will you put your left arm about your wife in a perverse embrace? Now why do I go on? Behold! From now on you must do everything with the left hand!" Walter answered him thus: "Why are you so boastful, I wonder, my one-eyed Sicambrian.[335] If I shall hunt stags, you will avoid boar meat.[336] Henceforth in fear you will order your servants—greeting the crowds of heroes with a sideways glance.[337] But, mindful of our old pledge, I will give you counsel: Now, when you come home and near your household, make a larded poultice of barley and milk. This will give you both sustenance and healing."

Heroum turbas[655] transversa[656] tuendo[657] salutans.[658]
Sed fidei memor antiquae tibi consiliabor:
1440 Iam si quando domum[659] venias laribusque propinques,
Effice lardatam de multra[660] farreque pultam:[661]
Haec[662] pariter victum tibi conferet[663] atque medelam."

His[664] dictis pactum renovant iterato coactum[665]
Atque simul regem tollentes valde dolentem
1445 Imponunt equiti et sic disiecti redierunt
Franci Wormatiam patriamque Aquitanus adivit.
Illic gratifice magno susceptus honore
Publica Hiltgundi[666] fecit sponsalia rite[667]
Omnibus et carus post mortem obitumque parentis[668]
1450 Ter denis populum rexit feliciter annis.[669]
Qualia bella dehinc vel quantos[670] saepe triumphos
Ceperit,[671] ecce stilus renuit signare retunsus.[672]

---

[655] heroum turbas] turmas heroum V
[656] transversa] transverso T; torveque V
[657] tuendo] tuenda K; inuendo T
[658] salutans] salutas V; saluta T
[659] domum] domi V
[660] multra] BV; mul^cra with "c" over erasure K; mulctra T
[661] pultam] pultim V; pultem T
[662] haec] hoc K; quae V
[663] conferet] BT; confert K; conferat V
[664] his] initial h om. PV; hic B
[665] coactum] γV; cruentum K
[666] Hiltgundi] Hiltgunde V
[667] publica … rite] om. K
[668] parentis] paratur T
[669] ter … annis] KV; rexit ter denis populum … B; feliciter populum ter denis rexerat annis P; om. 1450–6 T
[670] quantos] quantis K
[671] ceperit] Str. reads cepit for V, but he misses a mark through the tail of p that indicates cep[er]it for V.
[672] retunsus] PB; retusus KV

[1443] This said, they renew their pact with repeated pledge; and, together lifting the king, who was in great pain, they put him on his horse; and thus separated,[338] the Franks returned to Worms, and the Aquitanian came to his homeland. There, received gratefully with much honor, he made the customary public vows of betrothal to Hildegund;[339] and, dear to all after the death of his father, he ruled the people happily for thrice ten years.[340] What kind of battles and what great triumphs he often received hereafter ... well, my blunted pen refuses to write any more.

Haec quicunque legis,[673] stridenti ignosce cicadae[674]
Raucellam nec adhuc vocem perpende, sed aevum,
1455   Utpote quae nidis[675] nondum[676] petit alta relictis.[677]
Haec est Waltharii poesis. vos[678] salvet Iesus.[679]

FINIS[680]

---

[673] legis] leges K
[674] cicadae] cycadae V
[675] nidis] nidum K
[676] nondum] necdum B
[677] relictis] relictis perhaps corrected to relictum K
[678] vos] nos K
[679] Iesus] ihs (K in capitals) BK; iesus P; IESVS V
[680] finis] Ring; Waltarius clarus virtutibus at vir amarus K; TERMINAT LIBER DVORVM SODAL-
IVM WALTHARII ET HAGANONIS B

[1453] You whoever read this poem forgive the strident cicada.[341] And consider not its shrill little voice but its age, for it has not yet left the nest[342] to seek the sky.[343] This is the *poésie*[344] of Walter. May Jesus save you![345]

THE END

Notes

1. The prologue does not appear in all manuscripts, and many scholars do not think that it is by the same author. See the introduction on "The Authorship and Dating of the *Waltharius*" for more information about the relationship of the prologue to the epic.

2. That is, Christ, the second member of the Trinity.

3. That is, the Spirit has equal right or power with the Son and the Father.

4. The Latin phrase *vita vivens*, literally "living in life," an instance of *figura etymologica* (the juxtaposition of two etymologically related words for literary effect), seems to allude to God being the source of life or perhaps being its perfect manifestation. Etymological word play is found in both the prologue and the poem. While some of the word play seems to be inspired by a Germanic source (for example, "thorny Hagen," l. 1421), the poet also may have imitated etymological play in one of his Latin models such as Vergil. For Vergil's word play, see O'Hara, *True Names* (1996).

5. See below on "holy priest" (*praesul sancte*, l. 9) for the significance of Gerald's forms of address. On the prologue's use of traditional forms of praise for bishops, see Haefele, "Geraldus-Lektüre" (1998).

6. This Erkambald is often identified with either a bishop of Eichstätt in Bavaria (884–912) or with a bishop of Strasbourg (965–991). See the introduction on "The Authorship and Dating of the *Waltharius*."

7. Here the poet may draw attention to a flattering etymology of "Erkambald." In Old High German *erchan* means "genuine, true, or noble." The ending *-bald/-bold* is from the Germanic root seen in the modern English word "bold," meaning "courageous." Bate in his commentary, *Waltharius of Gaeraldus* (1978), calls this "a bilingual pun" (52), although it does not seem to be a strict pun since the Latin words *claro* and *fulgentem* do not correspond exactly (or even closely) to the sense of the Germanic name "Erkambald." Bate further suggests that *infictum* (in l. 8), translated loosely as "prepared," is not a participle of *inficio*, but a poetic invention meaning "not false" (*non fictum*). This suggestion is somewhat tempting and, if accepted, would make a true pun on *Erkam-*. If so, the translation should read: "… may be an *unfalse* medicine for many men…."

8. See the previous note.

9. The Latin *praesul* ("priest") by itself provides no clear indication of office, although it is commonly applied to the highest church officials (see, for instance, Gregory of Tours, *Hist.* 1.36, 5.49; Bede, *Hist. Eccl.* 2.17–18, 2.20, 5.2) and to God himself (for example, *Continuations of the Chronicle of Fredegar* 737; Paul the Deacon, *Hist. Long.* 1.26). However, along with *summus pontifex* ("highest priest") it ought to indicate at least a bishop or archbishop, as argued by Schaller, "Ist der *Waltharius* frühkarolingisch?" (1983), at 67–8, n. 24. For the alternate possibility—which seems highly improbable—that Gerald here refers to a chancellor or archchancellor, see von den Steinen, "Der *Waltharius* und sein Dichter" (1952), at 34–5.

10. As with the name "Erkambald" above, the poet here may point to the significance of the name "Gerald" (*Geraldus*). In *Waltharius of Gaeraldus* (1978), Bate notes on this line that *Ger-* represents Old High German *gaer*, meaning "spear shaft," and that *-aldus* is an "often derogatory adjectival ending" (53). For the derogatory nature of *-ald* he cites French *salaud*, *ribaud*, and *lourdaud* (French *-aud* being derived from Latin *-ald-*). However, the common modern etymology of "Gerald" gives the meaning "spear-ruler" or "spear-warrior," where "Gerald" = OHG *Gerwald*, and *-wald* is from the Germanic root from which modern English "wield" derives. Perhaps the contrast between the two names is best

indicated by the descriptions of the persons who hold them. Gerald describes himself as either a "feeble and trivial sinner by the name of Gerald" (*peccator ... vilis*) or, following Bate's suggestions, perhaps "a feeble sinner, Gerald, basely named." However the line is construed, it is clear that Gerald is being self-deprecatory while praising Erkambald. Therefore, if he intended the reader also to see a contrast between their names, it was perhaps that <u>Erkambald</u> was the true or genuine spiritual warrior, whereas Gerald, as his name indicated, was more of a worldly sinner, like the spear-wielding Germanic heroes who are described in the following poem.

11. I have translated the phrase *de larga cura* ("from his generous devotion") as causal, which seems the most natural rendering here, but it could also describe the manner of his composition, that is, "with generous devotion"—although this would be a non-classical construction. Other translators, wanting to make the case that the prologue's author is not the same as the author of the poem, have tried to make this phrase indicate that the prologue's author is old. However, *larga cura* more naturally means "bounteous" or "generous" rather than "long-standing" care.

12. Bate, *Waltharius of Gaeraldus* (1978), notes (53) that "pupil" (*alumnus*) suggests that Gerald is younger than Erkambald. This does seem the most natural way to take it, and it would fit with the final lines of the *Waltharius*, where the poet asks the reader to pardon him for his age as he is like a cicada which has not yet left its nest. However, those who argue that the prologue and poem are by different authors would no doubt point out that Gerald being the *alumnus*—that is, "pupil" or "ward" of Erkambald—in no way proves that Gerald was young: both could have been old men. In fact, Gerald could have described himself as the spiritual *alumnus* of a physically younger man. Even if Gerald and the poet of the *Waltharius* are both young, this provides no proof of the identification.

13. This line "May the Father ... grant" (*Det pater ex summis caelum terramque gubernans*) closely resembles Theodulf of Orléans, *Carmen* 71.91: *Det pater altithronus caelum terramque gubernans.* Orchard, *A Critical Companion to Beowulf* (2003), 135 n. 36, cites this resemblance as possible evidence for an early date, but nothing would prevent a much later poet from echoing Theodulf.

14. I follow MSS. B, P, and T (see "On the Manuscript History and the Latin Text" in the introduction), which read *omnitonantem* ("who thunders through all the heavens"), a pagan-sounding epithet similar to *altitonans*, found in Cicero, *Div.* 1.19; Lucretius, 5.745; and Varro, *L.* 7.7. In *Die Ottonenzeit* (1937), 407, Strecker mentions but rejects Meyer's suggestion to emend this unique word with the more Christian-sounding *omnitenentem* ("holding all creation"), which Gerald might know from Prosper of Aquitaine, *Sententiae* 278, or St. Augustine, *Confessions* 7.15.21, 11.13.15.

15. The phrase "in action" translates *factis* so as to make it functionally parallel to *loquelis* ("in speech"), since the number, case, and sense of the two Latin words indicate a contrasting parallel. Kratz, in *Waltharius and Ruodlieb* (1984), also makes the two parallel with his translation: "that you perform <u>in deeds</u> what I express <u>in words</u>" (3). Compare the contrast between *factis* and *dictis* at l. 135 of the *Waltharius*.

16. *Waltharius resectus* is presented illogically in the nominative, although it would be expected to agree with the genitive *tironis* ("of a young warrior"). MS. B alone has the expected genitives *Waltharii resecti*. However, the unexpected nominative is probably right. It is either an ungrammatical slip or an intentional instance of anacoluthon which highlights Walter, the subject of the following poem. The choice, of course, is tied to one's judgment of Gerald's skill.

17. The Latin *resectus* usually means "trimmed" or "cut off." Therefore, it may be proleptic, looking toward the end of the poem, when Walter will have his arm cut off. Kratz, in *Waltharius and Ruodlieb* (1984), seems to take it in a more general sense; he translates: "he was slashed in many battles" (3).

18. The key adjectives here are *inampla* ("undistinguished") and *longaevi* ("long-aged"). The second commonly describes aged people and rarely describes old things. The first, *inampla*, seems to be the poet's own formation meaning "not great" or "not impressive" (*non ampla*). Apparently the idea is that reading the poem will provide entertainment to shorten the run-of-the-mill times of an aged day.

Whether the day is "long-aged" because it wears on interminably or because the adjective has been transferred poetically from the reader (Erkambold) to his day is unclear. The former seems easier to understand, but in *Waltharius of Gaeraldus* (1978) Bate translates according to the latter interpretation: "when read through it shortens the unfilled time of a day in your old age" (53). If one views *longaevi* as a transferred epithet, perhaps Gerald uses it to mean "learned" (*doctus*), as suggested by Servius, *ad Aen.* 8.498. Certainly the poet of the *Waltharius*, whether Gerald or not, often displays knowledge of Servius.

19. That is, "brother." The French *frère* represents the Greek *adelphus*. The use of *adelphus* here as that of *fratres* in line 1 of the following poem refers to spiritual brotherhood, possibly in reference to fellow monks. Whether or not the dedicatory prologue is by the same poet as the main poem, the *Waltharius* certainly displays similar use of Greek loan words—see the introduction, "Stylistic Features, Meter, and Language."

20. Instead of starting *in medias res* like Vergil, the author of the *Waltharius* starts with an address to his "brothers" and a miniature lesson in geography and history that sounds like the introduction to Caesar's *Gallic Wars*. For the common ancient division of the earth into three parts, see Sallust, *Jug.* 17.3; Pliny, *Nat.* 3.3; Hyginus, *Astr.* 1.8.1; Servius, *ad Aen.* 1.385; Velleius Paterculus, 2.40.41; and Isidore, *Etym.* 14.2: "[orbis] divisus est autem trifarie: e quibus una pars Asia, altera Europa, tertia Africa nuncupatur." For the closest poetic parallel, compare Lucan, *BC* 9.411–17. In *Waltharius of Gaeraldus* (1978), Bate notes on this passage (53) that another medieval epic, *Within* by Letaldus of Micy (late 10th to early 11th c.), has a similar geographic beginning—this might indicate Letaldus's readership of the *Waltharius*.

21. This appears to be an address to fellow ecclesiastics, either monks or, perhaps, canons. Kratz, *Waltharius and Ruodlieb* (1984), xiii, says that this is the only sure indication of the author's identity, since the dedicatory prologue may have been written by someone else. However, I would agree with Ursula and Peter Dronke, who in *Barbara et antiquissima carmina* (1977), 69, argue that even this expression is inconclusive, though highly suggestive, since *fratres* ("brothers") was also a common address for the entire Christian community.

22. These people are called "Pannonians," "Huns," and "Avars" by the poet. Compare Isidore, *Etym.* 9.2.66, possibly known to our poet: *Hugnos antea Hunnos vocatos, postremo a rege suo Avares appellatos qui prius in ultima Maeotide inter glacialem Tanaim et Massagetarum inmanes populos habitaverunt. Deinde pernicibus equis Caucasi rupibus, feras gentes Alexandri claustra cohibente, eruperunt, et orientem viginti annis tenuerunt captivum, et ab Aegyptiis atque Aethiopibus annuum vectigal exegerunt.* The poet is obviously not concerned with historical distinctions between the Roman province *Pannonia* (roughly modern Hungary) and the separate peoples, the Huns and the Avars, who occupied the territory at different times. For the poet's connection of the Huns with *Pannonia*, see Gregory of Tours, *Hist.* 2.6 and Einhard, *Vita Karoli* 13, and the discussion of Schütte, "Länder und Völker" (1986), 72. For Attila and the historical Huns—who have little relationship to the literary constructions of this poem—see Gordon, *The Age of Attila* (1960); Mänchen-Helfen, *The World of the Huns* (1973); Thompson and Heather, *The Huns* (1996).

23. Learned, *The Saga of Walther* (1892), 163, shows that "Gibica" was the name of a Burgundian king mentioned in the *Lex Burgundionum* 3. See also Gillespie, "The Significance of Personal Names in German Heroic Poetry" (1965). The most recent treatment of Germanic history in the *Waltharius* is by Florio, "Literatura e historia en el *Waltharius*) (2009).

24. The poet hints that this son, Gunther, will play a major role in this story, since his greed will motivate the course of much of the poem, beginning at l. 470.

25. The legendary Gunther is usually and credibly identified with the historical Burgundian ruler *Gundaricus* or Γυντιάριος mentioned by Olympiodorus (in Photius, *Bibliotheca*, Codex 80, p. 58b,

ed. Bekker)—see Learned, *The Saga of Walther* (1892), 163–5. See also Grégoire, "La patrie des *Nibe-lungen*" (1934) and "Le *Waltharius* et Strasbourg" (1936). Grégoire suggests that Hagen's name comes from the title *Khaganos*, since Olympiodorus mentions Goar, a *Khaganos* or Khan of the Alans, along with Γυντιάρος. Gunther (*Guðhere*) and Hagen are both named in the fragments of the Anglo-Saxon *Waldere* (fr. A 25, B 15), dated between the 8th and 10th centuries. These fragments make it clear that in the *Waldere*, as in the *Waltharius*, Gunther was Hagen's overlord and tried to get him to face Wal-ter. However, in the *Waldere* Gunther and Hagen are Burgundians, not Franks. The author of the *Waltharius* has strayed from the facts by making them Franks, since Gunther is surely to be identified with the Burgundian *Gundaricus*/Γυντιάρος. Just as the poet has clearly reworked or altered the Ger-manic saga elsewhere, so in this detail he is probably altering his material intentionally, not making a careless mistake. If so, their Frankish nationality could indicate that the author was trying to associate contemporary Franks with these two famous warriors, or rather specifically with Hagen, who is in many ways the second hero of this poem and who is magnified by the poet's claim that he had Trojan blood. In addition to literary considerations, political changes that had added Burgundian towns—including Gunther's Worms—to the contemporary Frankish domain might have encouraged the poet to alter Gunther's nationality anachronistically. For an analysis of the character of Gunther in the *Waltharius*, see Scherello, "Die Darstellung Gunthers im *Waltharius*" (1986).

26. That is, the Danube.

27. For the probable historical source of Hagen's name, see n. 25 above on Gunther. Learned, *The Saga of Walther* (1892), 167–9, presents two other possible historical sources for Hagen, the late Roman general Aetius and a Saxon leader named Aigyna.

28. *Troia* ("Troy") here may represent Troneg—a place name sometimes written as *Troja*—see Learned, *The Saga of Walther* (1892), 169. Indeed, the *Nibelungenlied* (1.9) says that Hagen was from Troneg. Wieland, *Waltharius* (1986), 49, endorses one of Learned's suggestions, namely, that *Troia* here and *Tronege* of the *Nibelungenlied* both refer to Kirchheim in Alsace, which was once called New Troy. Kiefer, "*Waltharii poesis*: Hagen von Tronje" (2001), suggests *Colonia Traiana* was corrupted into *Troiana*, also noting that under its medieval name, Xanten, the town was connected with the Trojan River Xanthus in the eleventh-century *Annolied*. Our author may have invented Hagen's Trojan origin in order to tie his work, a Germanic and Christian poem, to the pagan classical tradition of Greek and Latin epic, represented by Vergil's *Aeneid*, to which he often alludes. Furthermore, the conceit of Trojan origin could be flattering to Franks. Compare the verses addressed to Charlemagne by the poet called Hibernicus Exul: *O gens regalis, profecta a moenibus altis / Troiae ...* (2.85–6). Our poet and Hibernicus Exul both employ clear verbal echoes alluding to Vergil's connection of Rome with Troy, *Aen.* 1–7: *Troiae ... / ... altae moenia Romae*. The association of Troy with the Franks was current at least as early as the *Chronicle of Fredegar* (2.4–5). Of course, our poet's *de germine Troiae* ("from the race of Troy") might intentionally allude both to Troneg from a Germanic model and to Vergil's Troy. For a general treatment of Troy and allegations of Trojan heritage in the Middle Ages, see Graus, "Troja und trojanische Herkunftssage im Mittelalter" (1989).

29. For an analysis of Hildegund's character in the poem, see Lührs, "Hiltgunt" (1986).

30. The epic simile is one of the major stylistic features adapted from Vergil and other classical mod-els; see the note on the longest of these at ll. 1337–43. Strecker and Schumann, *Nachträge* (1951), 26, note Vergil, *Aen.* 1.399, as a parallel for "not unlike" (*haud aliter*), but it is a common enough phrase; so Ovid, *Met.* 3.661, or Lucan, *BC* 9.284, may be the more direct model because they also share a form of *aequor* ("sea") in the fifth foot. However, *Aen.* 1.399 may be the source for both Ovid and Lucan, since they all share a form of *puppis*. Finally, since the *Waltharius* and Vergil share an abundance of *p* alliteration not found in the other two sources, our poet may be alluding to Vergil and either Lucan or Ovid at the same time, a showy poetic technique called a "multiple reference," on which see Thomas,

"Virgil's *Georgics*" (1986), 195, and Nelis, *Vergil's Aeneid* (2001), 5.   The epic similes should be contrasted with the *Waltharius'* short poetic metaphors that apparently reflect the influence of Germanic kennings—for example, *viridem ... aedem* ("green house," l. 1036).

31. It is unclear whether Hereric was a standard part of the saga or was introduced by the poet. A Hereric appears in *Beowulf* (2206). However, Learned, *The Saga of Walther* (1892), 169–70, suggests a connection with the Chararicus whom Gregory of Tours, *Hist.* 2.41, mentions as a king.

32. Kratz, in *Waltharius and Ruodlieb* (1984), 201–02, considers this passage, which situates Chalon-sur-Sâone in Burgundy, to be historical evidence for placing the *Waltharius'* composition in the ninth century, although the contemporary status of the town need not have inspired the poet, who might have easily known about Burgundy's political and geographic changes over time. Kratz also notes that "the identification of Aquitaine as a *regnum* (line 77) and the reference to Metz as a *metropolis* (644)" may support the idea that the *Waltharius* belongs to the Carolingian period. In these chronological points, Kratz follows von den Steinen, "Der *Waltharius*" (1952), 41–2.

33. The poet's use of *ecce* and *en* (usually translated "behold") is more frequent than is common in classical Latin epic, although *ecce* is sometimes used with similar frequency in medieval authors. The *Waltharius* has *ecce* in about 1.6% of the lines (24 instances)—comparable to the 1.0% in Alcuin's long hexameter poem *De pontificibus et sanctis ecclesiae Eboracensis*—and *en* in 1.0% (15 instances), whereas the *Aeneid* and *Metamorphoses* show much lower instances (*Aen.*: *ecce* 0.4%, *en* 0.2%; *Meta.*: *ecce* 0.3%, *en* 0.1%). This practice may have been influenced by a similar interjection in Germanic epic; compare the common Old English *hwæt* and *huru*. In any case, *en* and *ecce* often introduce a new scene or a new section of a speech.

34. The meaning of the Latin word *seniores* ("elders") in the Middle Ages is far-ranging—old men, elders (as persons of authority), or lords. Bate, in *Waltharius of Gaeraldus* (1978), 55, suggests a biblical provenance for *seniores* meaning "elders" in this passage.

35. That is, Herericus.

36. Alphere is also the name of Walter's father in the Anglo-Saxon *Waldere*. *Alphere* is the nominative Germanic form of the name. There is a possibility that our poet interpreted Alphere (Anglo-Saxon *Ælfhere*) as "Elf-lord" and his son's name *Walthere* as "Wood-lord" because one of Walter's opponents seems to make a pun on Walter's name by calling him a "faun" (*faunus*) or "wood-sprite" at l. 763—see Morgan, "Walter the Wood-Sprite" (1972), on this word play. The closest Germanic equivalent of the Latin *faunus* here is probably the *Waldschrat*, whose name could be connected with *Walthere*.

37. In the Latin all these futures are a mixture of present and future tenses. Whether we should attribute this to Germanic influence or simple poetic license is unclear.

38. Whether our poet found the name "Hildegund" in his model is uncertain. Hildegund may be based partly on the third and last wife of Attila, Ildico, and the roots *hilde* and *gunde* are both popular in Burgundian-Frankish names of the Merovingian period according to Learned, *The Saga of Walther* (1892), 170–1. Learned even cites a historical Childechinda, a daughter of Chilpericus I, which indicates that "the name Hildegunde belongs to Frankish-Burgundian soil" and "need not be a poetic creation" (171). Later in the feast scene (l. 322) there may be an allusion to a story of Ildico burning the palace. See Jordanes, *Getica* 49, for Ildico and *Nibelungenlied* 36, for the burning of Attila's palace by his wife Kriemhild, who is often considered a literary analogue to Ildico.

39. The phrase "with happy hearts" (*pectore laeto*) is one of the rare borrowings from Lucan, *BC* 9.1039, where Caesar cries false tears over Pompey's death while rejoicing in his heart. The allusion raises some doubts about the sincerity of Attila's supposed preference for peace (l. 69).

40. The Latin *pietas* ("fatherly care") is hard to translate, but our poet would have known its manifestation in the *Aeneid* as a key trait of Aeneas, who displayed *pietas* in, among other things, his care and devotion to father and son.

41. The taunts and jokes of warfare are an important characteristic of the warrior in the *Waltharius*. For example, compare Walter's jibe at Hagen (l. 1351) and the jests exchanged by Ekerich and Walter (ll. 761–9). Such comments are called "flyting," a mocking method of exchange sometimes for fun ("ludic flyting") among members of the same social group and sometimes to set the terms of battle ("heroic flyting")—see Halama, "Flytes of Fancy: Boasting and Boasters from *Beowulf* to Gangsta Rap" (1996). This type of exchange is common in confrontations between Homeric warriors in the *Iliad*; and in Vergil's *Aeneid* a more refined, literary form of flyting occurs (for example: 10.440–81 Turnus and Pallas, 12.887–995 Turnus and Aeneas), but the flyting of the *Waltharius* seems to have more in common with that seen in Germanic poetry. Compare the exchange between Beowulf and Unferth in *Beowulf*, 499–558, and the mocking language of the *Waldere*, the Anglo-Saxon version of the story of Walter (fr. B 16b–17): "Snatch, if you dare, the hoary hauberk from [me though] so battle-worn!" (*Feta, gyf ðu dyrre, æt ðus heaðuwerigan hare byrnan*). For Germanic flyting, see also Anderson, "Flyting in *The Battle of Maldon*" (1970).

42. That is, "clever men." The French *sophistes* represents the Greek-derived *sophistas*.

43. Here it is not clear whether Walter knew of Hagen's departure. Later at ll. 1239–43 Walter speaks of Hagen's embraces before he left the Huns, and Walter's words to Hildegund at ll. 254–5 may indicate that he had contemplated leaving with Hagen. Compare Carroll, "An Essay on the Walther Legend" (1952), 157, who suggests that our poet has diverged from his source, in which Hagen had been sent out by Attila himself and so had time to meet with Walter before his departure.

44. It is generally assumed that the poet invented the name *Ospirin*, since no parallel has been found. Following Grimm and Schmeller, *Lateinische Gedichte* (1838), 119, Althof, *Waltharii Poesis* (1905), 53–4, suggests that the poet has translated the name of one of Attila's wives, *Helche*, which he erroneously—though someone else might say intentionally—equates with *Helike* (Greek for *ursa maior*), into the Germanic *Ospirin*, which means "divine bear." For other evidence of our poet's interest in Greek, see note 19 above.

45. As often, the poet has used a plural "Your" (*vestri*) for the address to the king in observance of court manners.

46. That is, "I myself." This is a honorific title like "Your Majesty."

47. Our poet makes explicit connections both forward (as here) and backward within the narrative; compare the brief comment about Gunther above (ll. 15–16).

48. That is, "man of authority." The Latin word *satrapa*, based on the ancient Greek for the title of a Persian governor, could refer either to Attila himself or to his underling, thus meaning "ruler" or "vassal." It appears in the Vulgate, Jgs 3:3, where it refers to important "lords" (equivalent to high-ranking medieval vassals). Either way Attila hears the rumor, but perhaps he heard it through his vassal. Compare l. 371, where *satrapa* clearly refers to Attila.

49. That is, "tyrants." The French here represents the Greek-derived *tyrannos*.

50. The exact phrase "with his usual virtue" (*solita virtute*, l. 177) comes from Prudentius's description of Suffering (*Patientia*). Thus the allusion may be ironic, since Suffering wins her battles by not fighting (*Psych.* 155–9). Compare also *Aen.* 11.415 and Servius's note on the similar phrase *solitae virtutis*.

51. Already Attila has instructed Walter and Hagen in the "jests" (*iocis*, l. 102) of war; here battle itself is portrayed as a sort of game (*ludum*, l. 186). These references foreshadow the wordplay and swordplay that dominate the middle and end of the *Waltharius*. The Latin root for play, *lud-/lus-*, appears many more times (ll. 541, 734, 740, 766, 782, 794, 903, 956, 1230, 1252, 1291, 1349, 1352, 1424) in the context of such competitive play, and the metaphor of athletic games is operative in such vocabulary as *certamen* and *certare* (ll. 611, 743, 908, 1003, 1301, 1424), *athleta* (ll. 962, 1046, 1411), and *agon* (ll. 1025). Modern scholarship has made much of play in the poem; see the introduction on "The Poem and its Hero." It is possible that at least some of this emphasis derives from Germanic culture

and oral tradition. Ziolkowski, "Fighting Words" (2001), 43–50, points out that Anglo-Saxon shows many compounds of *plega* ("play") that refer to battle, notably *sweordplega* (*Waldere* A 13) and *lindplega* (*Beowulf* 1073 and 2039) and that the Old High German *Ludwigslied* describes a battlefield-scene by saying that the "Franks played there" (*Spilodon ther Vrankon*, 49). The frequency of such "play" may even provide a metapoetic expression of the poet's own literary games, as he plays with his various classical, Christian, and Germanic sources. When considering the playfulness of the poet or this text, one should not forget Gerald's words from the prologue (l. 20): "It requires one to p<u>la</u>y rather than pray to the Lord." Whether one considers Gerald to be the author or only a familiar reader, he knowingly alludes to the poem's playfulness.

52. An epic simile—compare the note on the longest of these (at ll. 1337–43). The image of battle as a storm is common in classical epic; for example, Vergil, *Aen.* 11.610, which is possibly the immediate source of this simile. However, it is also found in Germanic poetry; compare *Beowulf,* 3117, and see Althof, *Waltharii Poesis* (1905), 67, on this passage for further examples.

53. Though scarcely understandable in English without the "as" that marks it as a simile, the Latin actually has a metaphor. The phrase "present death" (*praesentem mortem*), adapted from Vergil, *Aen.* 1.91, is there used rather literally to refer to the threat of death in a storm. Here the poet uses it boldly for Walter.

54. The strong alliteration reproduces the Latin *frontem festa cum fronde.*

55. Compare Vergil, *Ecl.* 8.12–13 and *Aen.* 5.71, 7.614, 4.459, for the source of this image.

56. The first of several examples where the poet uses *eques* (usually meaning "horseman") for horse, following Vergilian practice as explained by Servius in his commentary on *Georgics* 3.116. Compare ll. 460–1, which extensively rework the same passage from the *Georgics.*

57. Townsend, "Ironic Intertextuality" (1997), 70–80, examines this episode in detail with a postmodernist interpretation where Hildegund becomes a surrogate for the intended audience of male monks and a "resisting reader" who rejects the ideology of heroic masculinity. Townsend does well to point out the problems in Walter's heroism, since he has just deceived Attila and soon asks Hildegund to do the same—neither act being either heroic or Christian.

58. "Goblet" (*tallum*) may be a Germanic word, as suggested by Althof, *Waltharii Poesis* (1905), 81, although it appears also in the Vulgate, 2 Macc. 14:4.

59. The signing of the Cross is the first of the explicitly Christian actions of the hero, and this scene is important because it marks a formal, though private, engagement of Walter and Hildegund, whom the poet will often call *sponsus* ("betrothed" or "bridegroom") and *sponsa* ("betrothed" or "bride"). For Walter as a Christian hero, see Wolf, "Zum *Waltharius christianus*" (1954–55), Katscher, "*Waltharius*—Dichtung und Dichter" (1973), and Ernst, "Walther—ein christlicher Held?" (1986). Ward, "After Rome: Medieval Epic" (1993), argues that the poem's depiction of Walter and Hildegund's relationship reflects contemporary concerns about the sanctity of Christian marriage.

60. This translation connects the reference to their parents' pledges (ll. 78–82), but alternately one could translate: "they knew that they had made pledges of betrothal with each other."

61. The future here represents a Latin present, which may indicate influence from Germanic usage. The literal translation "palate" (*palato,* l. 234) reveals a rare instance of metonymy for "mouth" or "voice."

62. That is, "irony." The French equivalent here represents the Greek-derived term. *Ironia* is an ancient rhetorical term often defined as saying one thing while meaning another. The poet may have picked it up from Servius (*ad Aen.* 4.93, 6.520, etc.), Isidore (*Etym.* 1.37.22–25, 2.21.41), or a similar source. On irony in the poem, see Parkes, "Irony in the *Waltharius*" (1974). On medieval use of rhetorical irony, see Green, *Irony in the Medieval Romance* (1979), esp. 21–2. One fragmentary manuscript of the *Waltharius* glosses the Latin *hyroniam* with the Germanic word *spot* (whence the modern German

Spott), meaning "mockery" or even "sarcasm"—see Green, "*Waltharius* Fragments" (2004), 65. See note 41 above, on Attila's instruction of Walter and Hagen (ll. 100–02), for the poet's interest in mocking language.

63. This is a strong allusion to Vergil, *Aen.* 4.105, where Venus and Juno both speak deceptively about plans to wed Aeneas and Dido. Of course, the allusion might cause the reader, as Hildegund, to question Walter, since he might, like Aeneas, run off and leave her.

64. Here "triple-ply hauberk" (*trilicem … loricam*) recalls *Aen.* 3.467.

65. The shirt or hauberk does save Walter later, and it seems to have played a larger role in the Anglo-Saxon *Waldere.* Compare l. 965 below with note 216. The "maker" is apparently the famous smith of Germanic myth, Weland.

66. Kratz, *Waltharius and Ruodlieb* (1984), xxiii, suggests that these two coffers stuffed with gold are meant to be compared unfavorably with the recommendations of Good Works in Prudentius's *Psychomachia* (613), who exhorts her companions not even to take a wallet with them in their journey, echoing the words of Christ (Lk 9:3, 10:4, 22:35). The author of the *Waltharius* frequently alludes to the *Psychomachia*, so that this is a compelling suggestion.

67. Neither activity is typically heroic, but this need not mean that we should question his heroism. It is tempting to see the juxtaposition of "fisherman" (*piscator*) and "bird-hunter" (*auceps*) in l. 273 as derived from Horace (*Serm.* 2.3.227)—if so, it is evidence for the poet's familiarity with Roman satire, perhaps an influence on his playful style. Compare note 75 on *linge de table* (l. 300) for another image from Horace. For possible echoes of the satirist Juvenal, compare the notes on "Savage Desire" (l. 869) and "Numidian bear" (l. 1337).

68. That is, "within the week." My French phrase represents the Greek term *ebdomada.* Compare its use in the Vulgate, for instance in Ex. 34:22.

69. A Greek name for the sun god, usually equated with Apollo, "Phoebus" is here used as often in Latin poetry as an elegant way of referring to the sun.

70. The feast set by Walter is based on the poetic prototype of Dido's banquet for Aeneas (*Aen.* 1.637–756). Of course, this ironically puts Walter in the role of Dido.

71. Wieland in *Waltharius* (1986), 62, rightly notes on this passage that Luxury or Gluttony is best understood as personified. Our poet probably adopted the personification from Prudentius (*Psych.* 311), since the *Waltharius* is pervaded by systematic allusions to Prudentius.

72. The "purple and fine linen" (*bissus … et ostrum,* l. 293) is a biblical allusion to Lk 16:19—my translation echoes the King James Version here.

73. *Sodales* means "companions" or "comrades" and here the context tells us that they are the king's, not Walter's companions. Kratz strangely translates this word as "guests."

74. That is, "mixed wine." The French phrase represents the Greek term *migma.*

75. That is, "table cloth." The French phrase represents the Greek term *gausape,* which our poet probably takes from Horace, *Serm.* 2.8.11 (the satire on Nasidienus's dinner party).

76. That is, "bowls." The French phrase represents the rare Greek *crateres.* The poet's source is probably Statius, *Thebaid* 10.313 (cf. *Achilleid* 1.114), where the same form is found in conjunction with a reference to Bacchus. There the reference is to the destruction caused by the deceitful night raid of Agylleus and Actor. Since Walter is deceiving the Huns and does plan to run off with Attila's treasure, if not kill him, in the night, the allusion serves to problematize his heroism.

77. Compare Servius, *ad Aen.* 1.730 and *Ruodlieb* 5.76, 6.46.

78. *Nappa* (meaning "drinking bowl") is one of the few Germanic-derived words in the poem (see Niermeyer/Kieft, *Mediae Latinitatis Lexicon Minus* [2002], s.v. *nappa*)—see also *Wah!* (l. 1429) and *wantis* (l. 1426) . I thus render it with the Old High German *hnapf,* cognate with modern German *Napf* ("bowl" or "dish").

79. For classical models for this bowl, compare Statius's description (*Theb.* 1.539–51) of a *patera* ("dish" or "bowl"), Vergil's description (*Aen.* 1.640-1) of a silver serving dish, and Ovid's description (*Met.*13.679–701) of a *crater*. Makkay, *Iranian Elements in Early Mediaeval Heroic Poetry* (1998), 48–50, here sees a reference to the historical Hunnish use of ceremonial bowls or shallow cups made of gold and silver, such as the "Cup of Solomon." Legend says the cup passed through the hands of Charlemagne and Charles the Bald, but that need not be true—compare Shalem, "The Fall of al-Madā'in" (1994), esp. 77.

80. As noted above (note 71) on Luxury, the personification of vices—including Drunkenness (*Ebrietas*)—is no doubt inspired by Prudentius's *Psychomachia*, where Luxury herself is described as "drunken" (*ebria*, 320).

81. The alliterative repetition of *s* here seeks to convey the onomatopoetic effect of the Latin line. Note the preponderance of labial consonants (l. 316): *balbutit madido facundia fusa palato.*

82. This may be an allusion to the burning of Attila's palace as found in the *Nibelungenlied* 36, if such a tale was current in the poet's day.

83. The Latin *iteri*, translated here with an old spelling of "journey," is an anomalous form. Most likely, our author has been reading grammarians who cited similar forms from archaic Latin poetry. Priscian cites Naevius for the genitive *iteris*; see Keil/Hertz (ed.), *Grammatici latini*, vol. 2 (1855), 229. Charisius too mentions a genitive *iteris* and cites Pacuvius; see Barwick/Kühnert (ed.), *Flavii Sosipatri Charisii Artis grammaticae libri V* (1964), 60, 104, 171. Priscian is extant in MSS. St. Gall, *Stiftsbibliothek*, 903 and 904 (probably not in St. Gall until 10th c.)—possible evidence for the localization of the author. The codices are dated to about 800 and 845 respectively; see the *Virtual Manuscript Library of Switzerland* for details: http://www.e-codices.unifr.ch.

84. For the connotation of Walter's comparison with a giant, consider Vergilian giants at *Aen.* 6.584–6 (impious Aloidae in Hades), 10.565–9 (comparison of Aeneas with impious Aegaeon), and 10.763–8 (comparison of Mezentius with impious Orion). Compare also the biblical giants, Goliath (1 Sm 17) and the Nephilim (Gn 6:1–4, Nm 13:32–33); there is a similar comparison to a giant at 1 Mc 3:3. Moreover, giants are also common in early Germanic tradition (cf. *Waldere* B 10, *Wanderer* 87a, and *Beowulf* 113, 1562, 1690), so that it reasonable to assume that our poet would have been aware of the cross-cultural, negative implications of his hero being "like a giant." See Dickins, *Runic and Heroic Poems* (1915), 60, and Carlson, "The Monsters of *Beowulf*" (1967), 360. *Beowulf* explicitly connects Grendel with the biblical Nephilim or *gigantas* (102–14), who were thought to be descended from Cain. D'Angelo, *Waltharius* (1998), 16–17, explores Walter's connections to both David and his giant opponent Goliath.

85. The second sword proves to be important in the climactic battle—see ll. 1390–2. The Anglo-Saxon *Waldere* fragments may indicate that that version of the story included a similar incident involving a second sword. Fragment A begins with someone (possibly Hildegund) encouraging Walter not to worry about his sword failing him, and this concern is repeated in l. 24 of the fragment—perhaps to foreshadow the shattering of his sword (seen in the *Waltharius*, l. 1374). Fragment B of *Waldere* seems to begin with a reference to a sword hidden in a jeweled vessel (that is to say, a sheath), but it is unclear who is speaking and so whose sword it is. Ziolkowski, "Fighting Words" (2001), 38–9, suggests that the description of Walter's arms and armor may correspond closely to what early Germanic nobles actually used. The second sword is called a *semispata* (l. 1390), which might mean it is shorter or that is has only one edge. Isidore, *Etym.* 18.6.5, identifies *semispata* as a sword of half length. Nickel, "About the Sword of the Huns and the 'Urepos' of the Steppes" (1973), 138–42, argues that the *Waltharius* echoes a real fifth-century Hunnish custom of wearing a short sword on the right side.

86. Hazelwood is traditionally used for fishing poles. The poet's source for this rare term is Vergil, *Geo.* 2.396.

87. Instead of "following," *sectantes* might be translated "slicing" if the "uncut mountains" (*montibus intonsis*) are a sign of etymological word play here.

88. For "loosed by sleep and wine," compare Vergil, *Aen.* 9.189, from the deceptive and tragic night raid of Nisus and Euryalus—along with the allusion to the night raid from Statius's *Thebaid* (see note 71 above on *boules*, l. 301), it reflects unfavorably on our view of Walter.

89. The "duke" is apparently Walter.

90. In *European Literature and the Latin Middle Ages* (1953), 429, Curtius cites this scene as an example of comic elements in medieval epic. Whether or not one sees humor in Attila's hangover, there may also be a serious message in his pain. It is easy to take the scene simply as payback for Attila's early violence, but the poet has presented Attila as a sort of father figure to Walter who only wants the best for him (ll. 96–102). Thus Walter's complete betrayal, though somewhat understandable, is morally problematic. Perhaps the poet wants us to suspect that Walter and Hagen, having been raised and educated by Attila, are destined to inherit his faults.

91. The poet again employs the Latinized Greek term *satrapa* meaning "ruler" for Attila, as in l. 170.

92. For the description of Attila here (ll. 380–401) our author has adapted Vergil's depiction of Dido in *Aeneid* 4.1–89. On this, see Dronke, "Functions of Borrowing in Medieval Latin Verse" (1971). Although there may be a sort of humorous irony in this connection, we should remember that Vergil sympathetically presented Dido as a misused but virtuous woman and an almost masculine leader of her state. Certainly the poet is not nearly as critical of Attila as he might have been. For example, note his preference for peace (l. 69) and his Aeneas-like *pietas* toward the hostages (l. 97).

93. An epic simile—compare the note on the longest of these (at lines 1337–43). Although it sounds Vergilian (cf. *Aen.* 5.790–1), the direct source of the phrase "sand … stirred by Aeolian gales" (*ac velut Aeolicis turbatur arena procellis*, l. 384) is Venantius Fortunatus (*non sic Aeoliis turbatur harena procellis*, 7.14.31), who used the lofty phrase to describe digestive problems. Our poet similarly depicts Attila's passion in epic grandeur, yet the overblown language only emphasizes his pomposity, enhancing the oddly humorous atmosphere of the scene, especially if the reader knows Venantius.

94. The clause "when dark night had stolen color from the world" is a close adaptation of Vergil's description of Aeneas's descent into the underworld (*Aen.* 6.272). As mentioned in the previous note, such epic language is probably best understood as ironic—Attila is hardly acting heroically.

95. Kratz, *Mocking Epic* (1980), 31, suggests that this wound is modeled after Dido's passion (*Aen.* 4.69). However, there are no verbal similarities, and so the wound does not suggest that Attila is a "jilted, lovesick woman," as Kratz claims. Instead, the image seems to be drawn from one of two Ovidian passages, which have closer verbal parallels: Cyparissus's wounding of a loved and sacred stag (*Met.* 10.130) and Callisto's near wounding at the hands of her own son (*Fasti* 2.187). The allusion may therefore emphasize that the king's wound came from a loved one, a son, since Attila raised Walter and Hildegund as his own children (ll. 97–9).

96. Compare Vergil, *Aen.* 2.255, where the deceptive Greeks come to sack Troy in the "friendly silence" while the Trojans are in bed. Thus the allusion, if recognized, connects Attila with the Trojans and Walter with the treacherous Greeks, for whom the silence is friendly.

97. For the Greek *licisca* translated here by the French *chien-loup* ("wolf-dog"), compare Vergil, *Ecl.* 3.16, in a context that suggests the term is an insult. Servius, *ad Ecl.* 3.16, and Isidore, *Etym.* 12.2.28, define it as a mixed breed of half wolf and half dog. This recherché term connects our poet's heroic flyting with the insults of Vergil's rustics.

98. The poet seems to have incorporated part of a gloss by Servius into his allusion to Vergil. Compare *Aen.* 8.624 and Servius, *ad Aen.* 8.624: *recocto saepe purgato*.

99. The rendering "as I live" follows the most common interpretation of *vivo* as a shortened form of *si vivo* or *dum vivo*—see the note on the Latin text here for a manuscript annotation that supports this

reading. Kratz (1984), 22, Bate (1978), 24, Strecker and Schumann (1951), 41, and Peiper (1873), 25, accept this reading in spite of the strange syntax. The other possible interpretation is that *vivo* is dative referring to Walter. Magoun and Smyser (1950) treat it as a dative. I have translated "as I live" because I have not found a parallel for a shortened final *-o* in the dative case of an adjective or substantive, although shortened final *-o* is common in verbal forms. In spite of Bate's remark that the dative "fails to make any real sense" (58) it could be translated: "I would bury him alive with the treasure." A possible parallel for Attila's exuberant promise of reward occurs in Angantyr's speech in the *Saga of Hervör and Heithrek*, chap. XII (see Ebeling-Koning, *Style and Structure* [1977], 127). Kershaw, *Stories and Ballads from the Far Past* (1921), 131, translates the passage as follows:

> I will case thee all in silver
> As thou sittest on thy throne;
> And a third of the Gothic peoples
> Shall be thine to rule alone;
> With gold shalt thou be covered
> As thou farest through the land.—
> Thou shalt dazzle the sight
> As thou walk'st in the light
> Like the flame of a fiery brand.

Here we see the same hyperbolic reference to surrounding the recipient with treasure. Murdoch, *Walthari* (1989), notes that "promises of reward often carry the proviso that the claimant has to survive" (94); thus, "alive" (*vivo*) could properly describe the proposed recipient.

100. That is, "tyrant" or here perhaps "vassal." The French here represents the original Greek-derived *tyrannus*.

101. The phrase "to stuff his purse with treasure" alludes to Prudentius's description of Avarice (*Psychomachia* 459). Kratz, *Mocking Epic* (1980), 55, rightly says that the phrase serves to criticize such money-based motivations. Although Attila's men fail to act, the criticism can reasonably be transferred to Gunther and his men, who do act on such motives.

102. Apparently this refers to some kind of trap.

103. The poet may be sincere in calling Walter a "praiseworthy hero" for his virtuous abstinence from sexual contact, although his virtue is elsewhere questionable.

104. Althof, *Waltharii Poesis* (1905), 150, notes that forty days is long enough that it cannot be meant to be a quick journey. The emphasis is on the great distance that must have been covered. The number forty may well have been chosen by the Christian poet from the repetition of forty days as a significant length of time in the Bible, for example: Gn 7:4, 12, 17; 8:6; Ex 24:18, 34:28; Mt 4:2, Mk 1:13, etc. Often forty days represents the length of a time of trial, as in Christ's forty days in the wilderness (e.g. Mt 4:1–2). Walter's flight through the wilderness may therefore be compared with such biblical trials, although the comparison may be taken as either symbolic or ironic.

105. Worms was the historical seat of the Burgundian king Gundahar (Gunther), who was defeated by the Roman general Aetius and Hunnish mercenaries in 437 A.D.

106. Evidently he was eager to continue on his way home; alternately he may have still feared pursuit by the Huns.

107. This archaic-sounding phrase translates the archaic Latin *cuias*, which is rare in classical Latin except as a legalistic or purposefully archaic term. In the classical period, this specific form of the word is found only in Livy (27.19.9) and Valerius Maximus (*Mem.* 8.5.6). Servius (*Comm. Don.* 435) may be our poet's source.

108. A strange description because the author offers a window reference to Vergil (*Aen.* 4.554–5), as seen through Servius (*ad Aen.* 4.555: *nam et certus eundi fuerat, et rite cuncta praeparaverat*).

109. Compare the first mention of Hildegund's outstanding beauty at ll. 36–7.

110. Literally this means "to ball up haughty whirls of legs," but compare Vergil, *Geo.* 3.117, 192. Note that, though not here, the poet sometimes uses *eques* for "horse" (for example, at l. 216), as Vergil did at *Geo.* 3.116, which is explained in Servius's comment on that line.

111. Walter could easily have paid the ferryman in gold. If he had, the king would never have seen the odd fish and would never have chased him. Thus Walter's own greedy unwillingness to part with a bit of the treasure causes his problems.

112. Gunther's haughtiness is his chief trait in the poem. *Guthere*'s character in the fragmentary Anglo-Saxon *Waldere* appears to have been similar (cf. fragment A, ll. 25b–29a), although clearly the poet of the *Waltharius* has added depth through his allusions connecting Gunther (and Walter himself) to the character Haughtiness or Pride (*Superbia*) in Prudentius's *Psychomachia*.

113. Note how Gunther repeats and perverts much of Hagen's speech—replacing Hagen's display of loyal friendship with greed and selfishness. The dissonance of their words foreshadows the coming tension between Hagen and Gunther during the battle against Walter.

114. Twelve was an important number for several reasons, one being the biblical number of the disciples. But the number is found elsewhere in medieval Germanic poetry, where the hero must often fight twelve enemies in single combat, and in Charlemagne's legendary twelve peers; see Surles, *Roots and Branches* (1987), 133. One could further point to the use of twelve witnesses in the *Laws of the Salian Franks* as evidence for a Germanic source; see Drew, *The Laws of the Salian Franks* (1991), 130. However, in "*Waltharius, Carmen de prodicione Guenonis* und Rolandepos" (1969), 50, Wilhelm Tavernier suggests that the twelve peers are based on Gunther's twelve followers. Indeed, he argues that the early twelfth-century Latin poem *Carmen de prodicione Guenonis* and, to a lesser extent, the Old French *Roland* were significantly influenced by the *Waltharius*.

115. Apostrophe or prosphonesis, a narrator's direct address to a character often indicates sympathy for the character or at least expectation of trials or death to come. See Behr, "A Narratological Repraisal of Apostrophe in Virgil's *Aeneid*" (2005). Vergil's sympathetic use of apostrophe supplied our poet's model and, if he read his Vergil with Servius's commentary, he would have learned that prosphonesis enhanced the vividness of the scene (Servius, *ad Aen.* 4.408). Compare our poet's apostrophe to Pandarus at ll. 727–8.

116. The verb *fraudare* ("to cheat") foreshadows the thievery topos that recurs throughout the coming battle. The poet's playfulness, perhaps purposefully, makes it unclear who are thieves and who are victims of thievery.

117. The epithets *infelix* ("unlucky," "unhappy," or "unblessed") and *superbus* ("haughty") are often applied to Gunther. This could be the plan of the Latin poet, since his model, Vergil, often uses such epithets calling Aeneas *pius* and Dido *infelix*—or it could betray influence from an oral Germanic model which used standard epithets as part of its formulaic language.

118. Althof, *Waltharii Poesis* (1905), 164, suggests that the Vosges are the Wasgenwald (or Vosges mountains). He then remarks that the verbal similarity of *Wasgenwald* and *Waschenstein* to *Wasconlant* (Old High German for Basque-land or *Aquitania*) could have led to the confusion of place names connected with Walter. It should be noted that these place names alliterating with Walter's own name may suggest an alliterative Germanic source. Two of early manuscripts (namely, V and U) here read *Wasagum*, which alliterates with *Waltharius*, instead of the more common *Vosagum*. The forested Vosges mountain range runs along the west bank of the Rhine in north-eastern France. Compare the *Nibelungenlied* (39.2344, ed. Bartsch), which places the confrontation at Waschenstein. For the Latin name *Vosagus* (ll. 769, 946) or *Vosegus* (l. 823), see Caesar, *BG* 4.10.1; Lucan, *BC* 1.397; Pliny, *Nat.* 16.197; and Silius Italicus, 4.213. Note that the poet describes the place as a *locus amoenus*, a charming natural spot (especially with *specus ... amoenum*, "a cave quite pleasant"); the topos is classical in origin and much used in medieval literature;

see Curtius, *European Literature and the Latin Middle Ages* (1953), 183–202. Our poet may have known the *locus amoenus* from Servius, *ad Aen.* 5.734 or Isidore, *Etym.* 14.33

119. A perfect place for Walter, if we consider the poet's hint at the etymology of his name, *Walt* = forest (see ll. 761–5).

120. The phrase "fitting … for bloody bandits" (*apta … latronibus … cruentis*) might cause one to consider who the bandits are. Both Walter and his attackers will be depicted as thieves or bandits in the following narrative. Walter has already stolen treasure and armor from Attila and will be shown "stealing" life from his attackers, while Gunther and his men will try to steal the treasure from him. Verbally this "cave" (*specus*) as a "refuge" (*statio*) recalls the cave where Aristaeus fights the shapeshifter Proteus from Vergil's *Georgics* 4.418–21. The intertext is compelling since Walter too is portrayed as a magical being and a shapeshifter (ll. 761–3, 769, 790–4, 803–04), and both Proteus and Walter are described as deceptive or tricky.

121. Nickel, "About the Sword of the Huns" (1973), 141, compares this scene where Walter sleeps in Hildegund's lap with numerous similar scenes from European folk ballads, arguing that the motif ultimately goes back to what he calls a "Urepos of the Steppes." Though interesting, his argument is highly speculative.

122. The Latin word for cloud is *nebula*, and Bate, *Walharius* (1978), 59–60, suggests that this is a proleptic etymological play anticipating the *Franci nebulones* or "Nibelung Franks" (l. 555), who are, of course, making the cloud. Although the poet elsewhere engages in such word play, these words are fifty lines apart, so that it may be a stretch to connect them in this way. Still, it is tempting, especially since the German *Nibelungen* may be linked at least through folk etymology to *Nebel* ("mist").

123. Compare Ovid, *Met.* 4.105–07, for the footsteps in the dust: *serius egressus vestigia vidit in alto / pulvere certa ferae totoque expalluit ore / Pyramus.* If this is not simply a convenience borrowing, one might see a purposeful comparison between Walter and a wild beast such as the lion whose tracks Pyramus here sees.

124. The description of Gunther here alludes to Prudentius's image of Pride (*Superbia*) in the *Psychomachia*, just before she falls in the pit of Deceit (*Fraus*)—not a favorable model. Furthermore, deceit will be a major part of the action during the battles; the verb *fraudare* ("to cheat" or "deceive") appears at ll. 486 and 979, while the noun *fraus* ("deceit" or "deception") appears at l. 790 describing Walter. The exact wording of the line "he urged on his swift steed with sharp spurs" (*Cornipedem rapidum saevis calcaribus urget*) suggests that the poet alludes to both Prudentius (*rapidum calcaribus urget / cornipedem, Psych.* 253–4) and to Prudentius's source, Statius (*saeuis calcaribus urguent, Theb.* 11.452), one of many multiple references characteristic of the poem.

125. The Latin *euntem* ("going along") does not specify the manner of Walter's movement, although it may suggest that he is going on foot. Perhaps Gunther saw Walter's footsteps in the dust (cf. l. 513) and so knew that they would easily catch him, since they were on horseback. On the manner of Walter's travel, see the description of the his escape from the Huns (ll. 341–54), which seems to indicate that the horse was just used as a pack animal; see Strecker, "Vorbemerkungen" (1942), 42.

126. An instance of the thievery topos which runs throughout this scene. Here Walter seems to be the thief, although the treasure could be called "stolen" because Attila originally "stole" it from Gunther's father.

127. Literally, this is either "how high he jumps against a shield" or "how high he rises up into his shield." It is pertinent to note that this rather odd description may owe something to the custom of using a shield as an offensive weapon; compare Tacitus, *Agricola* 36, and the fragmentary poem *Finn* 31–2 (ed. Dickins).

128. The phrase "by a crazed mind" (*male sana mente*) has been adapted from Prudentius, *Psych.* 203, a description of Pride (*Superbia*)—an appropriate allusion since "proud" or "haughty" (*superbus*) often describes Gunther.

129. Here we see Hagen's opposition to Gunther's plan of attacking Walter. It is natural for him not to want to fight his friend Walter. However, in his refusal he fails to fight for his lord, an almost unthinkable prospect for a Germanic retainer; compare Tacitus, *Germania* 14.1, and Byrhtnoth's men in the *Battle of Maldon*. On this problem, see Ziolkowski, "Fighting Words" (2001), 40. Eventually Hagen will fight for Gunther after all others die.

130. That is, "troop." The French represents the Greek-derived *phalanx.*

131. That is, "blindness." Here the poet uses a rare Greek term (*glaucoma*) found in Latin medical writing; thus I translate with a medical term (cf. Serenus Sammonicus, *Med.* 13.220; Plin., *NH* 28.95, 28.117, 28.171, etc.). Our poet's immediate source may be Prudentius, *Ham.* 85.

132. In *Walther of Aquitaine* (1950), 16, Magoun and Smyser misleadingly translate *rigidos* ("stiff") here as "sinewy." Compare Prudentius, *Ham.* 284, where God makes men's limbs stiff with bones: *rigidos duraverat ossibus artus.* Either his limbs are stiff because he just awoke, or he makes them stiff (or tough) through the armor he puts on. If the latter, the adjective is proleptic just as in Prudentius.

133. Kratz, *Mocking Epic* (1980), 47, notes that "who" (*qui*) here may refer to God, who is not mentioned in the text, or more likely to Walter's sword, which is the subject of the previous passage (ll. 449–50). The poet seems to allude to 2 Cor 1:10: "he who has snatched us from such great dangers" (*qui de tantis periculis nos eripuit*), where "who" clearly refers to God. The biblical parallel highlights Walter's impiety, if he is invoking his sword. Compare *Waldere* (fragment B, 25–9) for a simple statement about God giving victory, where it seems that Walter is addressing Gunther.

134. It seems likely that the poet is connecting the Latin *nebulones*, which usually means something like "good-for-nothings," with the German *Nibelungen*. Note that MS. N reads *nivilones*, which may be seen as closer to the Germanic name. Thus we could translate *Franci nebulones* as "Nibelung Franks" or "no-good Franks." It also possible that the poet is further playing with the etymology of *nebulones* through his earlier reference to their coming in a cloud (*nebulam*, l. 505)—compare the similar sounds of German *Nibelungen* and *Nebel* ("mist"). Kiefer, "*Walthari poesis*: débuts d'un sentiment national dans la dépréciation de l'autre" (2001), 15–16, sees this reference as well as the later phrase "Celtic tongue" (*Celtica lingua*, l. 765) as signs of the author's nationalistic bias against East Franks (*Alemanni*). See Ziolkowski, "Fighting Words" (2001), 45 n. 69, for further discussion of this word.

135. Haughtiness is a key trait of Gunther's and clearly negative, so Walter's boasting is a fault. Moreover, he has an immoderate desire for both treasure and fame. The poet knows well that this is a sinful attitude, and Walter's immediate repentance for this boast does not fully erase the stains that have defiled his character.

136. This is one of Walter's most Christian actions. It is hard to say just how much of this Christian element has been added by the poet, since Germanic versions of the tale probably had Christian features too. Compare the very Christian praise of God's power in the *Waldere* (B 25–31). Still, our poet highlights Walter's explicitly Christian actions, few as they are (cf. ll. 225, 427).

137. My translation reflects the strong alliteration of the original Latin: *Hunc hominem! pergant primum, qui cuncta requirant.*

138. I have used an archaic spelling for "man" because *homonem* is an archaic Latin form. It appears also at l. 933. Priscian (extant in MS. St. Gall, *Stiftsbibliothek*, 904, perhaps at St. Gall by the 10th century) quotes an example from Ennius, but Servius (*ad Aen.* 6.595) also quotes an Ennian fragment containing the archaic form, and our author definitely knows Servius. See above note 83 (on l. 331) for another form possibly from Priscian.

139. That is, the report from the ferryman about Walter passing through with treasure.

140. The simile "racing very much like the East Wind" (*rapidoque simillimus Euro*) combines Vergil, *Aen* 12.733 (*fugit ocior Euro*) and Prudentius, *Apoth.* 611 (*rapidoque simillimus Austro*).

141. "I have absolutely no idea" (*Ignoro penitus*, l. 595) is also found in Walafrid Strabo, *Vita Blait-maici* 151 (dated about 830). However, neither poet had to take the phrase from the other, as it is found as early as the Vulgate (Prv 30:18) in the order *penitus ignoro*, which is simply rearranged for the meter.

142. The word "hostage-like" translates the reverse prepositional phrase *obsidis ergo*. This is a rare and archaic construction structurally like the more familiar genitive with *causa*. Our poet probably found it in Vergil, *Aen.* 6.670, where Servius explains the usage. In *Waltharius of Gaeraldus* (1978), 60, Bate incorrectly assumes that *obsidis* is a mistake for the nominative case.

143. The narrator reserves this term for Walter. Here Camalo, speaking in character, applies it to his king and lord, whom the poet calls "haughty" (*superbus*) and "unlucky" (*infelix*).

144. Notice the alliterative "life and limb" where the Latin has no alliteration. Alliterative pairs are common in Germanic languages; the modern German for this old pair is *Leib und Leben*. Althof, *Waltharii Poesis* (1905), 188, cites early Germanic examples of the pair. The occurrence of such phrases is a sign that the author spoke a Germanic language or even that he was translating some passages directly from a Germanic original. Compare Althof, *Waltharii Poesis* (1889), 49–50, for a list of Germanisms in the poem.

145. I translate *sophista*, a Greek-derived term for a clever man, with the French.

146. The fragmentary *Waldere* (A, 28–30) also tells that Walter had offered Gunther treasure, including both rings and a sword, which the king refused.

147. The phrase "fingers from the fight" translates the alliterative Latin *de pugna palmam* (l. 619). Such brief alliterative phrases are common in the poem and may betray influence from a Germanic source, as noted above (note 144). However, some Latin authors also favor alliteration, notably our poet's model Vergil (for instance, *Aen.* 1.55, 81, 124, 214).

148. This dream foreshadows the final battle, and the image of Walter as a bear is in a way fulfilled by the most elaborate simile of the poem, which compares Walter to a Numidian bear (ll. 1337–43). Animal dreams occur also in the *Ruodlieb* 17.89–102, and the *Nibelungenlied* 16. Note that l. 625 ("tore off … thigh") is exactly repeated at l. 1364, when the dream is fulfilled.

149. That is, he was not hot with courage.

150. Gunther's taunt about Hagen's father will be repeated by Hagen himself (1067-1072).

151. For Gunther's pride and his refusal of Walter's offer of treasure, compare the Anglo-Saxon *Waldere* (A, 25–31).

152. For *metropolitanus* ("metropolitan") Kratz has "prefect" in *Walthrius and Ruodlieb* (1984), 33. The adjective *metropolitanus* typically refers to a metropolitan church, a major regional church center. Although Metz was not an archbishopric at the time of Attila, Camalo—contrary to his negative portrayal—appears to be an ecclesiastic metropolitan, a sort of prelate or archbishop in charge of a region. However, he could be a secular official having a similar kind of regional authority, although I know no precedent for *metropolitanus* to designate a secular official. The anachronistic status of Metz here has been used by von den Steinen, "Der *Waltharius*" (1952), 41–2, and others as evidence for the poem's date.

153. I omit l. 652, which appears only in the margin of S as a repetition from l. 647, "Hand over all the treasure to the king of the Franks!"

154. An instance of the thievery theme that runs throughout this scene. Note that "from King Gunther" has been translated as if *Gunthario … regi* were a dative of separation, while the Latin would allow a second meaning as a dative of advantage, "for King Gunther." Whichever way one reads the phrase, the reader might well note Walter's sarcasm and then recall that Walter actually "stole" the treasure for himself from Attila. Ebeling-Koning, *Style and Structure* (1977), 220–1, suggests that the implication of thievery represents a veiled criticism of Walter. See also l. 517, where Gunther had already called the treasure "stolen" (*furata talenta*). Consider also the poet's apparent criticism in ll. 1401–05.

155. Here "bitt" translates the rare *mordit*, in place of classical *momordit/memordit* ("bit"); for a possible model for the spelling, see Isid., *Sent.* 1.9.9.a. I have retained the rare perfect in the Latin text because the poet, following Isidore and Latin grammarians, elsewhere employs such rare or unique forms, as in l. 331 (*iteri*).

156. In *Waltharius of Gaeraldus* (1978), 61, Bate notes that nephews became stock figures of medieval romances. For this character's double names Kimo and Scaramund, compare Eleuthir/Helmnod later in the poem (l. 1007). Here as elsewhere it is hard to tell which, if any, of these names the poet has taken from his Germanic sources.

157. Murdoch, *Walthari* (1989), 16, suggests that this vague reference to the poet's source, "some say" (*referunt quidam*, l. 688), provides evidence of a Germanic original with the character Scaramund.

158. Kimo seems to have dropped his sword when it rebounded from Walter's helm, and so Walter picked it up. Although it may seem odd for a Christian hero to decapitate his opponents, our poet knew Prudentius, who made his personified virtues do the same (for example, Humility decapitated Pride)—arguably providing an acceptable Christian model for Walter.

159. Kimo or Scaramund is Camalo's nephew, so that the two have "kindred blood" (*cognatus cruor*). The alliterative phrase is rare, elsewhere only in Seneca, *Oedipus* 627 and *De beneficiis* 5.15.5, the poem's only evidence of possible Senecan influence.

160. That is, skill in archery.

161. The poet explicitly connects his epic to the Greco-Roman epic tradition by making Evarhard descend from Homer's Trojan Pandarus; compare with the mention of Hagen's Trojan blood (l. 28). These lines recall Vergil's direct address to Pandarus (*Aen.* 5.495–6). Pandarus also plays a part in the so-called Latin Homer (*Ilias Latina* 346–453), where he is also directly addressed by the poet (449). Pandarus was the chief archer of the Trojans in the *Iliad*, but because of the truce-breaking shot, which the poet here alludes to, he is often seen as a rogue. Compare the poet's direct address to Walter at l. 485.

162. The poet uses *auster* ("south wind"), it seems, for wind in general. Compare Servius's notes on Vergil's similar use of the word at *ad Aen.* 1.9 and 3.70. This is part of the evidence that the poet read Vergil with Servius's commentary.

163. That is, "descendent of Pandarus." Compare the patronymic *Alpharides* ("son of Alphere") for Walter at l. 839.

164. I imitate the poet's archaic Latin *olli* by writing the old spelling "hym" instead of "him." For the Latin *olli*, compare Vergil, *Aen.* 1.254, 12.829, and Servius, *ad Aen.* 1.254.

165. Literally this is "just weight," referring metaphorically to a balance scale.

166. As often, here Walter is called *iuvenis* ("the youth").

167. The Latin *preces* ("prayer") can also mean "plea."

168. Walter's lack of mercy, particularly since his opponent was possibly praying or at least pleading for mercy, is thoroughly un-Christian. Moreover, the phrase "left a torso" derives from some less than glorious Vergilan models, *Aen.* 9.332 (Nisus and Euryalus killing sleeping opponents) and 12.382 (Turnus killing a helpless opponent). The chilling touch of the scene is reminiscent of Aeneas's killing of Turnus, who is described as "begging" (*Aen.* 12.930: *precantem*), but here Walter has no source of moral justification like Turnus's slaughter of Pallas.

169. It is unclear whether this means Saxony on the continent or Saxon holdings in Britain.

170. The Latin verb *vegetat* ("gives you vigor") and the rest of this speech indicate a etymological pun on Walter's name, which is from the same root as German *Wald* ("forest"). Compare the puns on Hagen's name, which means "thorn bush" (ll. 1351 and 1421). See Morgan, "Walter the Wood-Sprite" (1972), for a discussion of the poet's etymological plays.

171. Langosch, *Waltharius, Ruodlieb, Märchenepen* (1956), 378, notes: "'Celtica lingua' ist nicht sicher zu deuten, meint wohl Kauderwelsch" ("'Celtic tongue' is not clear, perhaps it means *Kauderwelsch*")

By *Kauderwelsch* Langosch intends a sort of confused mishmash of Celtic and Germanic languages, a vulgar dialect. Morgan, "Walter the Wood-Sprite" (1972), 17–18, suggests that *Celtica* may refer not so much to language as to wit, therefore meaning "clever tongue." He claims that Walter is acknowledging Ekerich's riddling, ridiculing etymology on Walter's name. Kiefer, "*Waltharii poesis*. Débuts d'un sentiment national" (2001), 16, sees the remark as indicative of a nationalistic bias against East Franks; cf. above on *Franci nebulones* (l. 555). On the interpretation of *Celtica lingua*, see also Ziolkowski, "Fighting Words" (2001), 46, and D'Angelo, *Waltharius* (1998), 187.

172. That is, "phantasm." The French equivalent represents the Greek *fantasma*.

173. Compare Vergil, *Aen.* 9.665, and Servius, *ad Aen.* 9.662, for the "throwing strap" (*amento*).

174. Ekerich did not plan to die, but to kill Walter. Compare Vergil, *Aen.* 11.881.

175. That is, "circle." The French represents the Greek-derived *girus*.

176. An instance of the thievery theme with Walter depicted as the thief of life.

177. Perhaps this is another riddling reference to Walter as a "wood-sprite," since woodland spirits might change into birds.

178. This invocation of his right hand recalls the godless Mezentius's invocation of his right hand in place of a god in the *Aeneid* (10.773–6). Mezentius's impiety and his later downfall make this an unfavorable parallel—Walter should be addressing God! It is pertinent to note that Servius, with whom our poet is familiar, comments on *Aen.* 10.773: "so that [Mezentius], being sacrilegious, does not think he has any other god besides his own right hand and courage" (*ut non alium sibi putet deum esse sacrilegus, quam dextram et fortitudinem*). Walter's right hand that has brought him so much glory will be cut off in the final battle, evoking Mk 9:42: "And if your hand causes you to sin, cut it off ...."

179. The invocation of his left hand has a similar impious connotation. Moreover, Walter's strong attachment to his shield, a material possession, is not in keeping with the conduct of a Christian hero. Furthermore, the poet's choice of "Avars" as the name for the Huns here could be because of its punning connection with *avaritia* ("avarice" or "greed"); see below note 323 on l. 1404.

180. The language here is hyperbolic, portraying the men as giants with the earth as their battlefield.

181. Compare Vergil, *Aen.* 12.788. This allusion aligns Walter with Aeneas and his opponent with Turnus, but this is not always the case.

182. This patronymic epithet meaning "son of Alphere" is part of the poet's connection to pagan epic—Vergil calls Aeneas *Anchisiades* ("son of Anchises," *Aen.* 5.407). Compare with "Pandarides" above (l. 737).

183. Kratz, *Waltharius and Ruodlieb* (1984), 41, here translates "Pick up your shield!" but the Latin *Accipe scutum!* gives no indication of whose shield is being talked about. Therefore, since Hadawart attacked Walter specifically to take his shield, it seems far more poignant to have Walter mock him by saying, "Come, take it!" This ironic taunt fits well the tone of the exchanges between opponents throughout the combat sequence. The mocking tone presents Walter in an unfavorable light, but we have already noted failings in his character from a Christian standpoint, notably his invocation of his right and left hands, rather than God, to save him. While the unspecified shield (*scutum*, l. 840) in Walter's mocking address recalls Hadawart's desire for Walter's shield, it may also look forward to Hadawart's own shield, which first clatters on top of him and then is torn aside, as Walter beats down his opponent. This line and l. 1043, about taking a sword, are similar in tone to the hero's taunt in the *Waldere* (B, 16b–17): "Snatch, if you dare, the gray hauberk from this battle-exhausted man" (*Feta gif ðu dyrre / æt ðus heaðuwearigan hare byrnan*).

184. Hagen's speech is almost a sermon on greed or avarice. Note that the whole of the poem can be seen as illustrating the vice of avarice, since Walter greedily steals two chests of treasure and Attila's armor and helmet (ll. 263–4) for his journey, and then further problems ensue when Gunther wishes to steal the treasure from Walter. This is not in accord with the exhortation of Good Works in the

Psychomachia (613), or of Christ to his apostles (Lk 9:3, 10:4, 22:35), both of whom say not even to take a purse on one's journey. Bate and others have seen this speech as inconsistent with the narrator's claim that Hagen's nephew was "lusting to seize glory" (*laudem captare cupiscens*), but "lusting" (*cupiscens*) indicates avaricious desire, and "glory" (*laudem*) is usually accompanied by material wealth. Whether Patavrid wants the treasure for its monetary value or as a glorious symbol of exacted blood vengeance, his desire is excessive and avaricious.

185. The phrases "Insatiate Hunger to Have" (*fames insatiatus habendi*, l. 857) and "thirst to have" (*sitis ... habendi*, l. 864) allude to Prudentius' description of Avarice in the *Psychomachia*—"insatiate love of having" (*amor insatiatus habendi*, 478)—although the second phrase (*sitis ardet habendi*, l. 864) appears too close, in both word choice and order, to Boethius, *Consolation of Philosophy* 2.2.18 (*sitis ardescit habendi*) to assume another allusion is operative here.

186. "Whirlpool of Greed" is an allusion to Prudentius, *Ham.* 255.

187. In an allusion to 1 Tm 6:10, *fibra*—technically referring to a smaller fiber sent out by a larger root—is substituted for the metrically unfeasible *radix* or root.

188. As Wieland suggests in *Waltharius* (1986), 84, "filthy" (*turpem*) is transferred from "lucre" (*lucro*) to "death" (*mortem*), since this line recalls the biblical injunction against desire for "filthy lucre" (cf. *turpe lucrum* at 1 Tm 3:8 and Ti 1:11), perhaps influenced by Prudentius's description of Avarice (*Psych.* 460).

189. That is, "Hell." The poet has combined the Greco-Roman Erebus (for example, Vergil, *Aen.* 6.404) with the Christian concept of a fiery hell (as in Mt 13:43).

190. For "Savage Desire" (*saeva cupido*), compare Statius, *Silv.* 2.1.214 and Juvenal, 14.175 (similar moralizing passages about the ills of mankind). Vergil instead has *dira cupido* (*Geo.* 1.37; *Aen.* 6.373, 721, 9.185).

191. Notice that Hagen here indicates that desire for praise or glory is, in fact, just another type of greed. Thus Hagen's nephew is acting avariciously even if he seeks glory rather than gold, as indicated above (ll. 853–4). In *Mocking Epic* (1980), 39, Kratz notes that Hagen's later reasons for attacking Walter hypocritically include glory (cf. ll. 1275–9).

192. This is a touching echo of Vergil, *Ecl.* 3.79, where the expression is an address of a woman to her departing lover.

193. This passage shows the more Christian side of Walter, who wants to spare the young man, although one might also find a literary model in Aeneas's desire to spare Lausus, whom he kills, arousing the wrath of Mezentius (Vergil, *Aen.* 10.809–12). The scene also illustrates Walter's loyalty to Hagen, whom he does not want to grieve.

194. That is, "tyrant." The French here represents the original Greek-derived *tyrannus*.

195. The phrase "whirling, windy dance" reproduces the one Latin word *choris* (l. 890). For *chorus* as a dance ring or the movement of a dance, compare *Oxford Latin Dictionary* under *chorus* 1a and b, as well as Isidore, *Etym.* 19.30.2, a source available to our poet. Kratz's translation in *Waltharius and Ruodlieb* (1984) equates *choris* with *Cauris*, the ablative plural of *Caurus* ("north-west wind"), and translates: "Propelled by *breezes* and the raging warrior's strength ...." The double alteration of the diphthong *au* to the simple vowel *o* and of unaspirated *c* to aspirated *ch* is quite possible; compare *chorum* for *Caurum* in Einhard's *Life of Charlemagne* 29. This alternate spelling appears to be inspired by the etymology given by Isidore, *Etym.* 13.11.10 (*Et vocatus Corus quod ipse ventorum circulum claudat, et quasi chorum faciat*). The poet thus appears to be playing on this etymologizing sense of *chorus*.

196. That is, Walter. For this phrase applied to Walter, compare l. 454.

197. At *Aen.* 2.529, Vergil uses *vulnus* ("wound") apparently to refer to a sword. Servius comments on this line: *'vulnus' pro 'telo'* ("'wound' in place of 'weapon'"). Our poet often uses *vulnus* in lieu of a word meaning "blow" or "weapon" (ll. 338, 671, 712, 897, 1382), adopting the usage either directly from Vergil or from Servius.

198. An epic patronymic meaning "son of Alphere."

199. That is, unable to inflict the intended wound. Kratz, *Waltharius and Ruodlieb* (1984), translates "tricked into a wild blow" (45), but *vulnere* is more naturally understood as an ablative of separation.

200. That is, "steel." The poet uses the rare Greek term *chalibs*, which I translate with French.

201. An epic patronymic meaning "son of Alphere."

202. That is, leaving his body to be devoured by the forest animals and his soul to Hell.

203. Consider the narrator's earlier remark about the Hunnish custom of wearing two blades (l. 337, see note 85 above) and Hagen's later remark that Walter would be breaking his people's custom by wearing his sword on the right (l. 1429). These comments display an anthropological or antiquarian interest, although they need not be more than poetic fiction. Compare Statius, *Theb.* 5.525–6, and Silius, 8.549–50, for this kind of comment in Roman epic. Kiefer, "*Walthari poesis*, nouvelles recherches: les armes des héros" (2001), explores the connections between the poet's literary references to armament and the historical realities. On the tactical use of weaponry in the *Waltharius*, see Bachrach, *Early Carolingian Warfare* (2001), 196–200. On historical Frankish weaponry, see ibid., 81–131, and Coupland, "Carolingian Arms and Armor in the Ninth Century" (1990).

204. As often, the emphatically used "man" (*vir*) refers to Walter, who is known for his *virtus* or heroic courage.

205. The poet uses the archaic form *duellum*, rather than the usual *bellum*, for "war." *Duellum* is not found in Vergil. The source may by Statius, *Theb.* 8.684, 11.282; Ovid, *Fast.* 6.201; Juvenal, 1.169; or Horace, *Carm.* 3.5.38, 3.14.18, 4.15.8 and *Ep.* 1.2.7, 2.1.254, 2.2.298.

206. Compare Vergil, *Aen.* 12.714, and Servius's corresponding note, which implies that *fors* ("luck") is Turnus and *virtus* ("courage" or "virtue") is Aeneas. This may be the correct way to take the passage here with Walter as *virtus* ("courage") and his opponent as *fors* ("luck"), but both attributes may also belong to both combatants.

207. That is, "man." This imitates the poet's archaic spelling of the Latin word. See note 138 above.

208. Strecker and Schumann, *Nachträge* (1951), 62, have no punctuation after *exitiumque dolens* ("grievous death," l. 938), which they connect with the rest of the line, but I follow MS. V in punctuating after *dolens*. Thus *prodidit* ("brought forth," l. 937) has two objects in mild zeugma. Here *dolens* has the rare meaning "painful" rather than "feeling pain." MSS. B, P, and T read *exivit* instead of *exitium*, probably a conjecture introduced by someone who did not understand the function of *dolens* here.

209. Compare note 168 above on "left a torso" (l. 753). The comment about the headless corpse having once been count of Worms seems to be inspired by Vergil's pathetic description of Priam being beheaded by Pyrrhus. If so, the allusion casts Walter as an impious murderer.

210. The phrase "as … as this" translates the Latin *sic sic*, which seems in turn to translate a Germanic idiom; see note 322 on l. 1404.

211. As Althof, in *Waltharii Poesis* (1905), notes (265), the poet is apparently adapting 2 Mc 7:2: "we are ready to die rather than to transgress the traditional laws of God" (*parati sumus mori magis quam patrias Dei leges praevaricari*). Since this passage represents the speaking Jews as nobly resisting Antiochus IV in the name of God, it is hardly consonant with Gunther's arrogant challenge. Thus the allusion highlights the base character of his actions.

212. This is an instance of the thievery theme that runs throughout the latter half of the poem.

213. This athletic metaphor is extended below.

214. The reference to a hero as an athlete (*athleta*)—my recognizable French translation showing the poet's use of a Greek-derived term—is part of a series of athletic metaphors in the last third of the poem: cf. ll. 1025, 1046, 1411. This agonistic language may be inspired by Prudentius (cf. *Perist.* 4.184, 5.135) or come directly from the New Testament (cf. 1 Cor 9:25, 2 Tm 2:5). However, neither

of these uses *athleta*, although the term joined the rhetoric of Christian Latin early on (consider, for example, *athletam Christi* in Augustine, *De civitate Dei* 14.9).

215. Compare Prudentius, *Psych.* 116.

216. Weland is a Germanic god or hero known as the supreme blacksmith. In the Anglo-Saxon poem *Waldere*, Walter's sword is called "Weland's work" (*Welande<s> worc*, A 2). Also in the *Waldere* Walter's hauberk or byrnie appears to have played a greater role than here, since fragment B 16–24 contains a scene where Walter taunts Gunther, who seems to have particularly wanted this heirloom of Walter's father. In the *Waltharius*, it is his shield which receives the most attention as a desired prize—compare Hadawart's request to have the shield (ll. 781–2 above) and Helmnod's plan to wrench it away (ll. 982–1017). The phrase "Weland's work" (*Wielandia fabrica*) may be a direct translation of an alliterative Germanic phrase. Besides the above-mentioned passage in the *Waldere*, compare *Beowulf* 455.

217. That is, "circles" or "rings." The French represents the Greek-derived *girus*.

218. The poet uses a very rare Greek term for steel, *chalibs*, which I translate with French.

219. An epic patronymic meaning "son of Alphere."

220. The verb "to cheat" (*fraudo*) is an instance of the thievery theme recurring in the battle scenes. Walter keeps stealing the life of his opponents, just as they try to steal the treasure, which he stole first. Note that here again Walter is proudly concerned with his reputation; compare his arrogant boast at ll. 561–3. His actions are far from Christian, especially since he shows no mercy to his opponent.

221. One could also translate *precantis* "as he pled." Compare the similar scene at ll. 751–2 and the note there.

222. Helmnod appears in a group of three in the *Nibelungenlied* 38.2261 (ed. Bartsch), perhaps a detail derived from our poem or its source. Here Helmnod, Trogus, and Tanastus similarly make a group of three further marked by their use of a trident (three-pronged spear). The poet probably chose the trident as a symbol for the combined three-person attempt.

223. Helmnod is, of course, taunting Walter for the lost locks of hair.

224. Compare Isidore, *Etym.* 12.4.29 and Lucan, *BC* 9.720 and the corresponding note in the *Commenta Bernensia* (a commentary on Lucan preserved in a tenth-century manuscript) for this odd bit of lore.

225. Eleuthir (Helmnod) was first introduced at l. 982. The name "Eleuthir" may be one of the poet's Greek-derived words, meaning "free" (*eleutheros*). Ziolkowski, "Fighting Words" (2001), 46, suggests that the poet may be punning on one meaning of *Frank*, that is, "free" or "unrestrained."

226. That is, Strasbourg.

227. The name may be Trogus or Trogunt—the latter has good manuscript support at ll. 1009 and 1021.

228. Epic patronymic, "son of Alphere."

229. The Latin *framea* ("brand") is a rare word meaning a short spear in Tacitus, although it apparently means "sword" here—compare below at l. 1376. Interestingly, Tacitus uses it often in the *Germania* for the weapons of the Germans (see especially 6.1, where he claims it is a Germanic word).

230. The use of "bronze" instead of "iron" or "steel" is an anachronistic, literary touch, being owed to the poet's models such as Vergil, who adapted these "bronze" weapons and armor from archaic Greek poets such as Homer, whose poetry preserved memories of the late Bronze Age.

231. Note the probable word-play in Helmnod's death through the splitting of his helm. In *Waltharii Poesis* (1905), 273, Althof connects *-nod* with a root meaning "trouble" or "danger." One could compare more explicit examples of such word-play in the case of Hagen's ("thorny Hagen," l. 1421) and Walter's ("faun" or "wood-sprite," l. 763) names.

232. The word *agonem* is Greek in origin, so I translate with the recognizable French *compétition*; the poet might have known it from Servius (*ad Aen.* 3.704, 5.370; *ad Geo.* 3.19). This is another instance of the athletic metaphor which runs throughout this scene.

233. This is an example of the thievery theme running throughout the latter part of the poem. As elsewhere when applied to Walter, it problematizes his heroism.

234. This is a kenning for "sheath"—a sign of Germanic influence as such riddling metaphorical language is more common in the Germanic heroic sagas than in classical epic. In the *Waldere*, a similar kenning for sheath, *stanfate* ("jeweled vessel," fr. B 3), reminds one of *Waltharius'* "green house" (*viridem aedem*, l. 1036), especially if we imagine the "green" to refer to gems on the sheath.

235. The Latin *virtutem* could also be translated "virtue" or "courage," and it is echoed in the Latin by the word play in *habitum ... virilem* ("manly manner"). In the company of this word play, the "green house" (*viridem .... aedem*) of l. 1036 may hold an additional pun. Calling a sheath "man-house" could allude to the sword as a symbol of the hero's virility.

236. This taunt recalls Walter's jibe: "Come get my shield!" (l. 840).

237. I translate "too" (*quoque*) here because ghosts already smiled at Trogus in the previous paragraph. The association of Walter with ghosts is rather gruesome. Compare the earlier reference to Walter as "present death" (l. 199). Alternately "too" may simply mark Walter's response to Trogus, that is, "Then, grinning, the hero spoke too."

238. Trogus loses his right hand just as Walter does later. This detail and the fact that both Walter and Trogus also lose their shields apparently indicate that the poet presents Trogus as a nobler rival than the other numbered combatants. All the words with the *vir-* root used in this scene—*viridem* (l. 1036), *virtutem* (l. 1038), *virilem* (l. 1039), *virtus* (l. 1042), and *virtute* (l. 1056)—further mark Trogus as a *vir* ("man"), a term which is often used to describe Walter (ll. 895, 920, 959, 1182, 1360, 1386) and once for Hagen (l. 1369).

239. This Greek-derived term (*athleta*), which I translate with a recognizable French equivalent, refers to Walter, continuing the athletic metaphor.

240. This feat of strength is paralleled in *Beowulf*, where the hero wrenches off Grendel's arm.

241. The depiction of Tanastus's final goodbye is sympathetic, especially since he was seeking to protect his friend.

242. The word *preces* ("prayers") could also be translated "plea."

243. An epic patronymic meaning "son of Alphere."

244. The combination of the two commands, to die and to take a message to the underworld, is highly reminiscent of Pyrrhus's impious taunts before he kills Priam (Vergil, *Aen.* 2.447–50). For other passages connecting Walter with Pyrrhus, compare notes 209 on "left a headless torso" (l. 939) and 295 on Guther's weak spear throw (ll. 1296–8).

245. This sentence has given translators and commentators much trouble. The problem arises partly from the fact that the Latin sentence does not specify whose neck receives the torque. In *Waltharius of Gaeraldus* (1978), 63, Bate follows Magoun and Smyser, *Walther of Aquitaine* (1950), 28, in seeing the line as a poetic way of saying that Walter cut off Trogus's head. Thus "golden torque" (*torquem ... aureum*) would be a kenning for the circular wound around his neck. In *Style and Structure* (1977), 126–7, Ebeling-Koning, following Wolf ("Der mittellateinische Waltharius" [1940–41], 80–9), compares a passage from the *Heimskringla* for a similar kenning. However, it seems a stretch to translate *aureum* as "bloody" instead of "golden." Other possibilities include reading the line as a description of Walter putting Trogus's torque around his own neck, or as a poetic description of Walter strangling Trogus perhaps with a neck chain. I suggest that Walter actually respects Trogus for his bravery (*virtus*). Therefore, although Walter's command to "die and take this message down to Tartarus!" seems harsh, he may actually feel that Trogus's manly behavior has in some way avenged his comrades. With this reading, it would make sense for Walter to actually put a golden torque around Trogus's neck, as he lay already in the throes of death, in order to mark his bravery in the face of death. This reading is strengthened by the fact that the language used here derives from the biblical description of honors

received by Joseph and Daniel (Gn 41:42: *collo torquem auream circumposuit*, Dn 5:29: *circumdata est torques aurea collo eius*).

246. This description is striking, eliciting sympathy for the two friends. The poet may have been inspired by the model of Vergil's Nisus and Euryalus episode in book 9 of the *Aeneid* or by Statius's Hopleus and Dymas episode in book 10 of the *Thebaid*. Although Walter's words are harshly ironic, this does not necessarily mean that he had no respect for Trogus, especially if Walter did place a torque around Trogus's neck—see the preceding note.

247. In *Waltharius and Ruodlieb* (1984), 53, Kratz translates *falerati* as "richly furbished," perhaps a typographical error for "furnished." The Latin term indicates that the horse has an ornament on his head or chest.

248. He is sad for the death of his friends and his nephew. This sadness foreshadows his choice to join Gunther against Walter.

249. See ll. 628–31 for Gunther's taunt. Apparently Hagen says this with bitter sarcasm to repay Gunther for his earlier insult, for Gunther soon asks Hagen to put aside his personal grudge against the king (ll. 1075–6).

250. That is, "tyrant." The French represents the Greek-derived *tyrannus*.

251. "Head of the World" is a title for the powerful Frankish kings beginning with Charlemagne; thus Gunther's use here is both anachronistic and presumptious. See Althof, *Waltharii Poesis* (1905), 291–3, for examples of the phrase, often as *caput mundi*, in Carolingian times. The statement is notably ironic, for the reader can hardly fail to laugh at Gunther calling Walter a tyrant and himself the "Head of the World." One might alternately understand "Head of the World" as a reference to God and read it as a general criticism of Walter: "You would have better grown angry with Walter, who alone today dared to defame God." However, this seems a weak alternative and, as Althof argues (292), with this reading the "alone" (*solus*) loses its rhetorical force.

252. The dishonor lies in their failure to take Walter.

253. That is, promises impossible things.

254. I translate the Greek-derived *baratrum* ("abyss") as French. For *baratrum* compare Lucretius, 3.966, and Jgs 5:15: *duces Isachar fuere cum Debbora et Barac vestigia sunt secuti qui quasi in praeceps ac baratrum se discrimini*.

255. For "the path of salvation" (*viam ... salutis*), compare Acts 16:17. Although Hagen clearly says that he will try to keep them safe, the biblical meaning of *salus* ("salvation") is common in Christian literature, and the phrase draws attention to the very un-Christian actions of the subsequent battle. One could also translate the phrase as "the path to safety," as Kratz does in *Waltharius and Ruodlieb* (1984), 55, since it is also found in pagan literature (Servius, *ad Aen.* 8.131, and Cicero, *Har.* 63). It is possible the poet intended a double entendre.

256. Kratz, *Waltharius and Ruodlieb* (1984), translates: "Which will reveal itself—if not at once, then never" (55). But *nusquam* (the *lectio difficilior* and so probably the right reading here) means "nowhere" rather than "never." Also, *coacte* must mean something like "under force" rather than "at once." The *sive*, then, is parallel to *aut*; that is, it means "or else" not "if not"—see the *Oxford Latin Dictionary* under *sive*, 5a.

257. Compare Hagen's contradictory words at 1265–79.

258. Kratz, *Waltharius and Ruodlieb* (1984), translates *speculis* as "caves" (55)—apparently confusing it with *speluncis*—but Niermeyer/van de Kieft, *Mediae Latinitatis Lexicon Minus* (2002), defines *speculum* as "watch-tower." Langosch, *Waltharius, Ruodlieb, Märchenepen* (1956), 65, has "auf die Lauer" ("on the lookout").

259. *Virtus* ("virtue") here might also be translated as "courage," but this would lose the ambiguity of the term, which ironically points to their very un-virtuous actions and motivations.

260. That is, "fierce." The Latin *acrum* is an alternate archaic second-declension form of the adjective *acer*, which is always third declension in classical authors. However, we should probably attribute this not to ignorance but to erudition. The alternate declension is found in the Carolingian *Karolus Magnus et Leo Papa* 286 and in Alcuin, *Versus de patribus, regibus et sanctis Eboracensis ecclesiae* 1.557. Orthographic manuals by Caper (Keil, *Grammatici Latini*, 7:94), Bede (Keil 7:264 = *Orthographia* 108, ed. Jones), and Alcuin (Keil 7:295) endorse the second-declension form, and Charisius (Keil 1:117) has a similar alternate form for *acer*. Note that MS. St. Gallen, *Stiftsbibliothek*, 249 (ca. 800 A.D.) contains both Caper's and Bede's treatises, providing possible evidence for the poem's localization at St. Gall.

261. That is, the "Evening Star."

262. That is, "western." The poet seems to have created this adjective from the Vergilian form *Ausonidum* (*Aen.* 10.564, 11.297, 12.121), which Servius (*ad Aen.* 10.564) explains as a special genitive plural of a first-declension noun, *Ausonida.*

263. For *arguta indagine* ("in a swift hunt"), compare Servius, *ad Aen.* 4.121 (*indagine ferarum inquisitione*) and *ad Ecl.* 4.34 (*argutos celeres dici*).

264. Perhaps an allusion to "thorny Hagen," as Kratz suggests in *Waltharius and Ruodlieb* (1984), 204. See l. 1351 for a pun on Hagen's name, which is etymologically related to the *haw-* in *hawthorn*.

265. That is, "sphere" of the sun. The French here represents the Greek-derived *sp(h)era*.

266. This is another instance of the thievery theme running throughout the latter half of the poem. Also note Walter's recurrent concern with his reputation, appropriate to a pagan hero, not to a Christian.

267. Compare Vergil, *Ecl.* 5.39 and Servius's corresponding note. *Paliurus* or "Christ's thorn" is one of several different thorny or prickly shrubs found in Palestine, including *Paliurus aculeatus*, *Zizyphus spina-christi*, and *Zizyphus vulgaris*. The last produces the jujube fruit and may have been most available for making the crown of thorns for Christ. It is ironic that Walter seeks safety in thorns since "thorny Hagen" (l. 1421) will be his downfall.

268. This care for the dead bodies seems to be a Christian detail, as is certainly the following prayer that Walter says over them.

269. Early Christians always placed altars at the eastern end of their churches, and those praying were supposed to face the altar or the East. This orientation may relate to the association of Christ, who rose again with the sun. Here the ritualistic prayer highlights Walter's at least nominal devotion to Christ, yet in the context of Walter's violence and boasting one wonders whether the poet expected his audience to notice the discrepancy.

270. The reference to being saved "from their insults" shows that, even in the midst of prayer, Walter remains concerned with his reputation—a concern more appropriate for a pagan hero than for a Christian. Nevertheless, Walter's prayer ends on a truly Christian note of forgiveness and mercy. In fact, the juxtaposition of earthly and heavenly values here is quite jarring.

271. Walter clearly recognizes that he and his opponents both have faults and that both need God's forgiveness. Despite many negative and ambiguous aspects of Walter's presentation, this passage is indicative of his honest attempts to improve himself.

272. This does not count the king's own and Hagen's horse, which would make the full total of thirteen.

273. Evidently he is hot and sweaty from fighting.

274. That is, the "Morning Star."

275. The island is an unusually erudite detail, which explains the confusion in the manuscripts here. Usually identified with Sri Lanka (Ceylon), Taprobane is mentioned several times by Pliny the Elder, *Nat.* 6.79, 6.81, 6.89, 6.92, 7.30, 9.106, 32.143, and by others, including Ovid, *Pont.* 1.5.80, and Servius, *ad Geo.* 1.48, who may be the most likely source for our poet.

276. That is, the "Morning Star." Compare Vergil, *Geo.* 1.288.

277. After his Christian prayer over the dead, Walter has returned to the ethics of the pagan warrior. The description of the despoiling seems ironic, since the phrase "only the armbands" (*armillas tantum*) is followed by a long list of other items. Moreover, the armbands in this list bring to mind the Hunnish gold armbands and their connection with the key theme of greed. When Walter is finished despoiling "*only* the armbands …," he needs four horses to carry all the loot (l. 1195). Finally, the somewhat obscure reference to belt bosses (*bullis*, l. 1193) is quite possibly an allusion to one or more of the following passages, all with negative connotations: Euryalus's ill-fated looting (*Aen.* 9.359), Aeneas's notice of the belt that Turnus looted from Pallas (*Aen.* 12.942), or Prudentius's macabre description of the children of Greed (*Avaritia*) looting each other's corpses (*Psych.* 475–6).

278. The odd phrasing here is due to the poet's adaptation of Vergil's choice wording *raptim et sine more*; compare *Aen.* 8.635 and Servius's corresponding note.

279. Again he speaks of his right hand as his source of glory and honor; compare his invocation of both hands above (ll. 812–17) and his loss of his right hand in the final battle (ll. 1380–5).

280. Walter's pagan heroic ethos again leads him to love of glory and of material wealth, both of which desires are aspects of avarice, as was seen in Hagen's central speech (ll. 855–75).

281. The phrase "of salvation" translates *salutis*, which may also be translated "of safety" or "of health." The poet may intend the ambiguity of the meaning to highlight Walter's own ambiguous nature.

282. That is, "wolf-dog." See note 97 above.

283. Kratz, in *Mocking Epic* (1980), 52, and likewise in *Waltharius and Ruodlieb* (1984), 204, notes that those who call on Fortune in medieval literature are often concerned with transitory values rather than permanent moral goods. The most famous and influential example of this theme is in the *Consolation of Philosophy* 2.1, where Philosophy warns Boethius about the wheel of Fortune (see our poet's adaptation of Boethius at l. 864). Here Trogus has already cursed Walter's luck (*fors*), which in the place of manly courage (*virtus*) brought him victory (l. 1042). Walter will betray his misguided dependence on Fortune, rather than on God, in a later statement (l. 1348). Compare the earlier passage (l. 930), where Walter was associated with *virtus*, not *fortuna*. The change displays the ambiguity of Walter's heroism.

284. An epic patronymic meaning "son of Alphere."

285. This question seems somewhat incongruous, if not exactly inconsistent, with Hagen's secret departure (ll. 119–20). Carroll, "An Essay on the Walther Legend" (1952), 157, suggests that the discrepancy is due to the poet's alteration of his source.

286. The Latin *scandala* ("stumbling block") is derived from the Greek *skandalon*, as used in the New Testament (Mt 13:41, 18:7; Lk 17:1), where the King James Version reads "stumbling block." The original Greek term, however, literally refers to part of a trap, probably the trigger on which the bait is placed. This meaning is metaphorically present in the word's use in the New Testament and was probably familiar to the poet.

287. That is, "praises." The French represents *eulogiis*, derived from the Greek.

288. The phrase "ruddy metal" (*rutilo metallo*) is apparently one of the poet's rare debts to Lucan (*BC* 9.364), where it describes the golden apples of the Hesperides retrieved by Hercules. The allusion suggests a comparison between Hagen and Hercules, the model of heroic virtue as well as vice.

289. That is, "speak cleverly." The phrase "play the *sophiste*" translates the Greek-derived verb *sophari*.

290. Hagen earlier told Gunther that he refused to fight in vengeance for his nephew (ll. 1112–13). Here he contradicts himself. We can see this change either as motivated by Hagen's different addressee or as required by the plot. As for the latter, Carroll, "An Essay on the Walther Legend" (1952), 159, claims that our poet introduced this contradictory speech because he needed to create a reason for Hagen to fight against Walter, since Hagen had remained faithful to Walter in the original story.

291. The adjective *maligeram* ("death-bearing") has the best manuscript support (B, P, T, and I), but the first *a* wrongly scans long. The reading of K and S, *maligenam*, may be understood as "ill-bearing" or as "[made of] apple-wood"—the latter would scan correctly. V's reading *malignam* does not scan. Compare Langosch, *Waltharius, Ruodlieb, Märchenepen* (1956), 369.

292. An epic patronymic meaning "son of Alphere."

293. The poet here adapts Vergil's description of Mezentius's unsuccessful spear-throw at Aeneas (*Aen.* 10.776–80):

> … dixit, stridentemque eminus hastam
> iecit. at illa uolans clipeo est excussa proculque
> egregium Antoren latus inter et ilia figit,
> Herculis Antoren comitem, qui missus ab Argis
> haeserat Euandro atque Itala consederat urbe.

("He spoke and threw the shrieking spear from afar. But flying, it was knocked aside by the shield, and far off it pierced outstanding Antores in between his side and his groin, Antores, Hercules' comrade, who, sent from Argos, had stayed with Evander and settled in the Italian city.") The allusion is structurally pertinent, since Hagen claims to be avenging his nephew Patavrid (as Mezentius was avenging his son Lausus), and Walter, like Aeneas, had not wanted to kill the youth. The verb "whirled" (*contorsit*) is probably modeled on *Aen.* 12.266, where the old Italian seer interprets Juturna's deceptive omens as favorable before he "spoke" (*dixit*) and "whirled" (*contorsit*) his spear. Perhaps Hagen, like the old seer, is well meaning but mistaken in his choice to attack Walter.

294. That is, up to the nails that hold the spear head to the shaft.

295. Gunther's weak spear-throw is modeled after Priam's pitiful attempt to fend off Pyrrhus (*Aen.* 2.544–6). Therefore, the allusion paints the Frankish king as an ineffective and pitiable character. If one completes the comparison, Walter then is associated with the blood-crazy Pyrrhus, which brings Walter's heroism into question.

296. Note the thievery theme recurring in the latter half of the poem.

297. Although African bears are not common in poetry, there are precedents: Vergil, *Aen.* 5.37 (the skin of a "Libyan she-bear," *Libystidis ursae*), and Juvenal, 4.99–100 (arena fights with "Numidian bears," *ursos Numidas*). Compare also Solinus, *De mirabilibus mundi* 27.

298. In *Waltharius and Ruodlieb* (1984), 65, Kratz translates *artubus* ("on his limbs") as "with claws," but I can find no such extension of the meaning of *artus*. Our poet seems to be following Servius's interpretation of the Vergilian phrase *inhorruit armos* (Servius, *ad Aen.* 10.711): "that is, bristled up on its shoulders; or rather bristled upon its shoulders and stood up its shaggy hair" (*id est armis inhorruit: aut certe in armos horruit et erexit saetas*).

299. Kratz translates "lowering" instead of "covering," but I can find no parallel for *occultare* in this sense.

300. Umbrian (from Umbria in Italy) and Molossian (from North Africa) hounds were two ancient breeds. Although the chief model for this simile is elsewhere (see following note), the reference to the Umbrian hound may allude to a simile from Vergil, *Aen.* 12.749–57, where Aeneas is hunting Turnus.

301. This is the longest of the similes in the *Waltharius*, its chief source being Vergil's comparison of Mezentius to a boar attacked by dogs (*Aen.* 10.707–15). There is a close verbal connection with Hagen's earlier dream (ll. 617–27), since he saw a bear tearing off Gunther's leg, and Walter is here compared to a bear.

302. I prefer the sense of "ninth hour" here to "ninth wave," the alternate reading of MS. P (cf. Ovid, *Trist.* 1.2.49–59), because it is clear from the immediate context that the battle has gone on for a heroically long time since it began at the second hour (l. 1285). Furthermore, there seems to be a biblical echo of Christ's ninth hour on the Cross (Mk 15:34). However, I should note that the poetic

verb "flowed" (*fluxerat*) fits well with "wave," which may be why a later reader decided to improve on the original text.

303. Walter mistakenly concerns himself with Fortune, not God. Compare the note on Fortune at l. 1235.

304. Christ's thorn (*paliurus*) is sometimes suggested to be the type of thorn used for Christ's crown on the Cross. This is a punning reference to Hagen's name, which means "thorn bush." See also l. 1421.

305. This line adapts Vergil's description of Allecto enraging Turnus (*Aen.* 7.421), problematically connecting Walter with Turnus (or even Allecto) rather than with the hero Aeneas.

306. The significance of this sentence is debatable. Kratz, *Waltharius and Ruodlieb* (1984), translates: "He was of course resplendent, clad in finest armor" (65) as a parenthetical explanation that Hagen had fine armor on when Walter hit him. This may be right; but perhaps Hagen no longer gleams in splendid armor (hence the past perfect "had stood gleaming") because his shield has been pierced and his hauberk torn and stained with blood.

307. The word *vir* ("man") is marked in the Latin because of its connection with *virtus* (here "manliness," but also "courage" or "virtue"). In the nominative it usually refers to Walter (ll. 895, 920, 959, 1182, 1360, 1386) but once to Hagen (l. 1369).

308. Note that l. 1364, *Crus cum poplite ad usque femur decerpserat omne*, exactly repeats l. 625 from Hagen's prophetic dream. This is the first of the three maimings that mark this climactic scene. In *Waltharius and Ruodlieb* (1984), xxi, Kratz notes that this part of the poem has often confused readers, some of whom have thought that the poet carelessly retained this horrific, pagan scene from his model, although it does not fit the Christian poem. However, there is no evidence that this scene existed in any of the other versions of the story, so it is also possible to see it as an invention. The maimings apparently allude to Ex 21:24: *oculum pro oculo dentem pro dente manum pro manu pedem pro pede* ("eye for eye, tooth for tooth, hand for hand, foot for foot"). Furthermore, the poet's listing of Gunther's foot, Walter's hand, and Hagen's eye (at ll. 1402–03) directs the reader to Mk 9:42–47: *et si scandalizaverit te manus tua abscide illam bonum est tibi debilem introire in vitam quam duas manus habentem ire in gehennam in ignem inextinguibilem ... et si pes tuus te scandalizat amputa illum bonum est tibi claudum introire in vitam aeternam quam duos pedes habentem mitti in gehennam ignis inextinguibilis ... quod si oculus tuus scandalizat te eice eum bonum est tibi luscum introire in regnum Dei quam duos oculos habentem mitti in gehennam ignis* ("And if thy hand offend thee, cut it off: it is better for thee to enter into life maimed, than having two hands to go into hell, into the fire that never shall be quenched .... And if thy foot offend thee, cut it off: it is better for thee to enter halt into life, than having two feet to be cast into hell, into the fire that never shall be quenched .... And if thine eye offend thee, pluck it out: it is better for thee to enter into the kingdom of God with one eye, than having two eyes to be cast into hell fire"). In *Waltharius of Gaeraldus* (1978), Bate points out (66–7) some verbal resonances in the *Waltharius* that recall the text of the Gospels. First, *nec scandala noscens* (l. 1255) recalls the noun *scandala* and verb *scandalizo*, which appear in Mt 5:29–30, Mt 18:7–9, and Mk 9:42, 44, 46. Secondly, *abscide* (l. 1259) echoes *abscide* from Mt 5:30, Mt 18:8, and Mk 9:42. Thirdly, *eruit* (l. 627, in the prophetic dream) recalls *erue* in Mt 5:29. Finally, *lusce* is from *luscum* of Mk 9:46.

309. An epic patronymic meaning "son of Alphere."

310. That is, "sword." The French here represents *spata*, derived from the Greek.

311. See note 307 above.

312. This scene, where Walter's sword shatters and is thrown away, alludes to scenes in Vergil's *Aeneid* (Turnus's sword shattering at 12.729–41) and Prudentius's *Psychomachia* (Anger's sword shattering at 132–44), and both scenes problematize our view of Walter's heroism. Note also the striking personification of the sword, which is *stupefactus* ("stunned" or "astonished"). Kiefer, "*Waltharii poesis*: les

fragments *Waldere*" (2001), suggests (58–9) that the scene is not historically accurate in view of medieval steel technology—the literary, not historical, background has informed the scene.

313. Compare note 85 above, concerning the sword in the Anglo-Saxon *Waldere* fragments.

314. I have imitated the striking alliteration of *framea fragmina* (l. 1376) with "broken brand." The Latin *framea* usually means "spear" in classical Latin, but Niermayer/van de Kieft, *Mediae Latinitatis Lexicon Minus* (2002), defines *framea* as "sword," citing among others Gregory of Tours, *HF* 3.15. Clearly here the word refers to his sword, but compare l. 1016.

315. Walter's anger here is described in nearly the same words as Attila's excessive wrath (l. 380) after discovering Walter's betrayal. As noted above (n. 312), the sword-breaking scene is at least partially inspired by Prudentius's depiction of Anger. Walter's rage is clearly a mistake (or even a sin) that foreshadows his coming loss.

316. That is, "tyrants." The French represents the Greek-derived *tyrannus*.

317. In *Waltharius and Ruodlieb* (1984), 67, Kratz translates *semispatam* ("half-sword") as "a dagger," but it clearly is the second "sword" mentioned in ll. 336–7.

318. The archaic English spelling of "his" in this sentence reflects the archaic Latin dative *olli* (l. 1395).

319. The phrase "thunderstorm of war" (*fulmine belli*) is only paralleled in Silius Italicus (16.625), where it occurs in the same verse position. See Schieffer, "Silius Italicus" (1975), for further parallels and for evidence that places the poem at St. Gall.

320. The Latin *palma* here can—just like the English "palm"—refer to a hand or palm frond. A palm frond is a decoration of victory (see *Oxford Latin Dictionary*, under *palma*, 4b, 5–7), as it was for Prudentius's martyrs (for example, *Perist.* 2.32, 4.77). Our poet uses the word in this sense at l. 928. Townsend, "Ironic Intertextuality" (1997), 82, is right to emphasize the punning ambiguity of *palma* in l. 1402. The metrical pattern of the literal *dextra* ("right hand") is identical to *palma*, which suggests the poet chose to use the ambiguous word. The pun underlines the problematic nature of Walter's heroism. He has constantly trusted in the power of his right hand (ll. 339, 767, 813, 1215, 1362, 1383) to earn him victory (ll. 813, 1215, 1383). At last the "palm" lies before him, but now he will have only a stuffed glove in place of his "palm" (l. 1427)! Townsend writes that "the price of phallic potency is amputation … the price of the phallus is the rest of the body or at least significant portions of it" (83). In addition to the mutilations of the three surviving heroes, one should recall that Walter's other opponents suffered various mutilations as well. The ideological conflict between the heroic ethos and Christian doctrine (see the following note) is an undercurrent throughout the epic.

321. This obvious allusion to Mk 9:42–8 ("And if thy hand offend thee, cut it off …"; cf. Mt 5:30) indicates that all three of the men, including Walter, were subject to vice. Perhaps the implication is that their loss will help them, since "it is better for thee to enter into life maimed, than having two hands to go into hell" (Mk 9:43), and "it is better for thee to enter into life with one eye, rather than having two eyes to be cast into hell fire" (Mt 18:9). Walter's loss of a hand makes sense because of misguided trust in his hand (cf. ll. 812–17). Hagen's loss of teeth and eye is fitting because of his desire for vengeance for his nephew (cf. ll. 1268–74). After all, the Old Testament's law of vengeance (Ex 21:22-25) tells us, "an eye for an eye, a tooth for a tooth." Gunther's loss of his leg may well be seen as a cure for his pride, since he will now have to hobble around, but most likely the poet chose it so that he could describe the three amputations as hand, foot, and eye—matching Mark 9:42–8. See Ward, "After Rome" (1993), who argues (at 281) that Walter's loss of his right hand reflects his contemplated betrayal of his betrothal to Hildegund, parallel to Aeneas's betrayal of Dido, whom he had given his right hand. Certainly the betrothal of Hildegund and Walter receives much attention from our poet, as Ward rightly emphasizes, but I do not detect any indication of Walter intending to betray Hildegund. Ward further suggests (at 282) that Hagen's loss of an eye and part of his mouth show that he saw the truth of the situation and had spoken his pledge to Walter, but failed to act in accordance

with these indications, and that Guther's loss of a leg, which left him lying on the ground rather than standing, proudly punishes him for his arrogance. For a completely different view, see Lincoln, "Rewriting the German War God" (1998), who connects the wounds, not with biblical examples, but rather with Germanic stories about kings, heroes, and gods who lose body parts. He sees the wounds as reflecting the "three functions" that Dumézil attributed to Indo-European society: the loss of a hand or arm always marks a warrior; the loss of an eye or another part of the head marks the ruler or sage; and the loss of a foot or lower part of the body marks the lowest subservient order. Thus Lincoln notes that, in the *Waltharius*, "one finds an interesting inversion of the pattern, since it is a king, Guntharius, who loses his leg and the king's liegeman, Hagano, who loses an eye .... The text explains this reversal, however, telling how Guntharius deserves demotion because greed and weakness made him unworthy, while Hagano's bravery and righteousness made him the king's superior" (200–01).

322. "In just such a way" translates *sic sic*, a collocation which is strange in Latin and seems to reproduce a Germanic idiom cognate with the Anglo-Saxon *swa swa*. Alternately, one may translate it "thus, thus" as an echo of Vergil's Dido at the time of her suicide: "Thus, thus I gladly go to the shades!" (*sic sic iuvat ire sub umbras, Aen.* 4.660). For this interpretation, which others will prefer, see Dronke and Dronke, *Barbara et antiquissima carmina* (1977), 62–3. However, such a transference from passionate character to moralizing narrator seems inapt and unlikely, especially since the phrase occurs in a different verse position here.

323. There is a probable pun on the Latin words *Avares* ("Avars") and *avaritia* ("avarice"), as I suggest with "Avarish."

324. An epic patronymic meaning "son of Alphere."

325. I imitate the Greek-derived *athleta* with the recognizable French *athlète*. Compare the athletic language in the "tug-of-war" scene (ll. 954–1049), where *athleta* was used twice.

326. In *Waltharius and Ruodlieb* (1984), xviii, Kratz suggests that the final scene in the *Waltharius* is based on a scene from Prudentius's *Psychomachia* where the Virtues rest and refresh themselves after combat (606–63).

327. An epic patronymic meaning "son of Alphere."

328. The word *senior* ("lord") could also be translated "husband" in this context.

329. There is an etymological play on Hagen and the Germanic root meaning "thorn bush." The English words "hedge" and "hawthorn" are related, as is the modern German *Hagedorn*.

330. The mocking conversation between Walter and Hagen is a kind of ludic flyting—see note 41 above. For the poet's playfulness and extensive use of irony, see p. 4 in the introduction of this volume. For the dark humor of the scene, Townsend, "Ironic Intertextuality" (1997), 81, suggests a Germanic color and compares *Beowulf* 445–51 (Beowulf telling Hrothgar the king will not have to bury him after Grendel devours him) and *Njal's Saga*, chap. 77 (Thorgrim's dying jest about Gunnar's halberd being at home). However, one also finds black humor in our poet's Latin models, for example: Vergil, *Aen.* 2.547–50 (Pyrrhus's mockery of Priam), Statius, *Theb.* 9.96–103 (Eteocles' jest about a corpse too disgraceful even to be eaten by animals or burned by fire), and Prudentius, *Psych.* 118–20 (Anger's jest that Patience must suffer the pain without complaint).

331. The poet uses the Old High German word *wantis* ("gloves"). Compare the cognate English "gauntlet." Compare also the poet's use of the Germanic words *hnapf* (l. 308) and *Wah!* (l. 1429).

332. This is a Germanic interjection (see preceding note). Compare the Old Saxon *Heliand*, 3950, 5573.

333. The Latin *dicis* literally translates "do you say," but context implies a future here. I could have retained the present because English, like German, can sometimes use presents in this way. It is rather uncommon to have present for future in Latin, so that this appears to be a Germanic feature. Compare "I shall cheat" for the present tense *fraudo* at l. 979, and "I shall hunt" for present *venor* in l. 1436.

Occasionally, Latin too can use a present in place of a future, so that Germanic idiom is not the only possible influence here; see Pinkster, "Is the Latin present tense the unmarked, neutral tense in the system?" (1998).

334. The dramatic interjection *euge* ("hey") indicates that Hagen is pleased with his own clever imagination.

335. The adjective refers to an ancient German tribe called the *Sugambri*. However, this name was anachronistically associated with the Franks. Gregory of Tours says that the Merovingian-Frankish King Clovis I was called a Sicambrian when he was baptized by St. Remigius (*HF* 2.31). Moreover, the early eighth-century *Liber historiae Francorum* (1) has Trojan outcasts found a city named *Sicambria*.

336. Apparently a joke. Obviously, Hagen with his missing teeth will have problems chewing boar meat.

337. His glance is *transversa* ("sideways") because he is suspicious and because he only has one eye. For the phrase *transversa tuendo*, compare Vergil, *Ecl.* 3.8 (and Servius's note), as well as Valerius Flaccus, 2.154.

338. The Latin *disiecti* ("separated") can refer both to the dispersal of the friends and to the dismemberment of their bodies.

339. Ward, "After Rome" (1993), emphasizes the importance of Walter and Hildegund's legitimate marriage in the context of contemporary Frankish views on marriage: "Hiltgunde is thus a classic illustration of our recent textbook accounts of Carolingian attitudes towards women and marriage" (283).

340. Compare Iulus's likewise fortunate thirty-year reign of Alba Longa in Vergil, *Aen.* 1.267–9.

341. The image of the cicada with its shrill voice is probably inspired by a rustic scene from Vergil, *Ecl.* 2.12–13. The allusion thus confirms the humble tone of the comparison. See Haug, "Die Zikade im 'Waltharius'" (2004), 31–3, for more on the significance of the image.

342. The image of the bird leaving its nest is inspired by Vergil, *Georg.* 2.210.

343. It would seem that either the author thinks of himself as young and inexperienced, or at least he wants us to think this. He was probably fairly young, but owing to the frequent exaggeration of poetic language, it would be rash to assume that he must have been a boy. The claim that he had not yet left the nest could mean that he had not yet achieved the age or ecclesiastical learning which would allow him to gain a greater position in the Church, permitting him to leave his home monastery or church.

344. That is, "poetry." As elsewhere, I here translate the Greek-derived word *poesis* with French in order to represent the Latin poet's usage of Greek-derived vocabulary.

345. Strecker and Schumann, *Nachträge* (1951), 83, cite Hrabanus Maurus (PL 107:36b) for a similar phrase, "may Christ save you" (*Christus vos salvet*). In Hrabanus it opens the final couplet in a short elegiac poem.

Indices

Modern Authors

Subjects

PRINTED ON PERMANENT PAPER • IMPRIME SUR PAPIER PERMANENT • GEDRUKT OP DUURZAAM PAPIER - ISO 9706

N.V. PEETERS S.A., WAROTSTRAAT 50, B-3020 HERENT